Language Acquisition and Language Socialization

Advances in Applied Linguistics
General editors: Christopher N. Candlin and Srikant Sarangi

This series offers a number of innovative points of focus. It seeks to represent diversity in applied linguistics but within that diversity to identify ways in which distinct research fields can be coherently related. Such coherence can be achieved by shared subject matter among fields, parallel and shared methodologies of research, mutualities of purposes and goals of research, and collaborative and cooperative work among researchers from different disciplines.

Although interdisciplinarity among established disciplines is now common, this series has in mind to open up new and distinctive research areas which lie at the boundaries of such disciplines. Such areas will be distinguished in part by their novel data sets and in part by the innovative combination of research methodologies. The series hopes thereby both to consolidate already well-tried methodologies, data and contexts of research and to extend the range of applied linguistics research and scholarship to new and under-represented cultural, institutional and social contexts.

The philosophy underpinning the series mirrors that of applied linguistics more generally: a problem-based, historically and socially grounded discipline concerned with the reflexive interrogation of research by practice, and practice by research, oriented towards issues of social relevance and concern, and multi-disciplinary in nature.

The structure of the series encompasses books of several distinct types: research monographs which address specific areas of concern; reports from well-evidenced research projects; coherent collections of papers from precisely defined colloquia; volumes which provide a thorough historical and conceptual engagement with key applied linguistics fields; and edited accounts of applied linguistics research and scholarship from specific areas of the world.

Published titles in the series:
Multimodal Teaching and Learning: The Rhetorics of the Science Classroom
Gunther Kress, Carey Jewitt, Jon Ogborn and Charalampos Tsatsarelis

Metaphor in Educational Discourse
Lynne Cameron

Language Acquisition and Language Socialization

Ecological Perspectives

edited by
Claire Kramsch

continuum
LONDON • NEW YORK

Continuum
The Tower Building, 11 York Road, London, SE1 7NX
370 Lexington Avenue, New York, NY 10017–6503

First published 2002

British Library Cataloguing-in-Publication Data
A catalogue record for this book is available from the British Library.

ISBN 0–8264–5371–6 (hardback)
     0–8264–5372–4(paperback)

Typeset by BookEns Ltd, Royston, Herts.
Printed and bound in Great Britain by
Bookcraft, Midsomer Norton, Bath

Contents

Contributors

Anne Bannink, Associate Professor, Department of English and Germanic Linguistics and Graduate School of Education of the University of Amsterdam. Research interests: ethnography of schooling, classroom discourse, and second language acquisition. Author of *Mixed Cultures in In-Service Training – The Case of Dutch Trainers in Vietnam* (2000).

Patricia B. Genung, Professor and Deputy Head, Department of Foreign Languages, U.S. Military Academy, West Point, N.Y. Research interests: second language acquisition, classroom research, language and gender, language pedagogy. Co-author of "L'acquisition scolaire d'une langue étrangère vue dans la perspective de la théorie de l'activité: une étude de cas." *Aile* 12 (2000), 99–122.

Claire Kramsch, Professor of German and Foreign Language Education, University of California at Berkeley. Research interests: discourse analysis, language and culture, subjectivity and social identity in language learning. Author of *Discourse Analysis and Second Language Teaching* (CAL 1981), *Context and Culture in Language Teaching* (Oxford University Press 1993), *Language and Culture* (Oxford University Press 1998). Co-editor of *Text and Context in Language Study: Cross-Disciplinary Perspectives* (Heath 1992). Co-editor of *Applied Linguistics*.

James Lantolf, Professor of Spanish and Applied Linguistics, Penn State University. Research interests: Vygotskian approaches to SLA, sociocultural theory, social cognition. Co-editor of *Second Language Research in the Classroom Setting* (Ablex 1987), *Vygotskian Approaches to Second Language Research* (Ablex 1994), *Sociocultural Theory and Second Language Learning* (Oxford University Press 2000).

Diane Larsen-Freeman, Professor of Education, Director of the English Language Institute, University of Michigan. Research interests: SLA, grammar in ELT, chaos/complexity theory. Editor of *Discourse Analysis in Second Language Research* (Newbury House 1980), co-author of *An Introduction to Second Language Acquisition Research* (Longman 1991), co-author of *The Grammar Book: An ESL/EFL Teacher's Course* (Heinle & Heinle, 2nd edn., 1999) and author of *Techniques and Principles in Language Teaching* (Oxford University Press, 2nd edn 2000) and *Teaching Language: From Grammar to Grammaring* (Heinle & Heinle, 2003).

Jonathan Leather, Associate Professor, Department of English, University of Amsterdam. Research interests: phonological acquisition, ecological modeling of language acquisition, language attitudes, and language planning. Co-editor of *Second Language Speech: Structure and Process* (Mouton de Gruyter 1997); editor of *Phonological Issues in Language Learning* (Blackwell 1999).

Jay Lemke, Professor of Educational Studies at the University of Michigan, Ann Arbor. Research interests: social semiotics, discourse linguistics, language in education, science education. Author of *Using Language in the Classroom* (2nd edn. Oxford University Press 1985), *Talking Science: Language, Learning, and Values* (Ablex 1990) and *Textual Politics: Discourse and Social Dynamics* (Taylor & Francis 1995).

Elinor Ochs, Professor of Anthropology and Applied Linguistics, University of California at Los Angeles. Research interests: cross-linguistic and cross-cultural language socialization and acquisition, discourse structures across languages and communities, problem-solving discourse in science and the family, grammar in context, language and affect, narrative and mental disorders. Author of *Culture and Language Development: Language Acquisition and Language Socialization in a Samoan Village* (Cambridge University Press 1988); co-editor of *Language Socialization across Cultures* (Cambridge University Press 1986) and *Interaction and Grammar* (Cambridge University Press 1996); co-author of *Constructing Panic: The Discourse of Agoraphobia* (Harvard University Press 1995) and *Living Narrative: Creating Lives in Everyday Storytelling* (Harvard University Press 2001).

Celia Roberts, Senior Research Fellow, Department of Education and Professional Studies, King's College London. Research interests: institutional discourse in multilingual settings, second language socialization, ethnography as research method, intercultural learning, and medical discourse. Co-author of *Language and Discrimination* (1992), *Achieving Understanding* (1996). Co-editor of *Talk, Work and Institutional Order* (1999) and *Language Learners as Ethnographers* (2001).

Srikant Sarangi, Reader in Language and Communication and Director of the Health Communication Research Centre at Cardiff University.

Research interests: discourse analysis and applied linguistics, language and identity in public life, and institutional/professional discourse studies. Co-author of *Language, Bureaucracy and Social Control* (Longman 1996), *Talk, Work and Institutional Order: Discourse in Medical, Mediation and Management Settings* (Mouton 1999), *Discourse and Social Life* (Pearson 2001), *Sociolinguistics and Social Theory* (Pearson 2001). Editor of *TEXT* and co-editor of the series *Advances in Applied Linguistics* and *Communication in Public Life*.

Ron Scollon, Professor of Sociolinguistics, Department of Linguistics, Georgetown University. Research interests: mediated discourse, intercultural communication, public discourse, critical discourse. Author of *Mediated Discourse as Social Interaction: The Study of News Discourse* (Longman 1998) and *Mediated Discourse: The Nexus of Practice* (Routledge 2001). Co-author of *Narrative, Literacy, and Face in Interethnic Communication* (Ablex 1981), and *Intercultural Communication: A Discourse Approach* (Blackwell 1995).

Jet van Dam, Professor, Department of English and Germanic Linguistics and Graduate School of Education, University of Amsterdam. Research interests: classroom discourse, organization of correction and repair, ethnography of schooling, diary studies. Author of *Participant Structure and the On-Line Production of Discourse Context* (1995) and *Where's the Lesson in All This Talk?* (1995).

Leo van Lier, Professor of Educational Linguistics, TESOL/TFL Program, Monterey Institute of International Studies. Research interests: classroom research, computer-assisted instruction, semiotics, ecological approaches to SLA. Author of *The Classroom and the Language Learner. Ethnography and Second-language Classroom Research* (Longman 1988), *Interaction in the Language Curriculum: Awareness, Autonomy and Authenticity* (Longman 1996).

Contributors to the Commentaries

Edward Bodine, doctoral student, Graduate School of Education, University of California at Berkeley
Christopher Candlin, Senior Research Professor, Department of Linguistics, Macquarie University, Sydney
Meg Gebhard, Assistant Professor, School of Education, University of Massachusetts at Amherst
Livia Polanyi, Senior Research Scientist, FX Palo Alto Lab, Palo Alto, California

Ben Rampton, Reader in Applied Linguistics and Sociolinguistics, King's College London

Steven Thorne, Associate Director of the Center for Language Acquisition, Penn State University

Greta Vollmer, Assistant Professor, Department of English, Sonoma State University, California

Amy Weinberg, doctoral student, Joint Program in Special Education, University of California at Berkeley and San Francisco State University

Kevin Wiliarty, PhD in Germanic Linguistics, University of California at Berkeley

Foreword

Claire Kramsch's edited volume *Language Acquisition and Language Socialization: Ecological Perspectives* derives from an invited colloquium held at the Berkeley Language Centre at the University of California. As such, it represents the first of what we hope will be a succession of publications in the *Advances in Applied Linguistics* series to make available, in closely edited form, coherent statements on current issues in the field, drawing on research and inquiry from major centres and scholars in applied linguistics internationally. The book represents what one might call *interdisciplinarity-in-interaction,* where the contributors come from diverse fields of practice, but are endowed with a sense of tunefulness as they move freely between the boundaries of language acquisition and language socialization. This is evidenced further by the retention of the dialogicity, inclusive of the mild disagreements, which characterized the colloquium. The commentaries which follow the paired presentations provide rich insights into the theoretical, methodological and educational concerns surrounding acquisition/socialization studies. The book is also exemplary in its attempt to extend such debates to other professional sites and out-of-class activities.

The title of the volume already stakes a position in its orientation towards language acquisition. The focus is on language learners as language users in natural environments where their active engagement in semiotic – not just linguistic – and interactional activity creates the affordances (or not) for language acquisition. Such an orientation represents something of a departure from mainstream studies of second-language acquisition with their preference for experimental designs in the instructed site, their focus on monologic or at best dyadic data, and their reduction of language – even where there is a consciousness of pragmatics – essentially to the mastery of forms. What we have here is an alternative view of the learner, as Kramsch indicates in her Introduction to the volume. The learner is not a *computer,* even less an *apprentice,* but more of a *negotiator,* principally of course, of meanings, but also of pathways, of stance and of identities. Here the view of the learner and of language happily coincide. As Rutherford (1987) pointed out more than fifteen years ago, learning and language learning is better captured by the *organic* metaphor than it is by the *mechanistic* (see also Rogers 1975). What is more, all the data from naturalistic language learning, and even from instructed language learning, bear this out (see, for instance, Bremer *et al.* 1996; Rampton 1995; Roberts 2001). Why then the insistence on machine?

The learner as apprentice poses more of a problem. After all, learners are peripheral participators in Lave and Wenger's (1991) sense in that they are learning *the ways of learning*. The problem resides in identifying the community of practice that they are being apprenticed into, and the sense also that apprenticeship implies the accompaniment of a *meister*. *Instructed* second language acquisition of course fits the apprenticeship metaphor exactly: the classroom contextualizes the community of practice, and the teacher provides the guide. However, the fact is that most second language learning takes place outside the instructional site. As Roberts (2001) unerringly points out, once we introduce socialization, and necessarily with that the invoking of the wider context of the social world outside the classroom, apprenticeship is less plausible as an explanatory metaphor. What is less apparent is how socialization also has limits as an explanatory metaphor in that it suggests a goal, it suggests participation as a prize, but both may be misleading. In multicultural and multilingual societies there can be only plural goals and manifold identities into which persons become quite variously socialized, and what, if in that increasingly xenophobic and intolerant wider world, the community is not exactly standing there at the finishing line with open arms?

We are already conversing in metaphors, and doing so inevitably forges a connection with another title in the *Advances in Applied Linguistics* series – *Metaphors in Educational Discourse* by Lynne Cameron. Cameron's book underscores the importance of the negotiation of metaphorical meaning as a defining characteristic of education, and lays emphasis on a constructivist view of language use and its link to learning. Here in Kramsch's volume we note its counterpart in a constructivist and negotiative approach to learning and to acquisition. Metaphors link worlds, and two such metaphors – acquisition and socialization – have long been married in first-language acquisition, notably of course in the work of Elinor Ochs, one of the authors in this collection, less so in second-language studies, although with notable exceptions, some of whom, like Lantolf, Larsen-Freeman and van Lier are included here.

There is, however, a third metaphor in the title, that of *ecology*. In part the ground has already been prepared for its unpacking, in the references above to language and learning as an organism, and the role of the learner as negotiator. One interpretation of ecology points us directly to the negotiative interaction of human persons with their environment. Socialization is in one sense also exactly that. Another interpretation, of course, is the interaction among those persons themselves within that natural environment, and the relative constraints on the necessary affordances for learning offered by that environment. Ecology in this sense is both reactive and creative: it suggests a system, and it makes us reflect on change within that system and between that system and others. Capturing the essence of this systemic dynamism is what this volume has as a principal objective. As persons in the street amply recognize, language, like life, is interactive and consequential. What an ecological perspective also suggests, though, is the implication of interventions into that system. Instruction is one such intervention, but so is any language-mediated encounter in the wider context of the social world. Seeing the system systemically is both the challenge for any teacher and a challenge for those analysts who would model the ecology in terms of language, in terms of action and behaviour, and in terms of learning. Thus ecology has implications for the way we construct our primes but it also impacts on the way we conduct our practice. For example, as a metaphor it helps to clarify relationships between partners in the system, between professionals who analyse discourse and interaction and those professionals for whom discourse and communication is at the heart of their practice.

Above all, however, ecology, as Cicourel (1992) reminds us, imposes its own conditions on research validity. He draws our attention to what he calls *interpenetration* of contexts which needs to be matched by an interdiscursivity of research methodologies and approaches to data. Capturing and recording that dynamism will not be easy, as the contributions in this volume indicate, but what they also indicate is that the field of language acquisition, and especially second-language acquisition in non-instructional settings, is a key critical site of research engagement for such a task. Such a site can be seen quite locally, but it can also be explored in a more macro sense, for example in the fields of language planning and language education policy. Indeed, no more important example might be found of the power of the ecological metaphor than to trace there the consequences of action and intervention.

What Claire Kramsch's volume does is to address these issues of research model and research practice, and to focus them on issues of educational success in terms of language acquisition. This is explicitly manifest in the commentaries. As Léger well knew in his paintings, one always can see the dancers through the dance, but the trick is to grasp how to represent them, and how to understand the complexities of the choreography. Hence the importance here of the characterizing of what

Kramsch refers to as the interdisciplinary, multimodal and multi-scalar nature of ecologically oriented research. It suggests interdisciplinary teams of researchers with multiple research skills and orientations towards language-in-action as data and its analysis, the consequent privileging of activity-based research, and a multi-modal perspective on methodology. What it also does is to realign our perception of research sites, seeing Rampton's (1995) border crossing not as a special case, but actually language- and language learning in use – as it *always* is.

References

Bremer, K., Roberts, C., Vasseur, M., Simonot, M. and Broeder, P. (1996) *Achieving Understanding: Discourse in Intercultural Encounters.* London: Longman.

Cameron, L. (2002) *Metaphors in Educational Discourse.* London: Continuum.

Cicourel, A. (1992) The interpenetration of communicative contexts: examples from medical encounters. In A. Duranti and C. Goodwin (eds), *Rethinking Context: Language as an Interactive Phenomenon.* Cambridge: Cambridge University Press, pp.291-310.

Lave, J. and Wenger, E. (1991) *Situated Learning: Legitimate Peripheral Participation.* Cambridge: Cambridge University Press

Rampton, B. (1995) *Crossing: Language and Ethnicity among Adolescents.* London: Longman.

Roberts, C. (2001) Language acquisition or language socialization in and through discourse. In C. N. Candlin and N. Mercer (eds), *English Language Teaching in Its Social Context.* London: Routledge, pp.108-121.

Rogers, S. (ed.) (1975) *Children and Language: Readings in Early Language and Socialization.* Oxford: Oxford University Press.

Rutherford, W. (1987) *Second Language Grammar: Learning and Teaching.* London. Longman.

Christopher N. Candlin
and Srikant Sarangi

Acknowledgments

This book is based on the papers given at a workshop on "Language Socialization, Language Acquisition: Ecological Perspectives" that was held March 17–19, 2000, at the University of California at Berkeley. An organizational committee, consisting of Jonathan Leather (University of Amsterdam), Elinor Ochs (University of California at Los Angeles), Steve Thorne (Penn State University), Jet van Dam (University of Amsterdam), Leo van Lier (Monterey Institute for International Studies) and myself, drew up a list of participants. The papers presented at this workshop, together with excerpts from the commentators' responses and the general discussion, form the basis of the present volume.

The workshop lasted two full days, with four half-day sessions, each organized around a single theme addressed by three speakers. Jet van Dam, University of Amsterdam, chaired Session I, *Ecological Models of Language Socialization*; Steven Thorne, Penn State University, chaired Session II, *Ecological Models of Language Acquisition;* Leo van Lier, Monterey Institute for International Studies, chaired Session III, *Language as Social Action*; Jonathan Leather, University of Amsterdam, chaired Session IV, *Instructional Environments.* In the spirit of ecology, current and former doctoral students from the Berkeley Graduate School of Education – the upcoming generation of scholars and teachers in educational linguistics – were asked to respond to the three papers given during that session from the perspective of their own research or expertise. This volume includes papers presented at the workshop, as well as the Commentaries, prepared by Ed Bodine and myself, based on the contributions not only from the authors included in the volume, but also from other workshop participants, such as Chris Candlin, Livia Polanyi, Ben Rampton, and graduate student respondents Edward Bodine, Meg Gebhard, Steven Thorne, Greta Vollmer, Amy Weinberg, and Kevin Wiliarty.

The workshop was sponsored by the Berkeley Language Center, and was generously funded by the University of California at Berkeley's College of Letters and Science, International and Area Studies, the Department of Linguistics, the Townsend Center for the Humanities, the Graduate School of Education, and the Office of Educational

Development, as well as by the University of Amsterdam. My gratitude goes to all these sponsors. Thanks to the assistance of Mark Kaiser, Director of the Language Media Center and Assistant Director of the Berkeley Language Center, and Alex Prisadsky, then recording studio supervisor, and his team, Gregory Duby, Carolyn Batauta, and Chris Lovett, we were provided with a good audio recording of the papers and discussions. The discussions were transcribed by Daniela Dosch-Fritz, then a doctoral student in the German Department at UC Berkeley. From these transcriptions, Edward Bodine and I selected and arranged the "Commentaries" to be found at the end of each section.

I wish to express my deepest gratitude to Jonathan Leather and Jet van Dam, who, in January 1999, invited me to a workshop at the University of Amsterdam on the *Ecology of Language Acquisition*, which formed the impetus for the Berkeley workshop (see Leather and van Dam, forthcoming). Without their inspiration this book would not have come about. I also wish to thank all the participants and contributors for their visible enthusiasm for the theme of this book and for their willingness to think boldly and off the beaten track. The California sun, and the spirits of Bateson and Goffman hovering among the redwood groves, energized our discussions and encouraged us to think ecologically about all aspects of language acquisition and language socialization. I hope that some of our enthusiasm and energy comes across in this book.

Introduction

"How can we tell the dancer from the dance?"

Claire Kramsch

Do we need another metaphor?

In his short essay, "For want of a metaphor," the natural scientist Stephen J. Gould writes:

> We often think, naively, that missing data are the primary impediments to intellectual progress – just find the right facts and all problems will dissipate. But barriers are often deeper and more abstract in thought. We must have access to the right metaphor, not only to the requisite information. (Gould 1985:151)

This book is an attempt to go beyond facts and information and to find a different way of talking about the interaction of language learners and language users with their natural environment. Research into the way children and adults relate to their environment through language has been inspired by two very different metaphors. The field of language acquisition, born out of psycholinguistics at the end of the 1960s, has been dominated by the LEARNER-AS-COMPUTER metaphor (Ellis 1997:37; Lightbown and Spada 1999:41) The language learner is seen as an information processor that receives input from caretakers, teachers and peers, processes this input into intake, and, ultimately, produces output of a measurable kind. Even though linguistic anthropologists like Dell Hymes (1972) and John Gumperz (Gumperz *et al.* 1979) showed the exquisite negotiation of meaning that is necessary for successful communication in social contexts, and even though applied linguists like Michael Breen and Chris Candlin (1980) considered this negotiation to be central to a communicative curriculum, the prevalence of the machine metaphor has channeled the imagination of many researchers and teachers alike into viewing the acquisition of a language as an information-processing activity where what gets negotiated is not contextual meaning, but input and output. Most of the efforts of second language acquisition (SLA) research have gone into elucidating how skills are *acquired*, and have excluded the *use* of these skills from the primary domain of inquiry of SLA (for other views, however, see Firth and Wagner 1997; Lantolf 2000; Rampton 1997).

The field of language socialization, born out of linguistic anthropology (Ochs and Schieffelin 1979, 1983; Schieffelin and Ochs 1986), has focused on how "children and other novices are socialized through language" (Ochs 1996:408) and thus learn to "use language meaningfully, appropriately, and effectively" (ibid.). The dominant metaphor here has been that of LEARNER-AS-APPRENTICE in a community of practice. Language is not seen as input, but as a tool for getting other things done. The focus is not on the way symbolic systems are acquired, and grammatical and lexical paradigms are used to encode reality, but on the way language practices are organized within members of a community of language users. As novice members learn from more expert members how to use language accurately and appropriately, they enact social relationships and other sociocultural phenomena that will make them into expert members.

Interaction between these two fields has been rare, in part because of their different research traditions and the relative value they give to social context. Language socialization researchers have traditionally been interested in the sociocultural phenomena at work when children learn their native language in distant or familiar cultural contexts (e.g. Ochs 1988). Language acquisition researchers have been interested in the linguistic processes at work in first or second language acquisition by children or adults in a variety of natural and institutional contexts (e.g. Leopold 1954; Halliday 1975; Ellis 1997). The lack of cross-fertilization between language acquisition and language social-ization research is also due to differences in the ultimate criteria of success. Whereas the success of language socialization is full acculturation and assimilation into the language-speaking community, the success of language acquisition is full mastery of the linguistic and communicative aspects of the language, not primarily assimilation into the relevant speech community.

The dividing line between the two, however, is not clear-cut. The more the goal of language acquisition is expressed in terms of functional, communicative competence, and appropriate social and cultural performance, and the more socialization is dependent on precise grammatical and lexical ability, the more difficult it is to separate acquisition and socialization (Leather and van Dam, forth-coming). Attempts have been made to bridge the gap between linguistic structure and social structure in language acquisition and use. Halliday's functional systemic linguistics shows how the structure of language can reflect, express, and enact certain patterns of socialization within a given society through the very plurifunctionality of language. Sociocultural theory based on Vygotsky's Soviet psychology shows that children and adults learn first on the social plane, then internalize the social onto the psychological plane, i.e. by placing cognition and the mind into the social (Lantolf 2000). However, the terms used by Halliday and Vygotsky, *plurifunctionality* and *internalization*, risk keeping intact the very dichotomy they strive to cancel. A functional description of language does not eliminate the distinction between the individual language user and the social environment; it only attempts to show how each co-constructs the other. A Vygotskyian theory of SLA does not necessarily change the core input/output metaphor of learning (Dunn and Lantolf 1998:428).

The realization that both language acquisition and language socialization research might be prisoners of their own metaphors has prompted some researchers to seek, not necessarily another overarching theory, but another way of framing the search for understanding. They have rallied around the "ecology" metaphor that emerged in the 1960s in a variety of fields, independent of one another, e.g. systems theory and cybernetics (Bateson 1972, 1979), psychology (Gibson 1979; Lewin 1943; Neisser 1976), educational development (Bronfenbrenner 1979), linguistics (Haugen 1972; Makkai 1993; Mühlhäusler 1996), and that was picked up recently by educational linguist van Lier (1996, 2000) and psycholinguists Leather and van Dam (forthcoming) for language acquisition research. The metaphor, which captures the dynamic interaction between language users and the environment as between parts of a living organism, seems to offer a new way of bringing together frames from various disciplines to illuminate the complex relationship under investigation.

The need to take this symbiotic relationship into consideration is prompted by two recent developments on the larger geopolitical scene: globalization and multicultural education. The scale of human communication has been drastically changed by global technologies. As Bruno Latour (1999) and Lemke (this volume) point out, a change in the speed, scope, and volume of communication is not just a change in degree, but a change in kind. The Internet revolution has made researchers and practitioners even more aware of the importance of context in language development. Context was always at the core of communicative language learning (e.g. Ellis 1987), itself born in the wake of the 1960s' societal upheavals and ecology movement, but it was reduced in the 1970s and 1980s to its minimalist social dimensions in one-on-one verbal interactions. The 1990s brought back the importance of context on a much larger cultural scale and, with it, a need to rethink the relation of language and other meaning-making practices in everyday life.

This need is nowhere more apparent than in one of the consequences of globalization, namely, the increased ethnic, social, and cultural diversity of industrialized societies. The human migrations that have resulted from global economic shifts have called for a multicultural education that takes into account differences in abilities, styles, preferences, and cultural traditions. It is no longer sufficient to talk about "individual differences" in SLA against the backdrop of a universal learner. Difference and variation itself have moved to the center of language acquisition research. Variation becomes the primary given; categorization becomes an artificial construct of institutionaliza-tion and scientific inquiry. A corollary of this trend is the diminishing importance of knowledge-based expertise in relation to interaction-related expertise, the increased demand for the flexibility to move in and out of frames within professional encounters and to deal with cross-cultural misunderstandings. The need for sound judgment and on-the-spot appraisal in local interactions is rising as a consequence. An ecological perspective brings into focus all those intractable aspects of language development that have not been the object of systematic inquiry, for example: environmental adaptation and transgression, i.e. the proliferation of learners' and novices' sanctioned and unsanctioned (standard and non-standard) meanings (e.g. Kramsch 1997); parody and language play (e.g. Crystal 1998); imagination and creativity (e.g. Kramsch 1994; Cook 2000); language and symbolic power (Bourdieu 1991).

What unites the chapters in this volume is a common dissatisfac-tion with the traditional separation between language acquisition and language socialization and their exclusive metaphors. But the authors of this volume are reluctant to replace them by yet another single model or metaphor that claims to provide the ultimate synthesis of the individual and the social in language development. The term "ecology" itself is not unproblematic. It evokes organic unity, and the complex balance of natural forces, as well as concern for the environment and its management,[1] but it can also evoke ruthless Darwinian selection and a certain utopian idealism. Researchers in language development are aware of the need, as Diane Larsen-Freeman put it during the workshop, to not lose sight of the whole and to "prevent premature closure" (Part Two: Commentaries), but they have conflicting views as to what would count as ecological validity (see Cicourel 1992). And yet they found in the notion of "ecology" a rallying framework to voice the contradictions, the unpredictabilities, and paradoxes that underlie even the most respectable research in language development. By embracing an ecological perspective they do not intend to replace existing metaphors. Instead, in an intellectual move that hails back to Bateson (1972:180), they place themselves on a level that is of a different logical type from either language acquisition or language socialization: they seek new ways of conceptualizing the relationship of the dancer and the dance.

Chapters in this volume

The contributors to this volume share a sense that the "ecology" metaphor is a convenient shorthand for the poststructuralist realization that learning is a nonlinear, relational human activity, co-constructed between humans and their environment, contingent upon their position in space and history, and a site of struggle for the control of social power and cultural memory. The four parts of this book move the exploration of an ecology of language development from the level of models and metaphors (Part I), to the level of social practice (Part II) and institutional history (Part III), and, beyond history, to the hybrid time and rituals of classroom practice (Part IV).

Part I: *Language Development as Spatial and Temporal Positioning* proposes various models and metaphors as a new vocabulary for talking about language research. In Chapter 1, Diane Larsen-Freeman first recapitulates current debates within the field of SLA which have pitted language acquisition against language use, the individualistic and mentalistic against the interactional and sociolinguistic dimensions of language. She offers chaos/complexity theory as a metaphor that encompasses both sides of the debate. It is not, according to the theory, that the language game has no rules; indeed, if it did not have any, transfer and translation between languages would be impossible. But playing the game has a way of changing the rules that made the game possible in the first place.

In Chapter 2, Jonathan Leather applies the tenets of chaos/complexity theory and connectionism to an understanding of language development in multilingual children. On the example of one six-year-old Caribbean child, Alvin, and his brother Gregory, he develops a phenomenological model of phonological development that resignifies traditional SLA nomenclature. The emerging phonology of second language (L2) is described as a composite of individual phonologies, with varieties based on individual "preferences," rather than differences; it is the nonlinear development of a "segmental repertoire" rather than the acquisition of rules and symbols; it shows evidence of "alignment" with a speech community, rather than conformity to native speaker (NS) use. Leather's model seeks to capture the "gradient" changes in a child's acoustic output, rather than categorial evidence of acquisition.

Jay Lemke's vision, in Chapter 3, adds historical and educational dimensions to the models proposed in the previous chapters. His notion of an "ecosocial system," based on dynamic systems theory and inspired by Bakhtin and Halliday, consists of social material processes and social semiotic practices, not individual organisms. His focal scale is a human being's total historical trajectory in interaction with his/her environment. Language learners develop multiple scale identities through the lower or higher scale-level responses they engage in with their environment. They create coherence in their lives through the continuity of their engagement with their bodies, with material objects, tools, and signs which nurture memory and the acquisition of contextual repertoires appropriate for various ages and various environmental conditions.

Part II: *Language Development as Mediated, Social Semiotic Activity* deals with first and second language acquisition as socialization into communities of practice through the mediation of material signs. In Chapter 4, Elinor Ochs uses her extensive research in developmental pragmatics and child language socialization to examine the case of two autistic children: Erin, learning how to "play softball" and Karl, learning how to do math. Ochs shows how Erin and Karl and the people around them use language and other symbolic tools to construct social situations, and to develop the ability to signal the actions they are performing, the stances they are displaying, the social identities they put forward, and the activities in which they are engaged. Failure to relate actions to stances, or to associate actions and stances with particular social identities, leads to miscommunication and, ultimately, to developmental dysfunction.

In Chapter 5, Ron Scollon uses an utterance by a one-year-old baby, Brenda, to problematize what it means to speak a "language." He builds on Suzanne Scollon's distinction between langue, idiolect, and speech community. Langue denotes the closed rule-based system equated with such labels as "Japanese" or "French;" idiolect refers to the full linguistic ability of the person, including the ability to translate from one language to another; speech community includes the histories of the various languages in use at the time in the community, including, for instance, the ability of interlocutors to each speak a different *langue*, but to understand the other's language. This distinction forms the basis for Scollon's model of mediated discourse analysis which includes objectivized, rule-based structures of systems of representation, practice-based structures of the habitus, and the dialectical interactions between them in social action.

In Chapter 6, Leo van Lier lays out his ecological–semiotic view of SLA. He first debunks traditional views of language as a collection of atomistic objects to be transmitted through schooling. Drawing on work done in psychology (Gibson, Vygotsky), philosophy of language (Bakhtin), and semiotics (C. S. Peirce), he argues for a view of language as a semiotic activity, i.e. a nonlinear, emergent process of meaning-making, based on the relationality between signs and the triadic interaction between the self, the other, and the environment, resulting in various processes of sign making (semiosis). What learners are exposed to is not "input," but "affordances," from which they select those that best fit their experience, and the activity in which they are engaged, according to the three basic principles of meaning making: mutuality/reciprocity, indexicality, and predication.

Part III: *Discourse Alignments and Trajectories in Institutional Settings* addresses issues of power and control in the regulation of institutional discourse, i.e. in historically bounded communities like universities and medical schools. Because signs, as nonarbitrary artifacts, are created by human motives and goals, their use is inevitably embroiled in conflicts of interest, status, and social face.

In Chapter 7, James Lantolf and Patricia Genung analyze in detail the complex case study of P.G., a learner of Chinese at an American university, using an activity theoretical framework. They show convincingly how students' and teachers' motives, goals, and behaviors are dialectically related to material conditions, which in turn determine roles and identities. The conflict over which discourse community teacher and student are expected to belong to, or, rather, their simultaneous membership in various, conflicting discourse communities, created material conditions that resignified P.G.'s motivation, and ultimately perpetuated the material conditions against which she had originally rebelled.

Chapter 8, by Srikant Sarangi and Celia Roberts, examines the misalignments at the discourse level between examiners and examinee during gatekeeping encounters. Candidates in the oral examinations at the Royal College of General Practitioners are expected to orient strategically to three different modes of talk – institutional, professional, and personal experience – corresponding to three different roles and identities that they are expected to put forth depending on the place and value of the questions in the unfolding discourse. For a non-native speaker of English, learning to manage the institutional activity of the gatekeeping interview is a far more complex achievement than simply acquiring the proper linguistic proficiency. It is a truly ecological feat.

Part IV: *Classroom Rituals and Their Ecologies* deals with the delicate ecology of the foreign language classroom. In Chapter 9, Jet van Dam uses Goffman's framework of interaction ritual to document in exquisite detail how a classroom community of practice is made to emerge in the first lesson on the first day of an English class. Through a sophisticated balancing of frames, footings, and face-work, Frederick, Hans, and the other participants in the "language game" of the classroom co-construct the ecological environment that will help them enact their respective roles as teacher and students over the course of the school year. Here, the attention to face and to the ecological equilibrium it requires serves to mediate between language acquisition and language socialization in the classroom.

The last chapter, by Anne Bannink, returns to the dilemma, stated at the beginning of the book by Diane Larsen-Freeman, of language acquisition versus language socialization, but this time in the form of the fundamental paradox of the language classroom. This paradox can be formulated in the following way: How can the teacher "plan" creativity and unpredictability, even in a communicatively oriented classroom? How can students learn to speak informally and genuinely in the formal, artificial setting of the classroom? How can they both talk spontaneously, and talk reflectively about talk? Using Goffman's interactional analysis, Bannink shows how these paradoxes play themselves out on the grid of turns-at-talk, participant roles, and discourse levels. These discourse features form the ecosystem that both enables and constrains what we call the lesson.

The general ecological perspective proposed in this book strives to encompass the totality of the relationships that a learner, as a living organism, entertains with all aspects of his/her environment. As such, it is a **relational** "way of seeing" that enables researchers and practitioners to account for phenomena that would otherwise go unnoticed or unaccounted for. But it also questions traditional notions of language acquisition research, like "linguistic code," and, in language socialization, notions like "stages" of development or "rule-based" behaviors. As such, it is a **reflexive** way of seeing, which takes into account the spatially and historically contingent way in which researchers and teachers relate to themselves and their environment as they study language development. That double stance of relationality and reflexivity is an eminently **phenomenological stance**. Ecumenical in its cross-disciplinary embrace, microscopic in its attention to detail, it strives to encompass phenomena on multiple scales, both global and local, both universal and particular, without losing sight of who does the seeing, the embracing, the encompassing, and against which horizon of expectations.

The phenomenological stance

The phenomenological tradition of thought was evoked several times during the discussions (see *Commentaries*, this volume).[2] A branch of philosophy dating back to the German philosopher Edmund Husserl (1859–1938), phenomenology strives to understand the world from the phenomena of local experience as seen from the perspective of the participants in relation to others' perceptions and experiences, and in locally contingent contexts, not through pre-established objective categories. Indeed, Husserl's concept of the "lifeworld," taken up later by Schutz (see p. 12), served in his mind as the very basis of scientific inquiry. Schieffelin and Ochs (1986) have acknowledged the contributions that phenomenologists like Berger and Luckman, Ricoeur, and Schutz have made to language socialization research, as well as ethnomethodologists like Mehan and Garfinkel who work in the phenomenological tradition. Several authors in this volume draw explicitly or implicitly on this tradition. Jonathan Leather's "phenomenological phonology" (Chapter 2) studies the acquisition of speech in a multilingual society by "factor[ing] into modeling of the acquisition process *the situated real-world experience of the acquirer*" (my emphasis). Jay Lemke's multiscale model of development (Chapter 3) proposes to push the notion of "contingent context" a step further and replace objective meaning categories by "meaning-by-degree" and "multiple time scales" of development. Other chapters, like those by Scollon, van Lier, van Dam, and Bannink draw implicitly on phenomenological thought through their conviction that meaning emerges from a person's engagement with the world, through "perception-in-action" (van Lier), and that language as a social semiotic has a constitutive role in this process.

Much of phenomenological thought in the twentieth century has been of the philosophical theoretical kind, without any of the empirical methodology that would make it researchable by social scientists. Ethnographers like Elinor Ochs (*Commentaries* I) and sociolinguists like Ben Rampton (*Commentaries* IV) are therefore understandably nervous at the risk of having to sacrifice methodological rigor for theoretical unity. Chris Candlin expresses doubts that any one phenomenological theory can bring together "as in a coherent system" all the ecological models proposed in this volume (*Commentaries* I). Indeed, the hallmark of an ecological perspective is differentiation, diversity, and adaptability, not one overarching theory. In no case do any of the authors affiliate themselves with the full phenomenological tradition of philosophers like Husserl, Heidegger, or Bakhtin. Rather, their contributions to this volume represent attempts to grapple with the tension between the need to stay rigorously close to the ground and attend to the minutiae of their local data, and the need to adopt, if not an overarching interpretive system, at least a "phenomenological stance" to make sense of these data. In the spirit of Stephen Jay Gould invoked at the beginning of this introduction, they are anxious to have access both to the facts and to a metaphor that will make sense of the facts. I would like to suggest that the tension between fact and metaphor is at the very core of any ecological perspective on language development. It is reflected in the sometimes passionate tone of the *Commentaries*.

What does a phenomenological stance consist of? Three social scientists in the phenomenological tradition offer a range of constructs that seem to underlie the authors' common stance *vis-à-vis* language development: Merleau-Ponty (1945), Schutz and Luckmann (1973), and Goffman (1974, 1981). For the influence of these scholars on the study of language as communicative practice, see Hanks (1996).[3]

In his *Phenomenology of perception* ([1945] 1962), the French phenomenologist Marcel Merleau-Ponty (1908–1961), an admirer of Husserl, takes the view that we cannot know anything but through a **corporeal schema** that is the convergence of our body as vantage point of perception and the world as perceived and mediated through the body. Our body is the anchor point or "indexical ground" (Hanks 1992) in reference to which participants position themselves in social encounters through the use of indexical expressions like "here," "there," "I," or "you." It provides the fundamental context or ground of ecological validity for the acquisition of language and knowledge. The models proposed by Larsen-Freeman, van Lier, or Leather (this volume) take a dynamic perspective on events that are experienced from the inside as ongoing processes, not as *a priori* concepts, which cannot be known separately from our perception of their emergence in the ongoing flow of experience. For example, in order to understand what happens on the first day of an English class, we have to understand the corporeal constraints of the imposed seating plan, which might separate or bring together friends and strangers on the same bench; the two large pillars in the middle of the room that might obstruct the view; the potential drowsiness of the students after lunch; the loudness or softness of voices; as well as the anticipations and apprehensions associated with the first day of class (see Chapter 9). We have to understand these constraints but, at the same time, understand that they do not necessarily determine the outcome of the lesson. What is important is not the constraints, but our engagement with them.

Our corporeal schema, which enables us to understand and communicate with the world, emerges from our engagement with the world, in **activity**. In this volume, Ochs, Scollon, Lantolf and Genung, van Lier, and Sarangi and Roberts take activity (e.g. Erin's learning to play baseball, three-month-old Brenda handing an object to her mother) as their unit of analysis, not their words or utterances; they conceive of language as emerging from a person's situatedness or participation in a physical and social world. This engagement constructs the **phenomenal field** that includes our senses, perceptions, and emotions, and the world as it is perceived by us and others. To speak is to take a position in a phenomenal field. This field is not prepackaged in cultural categories that pre-exist our perception, like *a priori* rules of a game; rather, it is constantly under revision, adjusted and readjusted to the indeterminacies of our language, the surplus and deficiency of our meanings, the ambiguities of our silences and actions.

A phenomenological stance is more concerned with describing the world in all its variability than in uncovering its objective laws, because the worlds it observes are **intentional worlds** i.e. they are perceived and mediated through human emotions, desires, and value judgments, and thereby are not predictable like physical worlds.[4] Ochs remarks that in communities of practice, events and behaviors are "weighted," i.e. valorized or given saliency *vis-à-vis* other, less valued, phenomena, and assessed as good or bad, beneficial or detrimental. If, as van Lier argues, the traditional notion of "input" should be replaced by that of "affordances," it is because of the phenomenological view that certain elements in the environment have been made salient, relevant to the personal experience of the learners, for whom they "afford," i.e. yield, meaning. As shown in Chapter 7, foreign language learners do not just learn the language, they are also constantly engaged in judging the relevance, validity, pertinence, or usefulness of this or that bit of knowledge, this or that assignment, thus staking out the phenomenological field of their learning endeavor. Personal judgment and a sense of what is good and beautiful enter into this endeavor and into the subjectivity of the learner. The fact that this subjectivity is by definition an intersubjectivity (Merleau-Ponty 1945:415) (i.e. we can only know who we are and what we are worth through the eyes of the others) finds its illustration in a teacher's efforts to make an autistic child, Karl, see himself as a competent "math student," despite his protests to the contrary (Chapter 4).

The rules that human beings seem to have an urge to create in order to encode individual and group behaviors have the purpose of regulating what Merleau-Ponty calls *l'espace vécu*, or lived space, by stabilizing social organization and ensuring institutional continuity. These are precisely the rules that autistic children like the ones in Ochs' study both need and ignore. They originate, according to Merleau-Ponty, in the fundamental moral nature of human perception that relates us to ourselves through the judgments we make about the physical and social places we are in. The chapters in this volume give many examples of the way knowledge of ourselves and others is **mediated** by this lived space, and by the material artifacts we create, and which should be seen as an extension of our bodies. For example, the orientation of the baseball bat mediates the orientation of one autistic child to the social organization of the game, the alignment of another with the math set in front of him mediates the institutional identity offered him by the school (Chapter 4), the timing of a musical spelling jingle in an English class (Chapter 9) mediates the acquisition of English orthography.

Typical of Merleau-Ponty's theory is the notion of a **horizon of non-actualized but potential phenomenal fields** that arise out of the reflexive activity of human consciousness. Awareness and reflexivity are built into the phenomenological project, and they form a recurrent theme of the *Commentaries* in this volume: the concern about being trapped in our research metaphors because they have become invisible; the awareness of the political implications of certain scientific research traditions, of institutional power; the plea for ecological humility, for retaining a critical awareness of one's own metaphors, and most of all for remaining open to seeing things from different angles and on different scales – all these ecological aspects of language development research are very much in the phenomenological tradition of Merleau-Ponty and others. The horizon of potential phenomenal fields extends to the work of memory and the imagination in understanding human activity. The teacher who has to bootstrap a classroom culture on the first day of an English class (Chapter 9) has to tap the good or bad memories of prior first classes experienced by her students; she has to create with them an imagined world of playfulness and collaborative learning. Teachers who teach to their students' potential rather than to their actual abilities (Chapter 10) find ways of teaching to that horizon through reflexive action research.

To understand the role of memory and imagination in language development I now turn to another phenomenologist who has greatly influenced the ecological perspectives taken in this book. Alfred Schutz (1898–1959) was also an admirer of Husserl, who offered to make him his assistant before Schutz decided to leave Austria for America in 1939. In *The Structures of the Life-World* (Schutz and Luckmann 1973), Schutz asks the same question as Merleau-Ponty: How can we know the world and ourselves? If we are to ground our understanding of phenomena without subjecting them to pre-existing categories of analysis, how are we to know which phenomena are relevant and worthy of our attention? Schutz brings to phenomenology the idea of **typification** and relevance. We perceive things in the world as instances of *types*, which are the result of sedimented individual experiences preserved in embodied memory. What we call *frame of reference* is the sum total of typifications, that, when they are distributed among members of a language community, form a *stock of knowledge*, a background of ready-made meanings or categories of "common sense" that enable us, as Garfinkel has shown, to interpret the usual goings-on of everyday life and to notice when someone breaches the participants' unspoken expectations (Garfinkel 1967). The categories of common sense form the implicit playing field for interaction, the vantage point from where shared social meanings are built through *indexicality* in language. Indexicality, in turn, makes *intersubjectivity* possible, i.e. "[the ability for] separate individuals to know or act within a common world" (Duranti and Goodwin 1992:27). In cases where interlocutors lack a common indexical ground of reference or are unable to co-construct one, as in the medical board's examination described in Chapter 8, it is difficult to establish a sphere of intersubjectivity, and the encounter is likely to end in failure.

However, it is not always clear which stock of common knowledge is relevant to a specific situation, for example, Which stock of knowledge should the researcher draw from to understand the predicament of a learner of Chinese who finds herself at odds with her teacher's methodology (Chapter 7)? The knowledge of the university as academic institution or that of the research field of SLA as a disciplinary institution? And which knowledge is necessary to understand the Chinese teacher: her experience as a native Chinese? Her expertise as a teacher? Her training in the audiolingual method? Another example: What knowledge of a candidate's life history is relevant to describe how this candidate understands the medical board examination? (Chapter 8). Her experience as a student, as a researcher, as a nurse practitioner? Which institutional scale is relevant to her in this situation: the academic institution and its testing procedures, or the institution of medicine, the discipline *per se*? And, from the perspective of the candidate, which knowledge should she activate at any given time? As Bateson (1979:105) would say, which differences make a difference?

For Schutz, knowledge (and the projected knowledge we call imagination) is always social and contextual. There is no knowledge without a knower, and what makes a difference is the **relevance** of the phenomena for the potential knower. Schutz identifies three ways of relating the perceived world to a person's perception of relevance: thematic relevance links objects in the world to a person's thoughts or themes at the time of perception; interpretational relevance links them to a person's beliefs and world views; motivational relevance links phenomena to a person's needs and purposes for action. A language learner finds the class relevant if it resonates with his/her beliefs about language acquisition and her reasons for learning the language. However, the same object might be relevant to a person in many different, and sometimes conflictual, ways. These different relevances compete for the person's attention and value judgments and enter into competition with other people's relevances. For example, a pedagogy that might be common sense for students, based on their sedimented memories of past experiences, might not be common sense for teachers, based on institutional frames of reference that are at odds with students' expectations (see Chapter 7).

Schutz inspired much of the work of the third phenomenologist, Erving Goffman, whose influence on the chapters in this volume is undeniable, especially from his books *Frame Analysis* (1974) and *Forms of Talk* (1981), two collections of essays on the social organization of talk. Goffman, observing how social space is organized and reorganized in verbal encounters, asks the question: "What is it that's going on there?" (1974:8). His crucial notions – framing, keying, footing, and alignment – are all ways in which participants in an interaction position themselves *vis-à-vis* others and see the world according to those positionings. In a phenomenological sense, such spatial, topological metaphors (even keying; see below) are an attempt to understand the *espace vécu* from the perspective of the participants rather than from some pre-established typology of words or behaviors.

The first notion, **framing**, is borrowed from Gregory Bateson's famous 1955 essay reprinted in "Theory of Play and Fantasy" (1972:177), where Bateson, visiting the Fleishacker Zoo in San Francisco, observed that otters not only fight with each other but also play at fighting. Which signal do they give one another that this is play and not fight? This kind of signal, or schema, within which the activity is to be interpreted, Goffman and Bateson call "frame." Frames, or schemata of interpretation, give meaning to what would otherwise be meaningless events. They offer "guided doings."

Within a given activity, frames can be "broken" and shifted, as when an otter ceases to fight and starts playing at fighting. Such shifts are called **keying**.

> A given activity ... is transformed into something patterned on this activity but seen by the participants to be something quite else. The process of transcription can be called keying (Goffman 1974:44).

Although the analogy is, according to Goffman, "roughly musical," the definition is again spatial, as it transposes one activity onto another level of musical notation. It is the same fight, but transcribed into a parody of a fight. Keyings are subject to rekeyings, or transcriptions in a different key; activities can exhibit multiple layers of keyings or "laminations." For instance, a medical board's examination question like: "How would you deal with the problem of teenage pregnancy?" (Chapter 8) may require several keyings at once: a display of academic knowledge, evidence of experiential expertise, and demonstration of professional know-how.

When a given activity, one already meaningful in terms of some primary framework, such as asking a student his name in class within a serious learning frame, is rekeyed into a different activity, e.g. through parody, it is a sign that the speaker has taken a different role *vis-à-vis* the other participants in the class (Chapter 9; see also Sullivan 2000). A change in frame can be marked by changes in the way the participants index time and space, as well as their own subject position, in the interaction. It can also accompany a change in **footing**, i.e. "a change in the **alignment** we take up to ourselves and the others present as expressed in the way we manage the production or reception of an utterance" (Goffman 1981:128). Speakers can take various footings, depending on whether they simply animate other people's words (animator), speak their own words (author), or speak as the voice of an institution (principal). The consequences of misalignments due to mismatches in indexicality are dramatically illustrated in Chapter 8.

Shifting frames and footings are crucial to understanding humor, play, formality, and informality in communicative events and learning situations. This is precisely what autistic children cannot do, and why they have such difficulty in learning to play softball or math through verbal events. Language acquisition and socialization are about navigating through often conflicting institutional and domestic spaces. The ability to shift frames can be crucial to learner development, as shown in Chapter 10 when students in an English class are prompted to shift frame from a role-play ordering Peking duck in a restaurant, to a discussion among themselves regarding the pronunciation of "Peking duck," to a public report to the class on what they have ordered.

The phenomenological stance in social science research discussed above provides the implicit (or sometimes explicit) underpinning for the ecological perspective on language development offered in this book. Indeed, ecology, understood merely as the interaction of an organism with its environment, does not in itself include human moral and esthetic judgment, values, beliefs, and subjectivity. But the concern for ecology, born of the human sense of responsibility for the ecological equilibrium of the planet, does include a moral imperative to protect and conserve the Earth on which we live. The chapters in this volume have explicitly or implicitly conceived of an ecological approach to studying language acquisition and language socialization and how these behaviors and events interact with various human and natural environments, not merely as the ethnographic, descriptive recording of verbal behaviors and events. They are also inspired by a phenomenological stance that accounts for how humans make meaning of these interactions and take responsibility for their actions.

An ecological perspective on language development

The contributors to this volume have attempted to answer three main questions: What conceptual models best capture the ecological nature of language learning? What research approaches are most likely to illuminate the relationship between language and social structure? How is educational success defined for both language socialization and language acquisition? Although the authors have found it difficult to keep these questions separate, especially the first two, I will consider each one separately here for clarity of exposition.

1. What conceptual models best capture the ecological nature of language learning?

Complex, nonlinear, relational models

Contrary to the linear models of language acquisition used both by SLA research and language education, which are predicated on a cause-and-effect relation between input and output, between teaching and learning, the models proposed in this volume all view language development as a complex, nonlinear system. Chaos/complexity theory, optimality theory and connectionism, ecosocial dynamics, dissipative systems theory, activity theory, and interaction theory all espouse the view that new order can emerge from disorder (Larsen-Freeman, van Dam), effects are not proportional to nor directly attributable to causes (Lantolf and Genung, Bannink), meaning emerges at multiple levels of detail (Ochs, Sarangi and Roberts), on multiple timescales (Lemke), and in multiple semiotic and idiolectal forms (van Lier, Leather, Scollon). These models all stress the **relationality** of hierarchical organizational levels, from the emotional and motivational make-up of the individual learner, to the social/professional community of language users, to the larger institutional framework endowed with institutional memory, power, and authority.

Interaction and emergence

The models proposed here each have their own ways of explaining the various levels on which language, learners, and language learning environments interact. In the complex, nonlinear systems of *chaos/ complexity theory* (Chapter 1), only **the interactions** of the individual components are meaningful, not the components themselves. For example, the failure of the candidate in the oral examination described in Chapter 8 is not due to her deficient English, even though English is not her native language, but, rather, to the position and the choice of her modes of talk *in relation to* the examiners' questions and to her prior answers. **Fractal patterns** replicate phenomena and events at various levels of scale. For example, in Chapter 2, the two different lexical and phonological variants used by the six-year-old Dominican child Alvin to ask his mother why they don't have a car ("vwati") and by his 13-year-old brother Gregory to brag about his dream car ("motoka") play out on the microlevel of utterances the sociolinguistic dimensions of lexical variation in Kwéyòl in Dominica, and show the symbolic value of English to Dominican Kwéyòl speakers. Local phenomena interact in the inorganic, organic, biological, psychological, or social spheres and **emerge** as global patterns. For example, the exaggerated elongation of Gregory's [a] vowel in "motoka," indexing locally a Caribbean English parody of a British English stereotype of a "class" vowel, emerges as a global historic pattern of distance to the ex-colonizer of this Eastern Caribbean island state.

Constraints and equilibrium rather than rules

Grammar and phonology in such systems are both rigid enough to ensure stability, continuity and intelligibility from context to context, and flexible enough to adapt to innovation and to the unpredictability and ambiguity of new contexts. This view of grammar and phonology is well captured by *optimality theory* (Chapter 2), which is based on **constraints** rather than rules. Complex systems, like learners in complex learning environments, do the best they can under the circumstances within violable constraints, and settle into a temporary equilibrium. For example, in Chapter 9, Hans responds to the teacher's prompt "What's your name?" with a simple "Hans," a correct but inappropriately short response, that puts the ongoing classroom dialogue off balance. By correcting himself, but at the same time metacommunicating about his "error" through parody: "O-oh! My name is Hans," he manages to reestablish the delicate face-saving equilibrium of the classroom. Conversely, the teacher on this first day of a language class has to establish the linguistic and other constraints that will bring the potential community of practice into an equilibrium propitious to learning in future lessons. Through careful attention to the abilities and expectations of the students, she can model constraints which will allow for both predictability and innovation within the system. The situated, real-world experience of the acquirer is thus factored into the modeling of the acquisition process.

Mental processes themselves are, according to another ecological theory, *connectionism* (see Chapter 2), the gradual, experience-driven adjustment of connection weights between levels of "distributed" processing, i.e. processing that not only takes place between the "input" and the "output" in the individual's mind, but is distributed across neurons in an individual's mind and across individuals. Adaptive responses to changing inputs have the appearance of being rule-governed, but in reality they do not embody any explicit rules, only constraints on what is biologically feasible, socially acceptable, and politically legitimate in a particular context. The acquirer is approached as a complex adaptive system in his/her social environment, neither completely random nor completely deterministic. This is nowhere better illustrated than in the case of Erin, the autistic child learning to play softball in Chapter 4. By taking the perspective of the child, a developmental pragmatics model of language development is able to situate language practices in the concrete real-world experience of the child. It can show how veteran and novice participants coordinate modes of communication, actions, bodies, objects, and the built environment to enhance their joint knowledge and skills. Erin only appears to learn the rules of softball; in reality, she wouldn't be able to "play" softball if she had only learned the rules. She also needs to learn to adapt her responses to the totality of her environment, including her teacher and her peers.

The representation–action continuum

Thus, in a phenomenological view of language acquisition, representations are not the basis of social processes but their product (see Brenda's socialization into the "Japanese" language in Chapter 5). Traditional models maintain a strict distinction between universalistic or objectivistic analyses of representation and "analysis in use," i.e. a distinction between systems of representations (e.g. the Japanese language) and social organization (e.g., Japanese society, culture). An ecological perspective considers knowledge and awareness, not as being exclusively propositional and representational, but, rather, as being motivated, action driven, the motives frequently being established in the process of the activity itself (see also Chapter 7). If we take a fractal view of learning environments as complex systems, we can no longer think in categorial terms – here acquisition, there socialization. Rather, as Lemke argues in Chapter 3, we are led to view both linguistic systems and their use on a continuum operating on multiple timescales.

Multiple timescales

By introducing the notion of **timescale**, ecologically oriented research recognizes not only that linguistic phenomena are inextricably linked to other, nonlinguistic, semiotic systems (e.g. Chapter 6), but that they are also indissociable from an individual's memory of past phenomena and his/her anticipation of future ones; they retain the sedimented traces of experiences that a person's body has given meaning and relevance to. Learner development is not run by clock time, but by many different timescales cycling at various rates (school calendar, family gatherings calendar, family deaths, births, and marriages calendar, personal retrospective calendar, calendar of encounters with personal successes, failures, disillusions). People live on different timescales: on the immediately present timescale of an unfolding conversational interaction, people display their affective sensibility to language use. On the longer-term timescale of their professional or social life, they display their ability to deal with language in multi-lingual and multi-idiolectal situations, they make meaningful use of their code-switching and code-mixing skills, and their functional integration of languages, dialects, and sociolects. On the longest timescale of their entire lifetime, they show evidence of multi-lingualism, linguistic diversity, and style.

Hierarchies of organizational levels

Ecological models of language development view language learning systems as a blend of social semiotic and ecosystem dynamics, or "ecosocial dynamics" (Chapter 3). As the hybrid activation of linguistic and social systems, semiotic practices are conceptualized as material processes at various low and high scale levels. For example, candidates to formal examinations, who have been trained into a linear view of learning as input/output, fail when they are expected to display a complex, multilayered response to an examiner's questions (Chapter 8). What an ecological research perspective does is shift from an organism-centered to a multiple-timescale system view of development. Where we are used to seeing a learner's development as that of an individual inscribed within the 12 weeks of a semester, the 50 minutes of a lesson, or the 30 minutes of an exam, a multiscale model of development enables educators to imagine and to address the competent adult in the autistic child, and the competent physician in the medical student – focusing, as Merleau-Ponty would say, on their horizon of potential abilities.

The dissipative system model (i.e. a system not in equilibrium) proposed in Chapter 5 takes into account the fact that systems fluctuate internally due to all sorts of external factors precisely because they are open, or "dissipative," not closed systems. For example, instead of seeing languages as **langues**, i.e. closed, rule-based standardized systems, which operate quite independently of their sociocultural and biological environments, Scollon considers a language as an **idiolect**, i.e. the whole language of the experience of the person, including the ability to translate from one language to another. An idiolect is a system far from equilibrium, because it carries with it traces of past experiences and their emotional resonances that have gone into the constitution of the speaker as a subject (Benveniste 1966; Kramsch forthcoming). For example, in Chapter 9, when Freek answers "My name is Frederic," with a low fall, caricatured British voice and phonology, to the prompt by the teacher, he does not merely produce a sentence that conforms to some stable rules of English grammar and phonology. He injects his own destabilizing humor into it. As W. B. Yeats' poem suggests, the dancer is inseparable from the dance (see *Commentaries* I).[5] One could go even further and ask, Is the English that Freek is speaking: "English"? Or a parody of English? Or Freek's own idiolect? In Chapter 5, why is Japanese *chodai* (English boat), said by one-year-old Brenda, a "Japanese" word, rather than part of an idiolect shared by Ron Scollon, Brenda, and Brenda's mother? As suggested in Chapter 3, what linguists call "language" might be too narrow a definition: it has to be defined more functionally out of the flow and patternings of communicative–interactive–motor behavior and the multifarious modes of meaning making of everyday life.

Mediation through material, social, and discourse processes

One of the most important insights that ecological models of language development can offer is the concept of **mediation**. Because, as we have seen, meaning lies in relationships between artifacts, persons, and events, not in the objects themselves, language, as one of many semiotic systems, emerges from semiotic activity through affordances brought forth by active engagement with material, social, and discourse processes (cf. Vygotsky 1978; van Lier 2000). Rather than conceive of teaching and learning as the transmission and reception of a closed system of knowledge, ecological models of language development see it as an open process mediated by various semiotic tools in various activities.

Activity theory, discussed in Chapter 7, explains that understanding and communication are constructed through social relationships at work in the community and through engagement with culturally mediated artifacts, as well as through the life history of individuals and the history of particular psychological functions over relatively brief spans of time, such in classroom language learning. Lantolf and Genung show how activity theory can accommodate issues of power and conflicts of authority in the course of this mediation. Scollon's model of mediated discourse analysis proposed in Chapter 5 identifies five basic conceptual tools with which to capture the notion of mediation in language development: mediated action, social practice, site of engagement, mediational means (physical, external material objects by which we take action), and nexus of practice. The last three chapters in this volume give convincing illustrations of the value of Scollon's model to account for what is required to become a competent member of a particular institutional community.

Mediated action leaves space for newness and transformation. For example, unplanned activities may often be more successful in the classroom than planned ones, because students interact more actively with affordances that occur in the interstices of planned lessons than with goal-oriented exercises (Chapter 10). Both Larsen-Freeman and van Lier point to the transformational potential of ecological systems. Learners can learn things that were unintended by the teacher by engaging with their primary symbolic system – shapes and sounds of language, words on the page of a textbook, and with the other material constraints of the classroom.

In all these studies, an ecological research approach resists the reduction of symbolic or semiotic activity to the analysis of systems of representation, as well as the reduction of language to a social habitus. Scollon, in particular, argues for a dialectical interaction of representations and activities within an open systems model. Language, he argues, is representation and action, associated with emotions, memories, and imaginations that need to be documented and described.

2. What research approaches are most likely to illuminate the relationship between language and social structure?

Research sites

Many of the researchers in this volume seem to favor research sites that offer insights into border crossings of various sorts: a multilingual Dominican child navigating across various idiolects (Chapter 2), a rite of membership into a softball-playing school community (Chapter 4), a one-year-old child's first crossing into a recognizable standard national language (Chapter 5), a U.S. army colonel becoming a language learner again (Chapter 7), a gatekeeping examination or rite of passage into the medical corps (Chapter 8), a lesson on the threshold of a new term (Chapter 9), the transformation of pedagogical failure into pedagogical success (Chapter 10). Each of these studies focuses on the potential paradoxes and ambiguities of border crossings between various discourse worlds and how the participants negotiate these paradoxes. This is not surprising, since an ecological perspective on language development opens up possibilities of embracing the paradoxes, contradictions, and conflicts inherent in any situation involving semiotic activity, rather than rushing to solve them. The role of research is to identify and describe the affordances that emerge from these very paradoxes. If, in addition, the teacher is herself the researcher, as in Chapter 10, action research can serve as yet another source of affordances in the ecologically open system of teaching and reflection on teaching.

The evidence: interdisciplinary, multimodal, multiscalar

Ecologically oriented research is by nature interdisciplinary, multi-modal, and multiscalar. Interdisciplinarity is apparent in the variety of the fields from which the authors of this book draw their models: physics (chaos/complexity theory, dissipative systems theory), psychology (connectionism), biology and physiology, semiotics, social psychology, philosophy, sociology, and ethnomethodology. Ecology-conscious research is also multimodal. Many of the authors consider linguistic evidence to be embedded in and supported by other signifying material (gesturing, drawing, facial expression, objects of joint attention, etc.), in which body, object, and language all interact. Finally, as we saw in the previous section, all the contributors to this volume advocate using, and use themselves, methods of research that strive to account for multiple scales of phenomena, captured normally by various disciplines, over longer periods of time or across various levels of complexity. For example, Ochs' study is a long-term, rigorous ethnographic study over several years, "getting down to children's level and viewing situations as they do, stepping into their shadows," trying to understand children as social creatures, i.e. as members of culture. Evidence is sought at various levels of perception, action, discourse, and beliefs. Many of these beliefs are sedimented traces of past behaviors in present behaviors. Chapter 7 offers a good illustration of the benefit of going beyond the here-and-now data and considering the traces of past behaviors and experiences as they are reflected in the present social structure. The expectations of P.G. in her role as Chinese language student echo, in increasing length of timescale, her expectations as a researcher in applied linguistics and those she held as a colonel in the US Army. When these multiple expectations are thwarted, she feels naturally reduced to a unidimensional social actor – a reduction that does justice neither to her as a student nor to her as a competent researcher and person-in-command.

Units and tools of analysis and interpretation

To account for these multiple levels, the unit of analysis has to be not a component, but a fractal of the larger complex system itself. However, the term "unit of analysis" is not really appropriate for an approach that attempts to distance itself from that of the experimental sciences. It is better replaced here by "focal scale." For the authors of this volume, the focal scale is the social activity in which more or less experienced persons participate. It is generally studied over long periods of time, using micro-observations, video recordings, descriptions, and analyses.

The elicitation tools advocated here range from collaborative research practices to activity-based research (Chapter 7), action research (Chapter 10), diaries (Chapter 7), introspection (Chapters 7, 10), ethnographies (Chapter 4). They advocate using a wide range of analyses: ethnographic analysis (Chapter 7) semiotic analysis (Chapter 6), discourse and interaction analysis (Chapters 4, 8–10), and even post-structuralist, cultural studies analysis (Chapter 8). For example, ethnographic discourse analysis, using indexicality, footing, and face can signal alignments and misalignments, whether in learning how to play softball, orchestrating English lessons, or displaying one's knowledge in important examinations. Ecologically oriented methodologies are typically descriptive, analytical, and interpretive. They recognize the rhetorical bias built into ethnographic reports – what James Clifford (1988) calls "the predicament of culture." By not wanting to constrain the evidence, their problem will always be a problem of relevance (see Schutz, above), hence the ever greater need to make explicit the subject position of the researcher.

Ecological research approaches have in common that they resist the usual dichotomies, or clear-cut categories of meaning used by traditional approaches, i.e. individual versus social, representation versus action, not knowing versus knowing, non-native versus native speaker. Rather, words like "continuum," "dialectics," "hybridity," "affordance," and "mediation" are attempts to focus on relationships and contingencies, not on objects, on differences in degree, not in clear-cut categories. But such new metaphors risk creating their own obscurities: How are we to conceive of a "continuum" across multiple timescales? What provides the continuity of our engagement with the world? How is knowledge acquired in one situation or activity transferrable to another (Kirschner and Whitson 1998)? What exactly is the meaning of "mediation" if used as a synonym for "engagement"? How is the notion of "timescale" realized linguistically in discourse?

As van Lier argues in Chapter 6, ecological approaches require a great deal more conceptual clarification than traditional approaches, precisely because the language of research is traditionally categorial. They require also the location of new forms of (relevant) evidence through description and analysis, the elaboration of contextual research procedures, and plausible documentation. The chapters in the present volume constitute an agenda for future research in this regard.

3. How is educational success defined for language socialization and language acquisition?

Traditionally, language acquisition defines success as the ability of the learner to produce target-like forms of the language, in all dimensions of communicative competence. Language socialization, by contrast, defines success as the ability to communicate in the language of a particular community and to act according to its norms. In an effort to reach an ecological perspective on both acquisition and socialization and to avoid restrictive notions like "target" and "norm," the authors of this volume measure success in various ways. In all cases, success is defined not only by external measures of individual achievement but also according to subjective and relational criteria.

Success is aligning oneself in the social space

For Leather (Chapter 2), success in language development is the ability to locate oneself through one's lexical and phonological choices in a multidimensional social space, and to exploit the symbolic value of various linguistic repertoires for one's own "profit of distinction" (Bourdieu 1991:18). For example, success for Alvin and Gregory is the fit between their phonology and their ability to both meet and make fun of the expectations of their bilingual and diglossic environment. For Ochs (Chapter 4), success for autistic children is the ability to link linguistic forms to stances and acts, and to activities and identities. In the case of the autistic child Karl, it means displaying a certain type of stance toward doing math and linking this stance to an identity as "a math person." For Sarangi and Roberts (Chapter 8), success in an important oral examination is the ability to not only display linguistic and communicative competencies in generic terms, but also to perform in institutionally and professionally ratified ways which align with the structure and rhetoric of the activity.

Success is using one's full semiotic potential

For Lemke (Chapter 3), success is the ability to use language across the full range of human timescales, including the learner's comparative ability in L1 and L2, and the ability to mix or to switch between languages. Van Lier (Chapter 6) defines success as the ability to resonate to and use language in the full range of semiotic activity, to express individual and mutual feelings, to index relationships, to predicate thoughts and representations. For Lantolf and Genung (Chapter 7), the notion of success itself is relative. Their example of the discrepancy between "doing–learning–Chinese" and "learning–Chinese" shows that activities and their outcomes are always embedded in relations of power and authority that are constantly challenged or accepted. Thus, institutional power defines what "success" may legitimately mean, for both learners and researchers. In the case of P.G., who was both a student and a researcher, success was doubly ambiguous. For there is a tension, inherent to academia, between the institutional structure that teaches and evaluates students, and the research community that legitimates researchers and holds them accountable intellectually. According to the criteria of the institution, P.G. had succeeded in passing the course. According to the criteria of her research community, P.G. had failed to learn Chinese.

Success is "seizing the moment" and negotiating paradoxes

For van Dam (Chapter 9), teachers and students define success as achieving a sense of community out of a diverse group of students on the first day of class. The ability of teacher and students to "seize the moment" and to make use of all the semiotic resources at their disposal (ritual, play, theatrical distance) accounts for a great deal of their sense of success. For Bannink (Chapter 10), this sense of community can only emerge from a teacher's tolerance of paradox and her ability to reflect upon it as teacher-researcher. In turn, students' success is measured by their degree of engagement in discovering unplanned affordances along the way (see Kramsch 1993).

It remains to be seen how such varied criteria of success can be accommodated within traditionally positivistic structures of education. But if, indeed, the essence of an ecological perspective on educational research is to acknowledge and live with paradoxes, one could argue, with Larsen-Freeman, that the major benefit of such a perspective is "to prevent premature closure," and to shape an attitude among teachers and researchers that there is more between heaven and earth than traditional research enables them to envisage.

Notes:

1. As Stephen Toulmin points out, the Greek root of the word *ecology* means "the science of household management" (1990:182).

2. For further readings in the phenomenological tradition and its influence on the study of language, thought, and identity, see Lee and Mandelbaum 1967; Taylor 1973, 1992; Ricoeur 1973; Kelly 2001.

3. Phenomenology is an epistemology based on phenomena (from the Greek *phainein* = to appear) rather than on noumena (from Greek *nous* = reason, mind). Whereas *noumena* are things known by reason, as they are, in their absolute truth, *phenomena* are things known by perception, as they appear, in their relative and contingent truths. Phenomenology is the philosophical study of how we come to know and understand things, based on our perception and human experience, not merely through the universal rationality of Descartes' *cogito ergo sum*. Phenomenological thought is recognizable in philosophy and literature in the work of existentialist philosophers like Martin Heidegger, Jean-Paul Sartre, Max Scheler, Hans-Georg Gadamer, Paul Ricoeur, Mikhail Bakhtin, Charles Taylor, and Ludwig Wittgenstein; of anthropologists like Gregory Bateson, Clifford Geertz, Paul Friedrich, William Hanks, and A. L. Becker; of sociologists like Maurice Merleau-Ponty, Alfred Schutz, Erving Goffman, and Thomas Luckmann; and of educational psychologists like Jerome Bruner.

4. The notion of "intentional worlds" used by Shweder (1990:24) indexes the phenomenological heritage of the new field of cultural psychology (Stigler *et al.* 1990). It is the topic of a contrastive analysis of intentionality in analytic and phenomenological philosophy by Sean Kelly (2001).

5. Merleau-Ponty (1945) shows that such a perspective has an esthetic dimension: "Esthetic perception opens in turn a new spatiality ... dance

unfolds in a space without goals and without directions, it is a suspension of our history; in dance, the subject and his world are no longer in opposition, one no longer stands out against the background of the other ..." (333; my translation).

Acknowledgments

I wish to thank Ed Bodine for thinking this introduction through with me at all stages of its development. I am grateful to Leo van Lier and Srikant Sarangi for their valuable responses to an earlier version.

References

Bateson, G. (1972) Theory of Play and Fantasy. In his *Steps to an Ecology of Mind.* New York: Ballantine.

Bateson, G. (1979) *Mind and Nature: A Necessary Unity.* New York: Bantam.

Benveniste, E. (1966) *Problèmes de linguistique générale.* Paris: Gallimard.

Bourdieu, P. (1991) *Language and Symbolic Power.* Ed. and Introd. by J.B. Thompson., trsl. by G. Raymond and M. Adamson. Cambridge: Harvard University Press.

Breen, M. and Candlin, C. (1980) The essentials of a communicative curriculum in language teaching. *Applied Linguistics* 1, 89–112.

Bronfenbrenner, U. (1979) *The Ecology of Human Development.* Cambridge: Harvard University Press.

Cicourel, A. (1992) The interpenetration of communicative contexts: examples from medical encounters. In A. Duranti and C. Goodwin (eds) *Rethinking Context: Language as an Interactive Phenomenon.* Cambridge: Cambridge University Press, pp. 291–310.

Clifford, J. (1988) On ethnographic authority. In *The Predicament of Culture.* Cambridge: Harvard University Press, pp. 21–54.

Cook, G. (2000) *Language Play, Language Learning.* Oxford: Oxford University Press.

Crystal, D. (1998) *Language Play.* Harmondsworth: Penguin.

Dunn, W. and Lantolf, J.P. (1998) "i+1" and the ZPD: incommensurable constructs, incommensurable theories. *Language Learning* 48, 411–42.

Duranti, A. and Goodwin, C. (1992) Rethinking context: An introduction. In *Rethinking Context. Language as an Interactive Phenomenon.* Cambridge: Cambridge University Press, pp. 1–42.

Ellis, R. (1987) *Second Language Acquisition in Context.* Englewood Cliffs: Prentice Hall.

Ellis, R. (1997) *Second Language Acquisition*. Oxford Introductions to Language Study. Oxford: Oxford University Press.

Firth, A. and Wagner, J. (1997) On discourse, communication, and (some) fundamental concepts in SLA research. *Modern Language Journal* 81(3), 285–300.

Garfinkel, H. (1967) *Studies in Ethnomethodology*. Englewood Cliffs, NJ: Prentice Hall.

Gibson, J.J. (1979) *The Ecological Approach to Visual Perception*. Boston: Houghton Mifflin.

Goffman, E. (1974) *Frame Analysis*. New York: Harper & Row.

Goffman, E. (1981) *Forms of Talk*. Cambridge: Harvard University Press.

Gould, S.J. (1985) For want of a metaphor. In his *The Flamingo's Smile: Reflections in Natural History*. New York: W.W. Norton, pp. 139–51.

Gumperz, J.J., Jupps, T.C. and Roberts, C. (1979) *Cross-Talk: A study of cross-cultural communication*. Havelock Centre, UK: National Centre for Industrial Language Training.

Halliday, M.A.K. (1975) *Learning to Mean: Exploration in the Development of Language*. London: Edward Arnold.

Hanks, W. (1992) The indexical ground of deictic reference. In A. Duranti and C. Goodwin (eds.), *Rethinking Context: Language as an Interactive Phenomenon*. Cambridge: Cambridge University Press, pp. 43–76.

Hanks, W. (1996) *Language and Communicative Practices*. Boulder: Westview Press.

Haugen, E. (1972) *The Ecology of Language*. Stanford: Stanford University Press.

Hymes, D. (1972) Models of the interaction of language and social life. In J.J. Gumperz and D. Hymes (eds.) *Directions in Sociolinguistics*. New York: Holt, Rinehart & Winston, pp. 35–71.

Kelly, S.D. (2001) *The Relevance of Phenomenology to the Philosophy of Language and Mind*. New York: Garland Publishing.

Kirschner, D. and Whitson, J.A. (1998) Obstacles to understanding cognition as situated. *Educational Researcher* 27(8), 22–8.

Kramsch, C. (1993) *Context and Culture in Language Teaching*. Oxford: Oxford University Press.

Kramsch, C. (1994) In another tongue. *Profession 94*. New York: Modern Language Association, 11–14.

Kramsch, C. (1997) The privilege of the non-native speaker. *PMLA* May, 359–69.

Kramsch, C. (forthcoming) The multilingual subject. In I. de Florio-Hansen and A. Hu (eds) *Mehrsprachigkeit und Identitätsentwicklung*. Tuebingen: Stauffenburg Verlag.

Lantolf, J. (2000) Introducing sociocultural theory. In J. Lantolf (ed.) *Sociocultural Theory and Second Language Learning.* Oxford: Oxford University Press, pp. 1–26.

Lantolf, J. (ed.) (2000) *Sociocultural Theory and Second Language Learning.* Oxford: Oxford University Press.

Latour, B. (1999) *Pandora's Hope: Essays on the Reality of Science Studies.* Cambridge: Cambridge University Press.

Leather, J. and van Dam, H.R. (eds) (forthcoming) *The Ecology of Language Acquisition.* Dordrecht: Kluwer.

Lee, E. and Mandelbaum, M. (eds) (1967) *Phenomenology and Existentialism.* Baltimore: Johns Hopkins Press.

Leopold, W. (1954) A child's learning of two languages. *Georgetown University Round Table on Languages and Linguistics* 7, 19–30.

Lewin, K. (1943) Defining the "field at a given time". *Psychological Review* 50, 292–310.

Lightbown, P.M. and Spada, N. (1999) *How Languages Are Learned.* Rev. ed., Oxford: Oxford University Press.

Makkai, A. (1993) *Ecolinguistics: Toward a New Paradigm for the Science of Language?* London: Pinter.

Merleau-Ponty, M. (1945) *Phénoménologie de la perception.* Paris: Gallimard.

Mühlhäusler, P. (1996) *Linguistic Ecology: Language Change and Linguistic Imperialism in the Pacific Region.* New York: Routledge.

Neisser, U. (1976) *Cognition and Reality.* San Francisco: Freeman.

Ochs, E. (1988) *Culture and Language Development: Language Acquisition and Language Socialization in a Samoan Village.* Cambridge: Cambridge University Press.

Ochs, E. (1996) Linguistic resources for socializing humanity. In J.J. Gumperz and S.C. Levinson (eds) *Rethinking Linguistic Relativity.* Cambridge: Cambridge University Press, pp. 407–37.

Ochs, E. and Schieffelin, B.B. (1979) *Developmental Pragmatics.* New York: Academic Press.

Ochs, E. and Schieffelin, B.B. (1983) *Acquiring Conversational Competence.* Boston: Routledge & Kegan Paul.

Rampton, B. (1997) Retuning in applied linguistics. *International Journal of Applied Linguistics* 7(1), 3–25.

Ricoeur, P. (1973) Human sciences and hermeneutical method: meaningful action considered as a text. In D. Carr and E.S. Casey (eds) *Explorations in Phenomenology.* The Hague: Martinus Nijhoff, pp. 47–101.

Schieffelin, B.B. and Ochs, E. (1986) *Language Socialization Across Cultures.* Cambridge: Cambridge University Press.

Schutz, A. and Luckmann, T. (1973) *The Structures of the Life-World*. Trsl. by R.M. Zaner and H.T. Engelhardt Jr. Evanston: Northwestern University Press.

Shweder, R.A. (1990) Cultural psychology – what is it? In J.W. Stigler, A. Shweder and G. Herdt (eds) *Cultural Psychology: Essays on Comparative Human Development*. Cambridge: Cambridge University Press, pp. 1–43.

Stigler, J.W., Shweder, R.A. and Herdt, G. (eds) (1990) *Cultural Psychology: Essays on Comparative Human Development*. Cambridge: Cambridge University Press.

Sullivan, P. (2000) Playfulness as mediation in communicative language teaching in a Vietnamese classroom. In J. Lantolf (ed.) *Sociocultural Theory and Second Language Learning*. Oxford: Oxford University Press, pp. 115–32.

Taylor, C. (1973) Interpretation and the sciences of man. In D. Carr and E. S. Casey (eds) *Explorations in Phenomenology*. The Hague: Martinus Nijhoff, pp. 13–46.

Taylor, C. (1992) Heidegger, language and ecology. In H. L. Dreyfus and H. Hall (eds) *Heidegger: A Critical Reader*. Oxford: Blackwell, pp. 247–69.

Toulmin, S. (1990) *Cosmopolis: The Hidden Agenda of Modernity*. Chicago: University of Chicago Press.

van Lier, L. (1996) *Interaction in the Language Curriculum: Awareness, Autonomy, and Authenticity*. London: Longman.

van Lier, L. (2000) From input to affordance: Social-interactive learning from an ecological perspective. In J. Lantolf (ed.) *Sociocultural Theory and Second Language Learning*. Oxford: Oxford University Press, pp. 245–59.

Vygotsky, L. (1978) *Mind in Society*. Cambridge: MIT Press.

Part One

Language development as spatial
and temporal positioning

Language acquisition and language use from a chaos/ complexity theory perspective

1

Diane Larsen-Freeman

Introduction

The field of second language acquisition (SLA) is in a state of turmoil. Heated exchanges are published in our journals, and internecine feuding is widespread. For while an individual/cognitive perspective on language acquisition prevails in SLA research, this "mainstream" view has been under increasing attack, and a more socially situated view of language use/acquisition is increasingly finding favor. At this juncture in the evolution of the SLA field, it would be worthwhile to examine the nature of the debate in order to truly understand what is being contested. This I do in two steps. In the first part of this chapter, I summarize two key issues as they have been put forth by some of the protagonists. Then, to contrast the two issues in a different way, I turn to the third question posed by the organizers of the workshop at which the chapters in this book were originally presented as papers. The question is: How is educational success defined?

Next, I propose that a way to deal with the conflict today is to do what the SLA field has always done on such occasions: to adopt a perspective that is large enough to accommodate the two competing points of view. In this chapter, I offer chaos/complexity theory (C/CT), not as a single grand unifying theory, but as a larger lens through which to view issues of interest to the SLA field. Finally, before concluding, I digress briefly to discuss a parallel debate ongoing in the field of linguistics.

The debate in SLA[1]

Firth and Wagner (1997, 1998) call for what at first appears to be a theoretically balanced approach to the study of SLA – one where both the social and the individual cognitive dimensions of SLA would be treated equally. In order to put forth their case for more representation for the social side, however, it appears that they are seeking to do more than redress a perceived imbalance. To this end, they urge the SLA researchers to reconsider "unquestioningly accepted and well established concepts such as learner, nonnative, and interlanguage." As they put it, ". . . we are unable to accept the premises of 'interlanguage' – namely, that language learning is a transitional process that has a distinct and visible end" (1998:91). They add that these problematic concepts are associated with the predominant view in the SLA field, which has been "individualistic and mentalistic," and that this view thus fails to account in a satisfactory way for interactional and sociolinguistic dimensions of language (Firth and Wagner 1997:285). Rampton (1997) calls this "disembedded cognition." Firth and Wagner contend that, since its founding by Corder, SLA has been much less concerned with what language is used for and much more concerned with individual acquisition and its relation to general human cognitive systems – the acquisition of L2 competence in the Chomskyan sense. "As such, it is flawed," they write, and "obviates insight into the nature of language, most centrally the language use of second or foreign language speakers" (1997:285).

The critics find further faults as well (for a discussion of these, see Larsen-Freeman 2000; Tarone 2000), but this brief recapitulation captures two of the most trenchant criticisms of mainstream SLA research: the imbalance between the psychological and the social, and the failure to consider language use. Let me now summarize what some of those invited to reply to the criticism had to say. First of all, they responded that a major flaw in Firth and Wagner's position is that they miss the point – that what SLA aims to do is to explain language *acquisition, not language use* (Kasper 1997; Long 1997; Gass 1998). According to Long (1997), "most SLA researchers view the object of inquiry as in large part an internal mental process: *the acquisition of new (linguistic) knowledge.* . . . The goal of research on SLA . . . is to understand how changes in that internal mental representation are achieved, why they sometimes appear to cease . . . and which learner, linguistic, and social factors . . . affect and effect the process" (Long 1997:319). Long goes on to say, because SLA researchers are concerned with mental processes, "cognitive variables are inevitably and justifiably a central focus" (1997:319). Gass (1998), acknowledging that perhaps some parts of language may be socially constructed, adds that SLA researchers subscribe to the view that language is an abstract entity residing in the individual. This position finds support, according to Gass, in the fact that ". . . there are parts of what we know about language (e.g. what is grammatical and what is ungrammatical) that cannot come from social interaction" (1998:88).

Apparently unconvinced, in the final exchange of this series, Firth and Wagner (1998) lament that "SLA seems to be dominated by Chomskyan thinking to such a degree that others' frames of reference for the understanding of language and cognition have become inconceivable" (1998:92).

Dealing with competing views

The fact that there are competing views in SLA is not remarkable. Indeed, some would find it a very healthy sign (Lantolf 1996). That there are at least these two major positions prevents either view from remaining or becoming hegemonic. Neither view can dictate what is normal SLA research and what is anomalous. Further, it is certainly not uncommon to find disciplines in which competing points of view co-exist. Thus, perhaps it is the fate of those interested in SLA to live with equally powerful contradictory views as well. However, before we accept this state of affairs as inevitable, it makes sense to see if the two points of view are reconcilable. They may very well be if the terms of a reconciliation would only require that we achieve a balance between psycholinguistic and sociolinguistic perspectives, although it turns out that even accomplishing this may be easier said than done.

For instance, Poulisse (1997) acknowledges that both psycho-linguistic and sociolinguistic approaches are important, but considers the psycholinguistic approach as primary and the sociolinguistic approach to be secondary, adding "you first need to describe the basic processes of learning and using language and then to discuss the contextual factors that influence these processes" (1997:324). Such a position is not going to satisfy the critics of mainstream SLA. Of course, even if a balance were achieved, we would need to be vigilant to ensure that the field does not move beyond the point of equilibrium, resulting in an imbalance in the other direction. With any dualism, hegemony can extend in either direction. As Kirshner and Whitson (1997) point out, "the Vygotskyan tradition is similarly weighted toward a deterministic social plane. The source of this weighting is the central tenet that 'social relations genetically underlie all higher [mental] functions and their relationships'" (Vygotsky 1981, in Kirschner and Whitson 1997:8).

Awarding either the psychological or the social primary status would do little to quell the debate or to advance the field. However, balancing the two would not end the debate either. This is because there is much more at stake than whether psychological or social factors are given equal attention. There is the second criticism with which to contend – that mainstream SLA has ignored questions of language use. This criticism highlights a fundamental, ontological difference between the two positions. Mainstream SLA makes a distinction between language acquisition and language use, and sees the former its rightful domain. As Gass (1998:85) puts it, "The research question central to SLA . . . is: How do people *learn* an L2? – The question is not: How do people *use* an L2, unless the latter is a means of getting at the former." While the mainstream view emphasizes the inward movement (acquisition process) of the object known as language (product) until some future point at which the product is isomorphic with a target, the newer view makes salient the discoursal nature of the learning interaction, with the dividing line between language learning and language use not easily drawn (Firth and Wagner 1998). This difference can best be appreciated by turning to the question of the definition of educational success, posed by organizers of the workshop.

A definition of educational success

For mainstream SLA researchers, success is defined as acquisition of the rules that bring the learner's performance into ever greater conformity with the target language – in terms of accuracy of production when compared with native-speaker performance. According to a more recent depiction, success is brought about by the acquisition of memorized sequences or chunks of language. Still, success is measured by the closeness of fit between the interlanguage that a learner produces and the corresponding baseline performance of the native speaker. Such a view of language success, Sfard (1998)[2] tells us, reflects an "acquisition metaphor" of learning, i.e. that human learning is conceived of as an acquisition of something, that something being an *a priori* category such as rules or sequences of language. Once rules or sequences are owned or acquired, according to the acquisition metaphor, they may be applied, transferred (to a different context), and shared with others.

A potential characterization of educational success presented by the challenger to this mainstream view can also be characterized by a metaphor. Sfard calls it "the participation metaphor." In the participation metaphor, rather than talking about acquiring entities, attention is paid to activities. "In the image of learning that emerges from this linguistic turn, the permanence of *having* gives way to the flux of *doing*. While the concept of acquisition implies that there is a clear endpoint to the process of learning, the new terminology leaves no room" (1998:6) for such.

This view leads to a different definition of educational success. According to the participation metaphor, learning a language is seen as a process of becoming a member of a certain community. "This entails, above all, the ability to communicate in the language of this community and act according to its norms ... While the AM [acquisition metaphor] stresses the individual mind and what goes 'into it,' the PM [participation metaphor] shifts the focus to the evolving bond between the individual and others" (Sfard 1998:6). Learning is taking part and at the same time becoming part of a greater whole.

It is important to note that the acquisition metaphor and the participation metaphor do not inevitably correspond to the psycho-logical–social dichotomy previously discussed. The reason for this is that the acquisition metaphor makes no distinction between the internalization of rules of language and the internalization of socially established concepts. Psycholinguistic rules and sociolinguistic con-cepts can both be objects of learning, something to be possessed. Furthermore, whereas the social dimension is salient in the participa-tion metaphor, it is not necessarily absent from research informed by the acquisition metaphor. This, after all, is what some of the mainstream SLA researchers have said in their responses to Firth and Wagner's criticism (see also the interactionist perspective in SLA, e.g. Gass 1997).

Instead, the acquisition/use division is ontological in nature, with the two positions reflecting fundamental differences in the way they frame their understanding of learning. Those that operate within an acquisition metaphor study the language acquisition of individuals, and evidence of the individuals' success is sought in their acquisition of target rules and structures. Those that operate within a participation metaphor study the language use of socially constituted individuals within groups, and seek evidence of success in the learners becoming participants in the discourse of a community. Distinguishing the mainstream and challenger views in this way is more illuminating than construing the dispute solely as a psycholinguistic versus socio-linguistic split.

It is, at the same time, more problematic, for it is far less obvious how such a fundamental difference can be resolved. Perhaps seeking a resolution is not necessary, of course, as I have already pointed out. One option, therefore, is for each side to pursue its own research agenda, providing the necessary checks and balances for the other. A second option for dealing with the dispute is to have it adjudicated through empiricism (e.g. Long 1997). However, Sfard (1998:12) warns that "empirical evidence is unlikely to serve as an effective weapon in [the SLA] paradigm wars" since the power of data to determine who is right may be confined to the paradigm within which they came into being.[3] Yet a third option exists, one to which the field of SLA has historically resorted.

When faced with challenges to prevailing views in the past, the field of SLA has not replaced a view with its challenger, but rather repeatedly broadened its domain of inquiry (Larsen-Freeman and Long 1991). When fault was found with the *a priori* contrastive analysis hypothesis, a view of learning was posited that aimed to explain the SLA process through an analysis of learner errors, appealing to contrastive analysis to account for some of them. In turn, error analysis was encompassed by a view that held that only a complete analysis of the learners' performance, including their errors, would suffice. Performance analysis was subsumed by discourse analysis when it became evident that attention needed to be paid not only to learners' performance, but also to what sorts of interaction they engaged in.

Thus, with an eye to our history, I suggest that the way out of the acquisition versus use/participation dilemma is to find a larger lens through which to examine issues in our field. And I offer chaos/complexity theory as a metaphorical means for doing so.

Chaos/complexity theory

Chaos/complexity science deals with complex, dynamic, nonlinear systems. It is the "science of process rather than state, of becoming rather than being" (Gleick 1987:5). Far more has been written about the new science than can be dealt with here. Therefore, let me just touch upon a few of its qualities germane to the present discussion (see for example, Haken 1977/1983; Odlum 1983; Prigogine and Stengers 1984; Gleick 1987; Salthe 1989; Stewart 1989; Waldrop 1992; Hall 1993; Lemke 2000).

Unlike traditional scientific approaches that analyze systems into their components and study them individually, chaos/complexity theory (C/CT) considers the synthesis of emergent wholes from studying *the interactions* of the individual components. Outcomes arise that cannot be anticipated from an examination of the parts independently. Neither is it the case that there is a central executive responsible for managing the discrete parts. Rather, the agents/elements act, react to, and interact with their environment (i.e. the other actors/elements and any features of their environment) without any reference to global goals – they are undertaking purely local transactions. The net result of these local transactions is a pattern that emerges at a global level. Thus, for example, the global pattern of a flock of birds emerges from the local behavior of the individual birds that comprise the flock.

In the abstract viewpoint employed in C/CT, it is assumed that the dynamic processes of systems are independent of their physical manifestation and depend only on the nature of their interactions. In this way, the findings are said to be equally applicable to all forms of systems – inorganic, organic, biological, psychological, or social. Of course, there are significant differences among these systems – agents are intentional and semiotic, for instance, whereas inorganic elements presumably are not. Nevertheless, in the case of both organic and inorganic systems, the emergent features will show equivalent properties relevant to the particular system.

Further, the emergent properties can themselves interact. For example, interacting molecules produce emergent cells; these interact to form organisms, which interact to form societies. In other words, there are a number of nested levels of detail, each needing a different type of label and description, but originating in the same way. The nested levels reflect a fractal pattern – each level of scale is self-similar. Importantly, a change at any one level will have implications for every level.

Complex systems that are open import free energy from the environment to reorganize themselves to increasingly higher orders of complexity. Thus, contrary to the second Law of Thermodynamics, in such systems, entropy, or lack of order, is not inevitable. Indeed, new order can emerge from disorder. When the dynamic systems are far from the point of equilibrium, spontaneous large-scale restructurings can take place. Conversely, when a system is near equilibrium, it displays a certain stability. Minor fluctuations are dampened.

These systems are dynamic. As they move through space/time, they follow a path, called an attractor – the state or pattern that a dynamic system is attracted to. A complex dynamic system exhibits a strange attractor, because its path never crosses itself. Although its cycle repeats itself (like a frictionless pendulum), no cycle ever follows the exact same path or overlaps any other cycle.

Finally, these complex, dynamic systems are nonlinear. This means that the effects resulting from a cause will not be proportional to the cause. Because of this, the effects of a pertubation bear no relation to its size – a minor change can have global effects, can throw the system into chaos, yet a major one may be absorbed without effect. Moreover, because of their sensitivity to initial conditions, there is an unpredictability inherent in these systems.

Lessons from a C/CT perspective

There are many lessons to be drawn for work in both the physical and the social sciences from the new sciences of chaos and complexity. I will limit my discussion here to three (for others, see Larsen-Freeman 1997). First, a C/CT perspective forces us away from reductionism and toward holism. From a C/CT perspective it is meaningless to attempt to understand something by taking it apart, explaining the behavior of the parts, and finally aggregating these partial explanations into an explanation of the whole. Behaviors arise that cannot be anticipated from examining the parts. Furthermore, the parts are interconnected. If one is affected, it will affect the other parts, although not necessarily in a predictable fashion.

A C/CT perspective also forces us away from easy distinctions, which may very well turn out to be false dichotomies (Larsen-Freeman 1999). For example, in the brief description above, we saw that complex systems are characterized both by a dynamic attractor path and by a fractal pattern. Instead of dichotomizing, we are encouraged to look for interconnections. What connects motion and pattern? Further, what connects the different levels of scale in the nested systems? How can we connect the micro-level of the individual organism with the macro-level of society? Is there a way to avoid a dualism between the individual and social, for instance?

A final lesson we can derive out of the brief introduction to C/CT is to entertain what it means to be dealing with open systems; systems that are not homeostatic, but, rather, grow more complex. How will conceiving of language as an open system and language acquisition as an open process influence our understanding?

Armed with this new perspective, let us now revisit the SLA controversy that I introduced earlier.

Controversy in SLA revisited

Although the SLA controversy has been depicted as pitting psycho-linguistic against sociolinguistic perspectives, neither side has claimed that it can account for the whole of SLA exclusively. This is as it should be, I believe. After all, if language and interlanguage development are (at least metaphorically) complex, dynamic, and nonlinear systems/processes, as I have previously suggested (Larsen-Freeman 1997),[4] then we would not be doing justice to the whole by singling out one part. It is not the case that we can figure out the cognitive acquisition process and then turn to the social use process, any more than it is the case that we can understand the whole of an organism by understanding its circulatory system. Instead, we should look for how to connect cognitive acquisition and social use, an aim that neither side of the SLA dispute would object to, I am sure.

One hint for how to connect them comes from Gleick's observation (1987:24) that with complex systems, "... the act of playing the game has a way of changing the rules." Of course, Gleick was not discussing matters concerning language. Applying his observation to such matters, though, could suggest that participation in a process and changes in the rules governing the process take place at one and the same time. Linguists have called this the Labov principle, acknowledging the intimate connection between (synchronic) variation and (diachronic) change (Givón 1999). Being inspired partly by connectionism, I suggest that language use and language acquisition are also synchronous: the act of using the language has a way of changing the language or, in the case of learners, their interlanguage.

At this point, it would be helpful to digress and consider a parallel, although not identical, controversy in the field of linguistics.

A digression to linguistics

Whether to treat language as a system to be acquired or a process in which to be engaged is not a controversy to which linguists are immune. As applied to the grammatical subsystem, a long-standing debate has been taking place, represented by the "*a priori* grammar attitude" and the "emergence of grammar attitude" (Hopper 1988). Viewed from the perspective of the *a priori* grammar attitude, grammar is seen to be a predetermined discrete set of generative rules, which are logically detachable from language use. The subscribers to the *a priori* grammar attitude conceive of grammar as a static entity, an object, which is fully present at all times in the mind of the speaker. It is therefore essentially atemporal.

In striking contrast, linguists who subscribe to the emergence of grammar position view grammar as a phenomenon "whose status is constantly being renegotiated in speech and which cannot be distinguished *in principle* from strategies for building discourses" (Hopper 1988:118). As Hopper (1998:156) puts it: "Its forms are not fixed templates, but arise out of face-to-face interaction in ways that reflect the individual speakers' past experience of these forms, and their assessment of the present context, including especially their interlocutors, whose experience and assessments may be quite different. From the emergent grammar perspective, "language is a real-time activity, whose regularities are always provisional and are continually subject to negotiation, renovation, and abandonment" (Hopper 1988:120).

Significantly (1998:163), "in emergent grammar, because the forms of language do not exist hermetically sealed in the mind of the individual speaker, but are instead distributed during acts of communication among speakers," it follows, according to Hopper, that the learning of language must be reconceived. "Learning a language is not a question of acquiring grammatical structure but of *expanding a repertoire of communicative contexts*. Consequently, there is no date or age at which the learning of language can be said to be complete. New contexts, and new occasions of negotiation of meaning, occur constantly. A language is not a circumscribed object but a loose confederation of available and overlapping social experiences" (1998:171).

It is clear that there is much in Hopper's view (in the emergentist perspective) that resonates with the participation metaphor. Grammar is regarded as epiphenomenal, a by-product of a communication process. It is not a collection of rules and target forms to be acquired by language learners. Language, or grammar, is not about having; it is about doing; participating in social experiences. Further, echoing Firth and Wagner's comment cited above, there is no point at which it could be said that the learning of a language is complete.

Likewise, we can find parallels between the *a priori* grammar attitude and the acquisition metaphor. While not all mainstream SLA researchers believe in an innate universal grammar (UG), the mainstream view does accept the existence of *a priori* grammatical rules and structures as rightful targets of an acquisition process. In addition, it sees the target rules and structures as detachable from language use. According to this view, the acquisition of a system allows one to apply it to contexts other than the ones in which it was learned. The knowledge of grammar can therefore be transferred.

Givón (1999), objecting to the absolutism of both the Platonic essentialist *a priori* and the Wittgensteinean emergent grammar viewpoints, asserts that both views represent extremes. Givón maintains that the facts of grammar in natural language use tend to uphold an adaptive compromise. Grammar is not totally flexible, always negotiated for the occasion, but it can be context-dependent and usage driven. Since language is constrained by its adaptive environment, it must possess a certain rigidity for rapid speech-processing purposes, along with a flexibility that allows for change, adaptive innovation, and learning, not to mention the need to deal with contexts of high informational ambiguity and uncertainty. Thus, any model of grammar must be able to accommodate both rigidity and flexibility.[5]

C/CT and the SLA controversy: Conclusion

There is much about the participation metaphor/language use/ emergent grammar position that fits with C/CT. From the participation metaphor/language use/emergent grammar standpoint, the view that language is not static can easily be accommodated within C/CT. Moreover, the mechanism for change, the interaction of the agents in real-world contexts, is common to all three perspectives and to C/CT. They also share the view that language is an open system, one that is evolving and changing. If this is true of language, it must also be true of its learning – it will never be complete if the target is always moving. However, recall that "the act of playing the game has a way of changing the rules;" thus, from a C/CT perspective, there is also room for a view of language as a set of rules or patterns. Indeed, without this perspective, how is it possible to address not only Givón's concern about rapid speech processing, but also the fact that there is carry-over in use from one context to another?

Indeed, it is difficult to deny that something does keep repeating itself as we move from situation to situation, context to context (see Long 1997 on this point). Being prepared to deal with novel contexts that are going to be encountered beyond the classroom is the very purpose of learning. And what about the ubiquitous evidence of the role of L1 transfer in L2 acquisition? How is this accounted for if we are not allowed to talk about carrying anything with us from one situation to another – if each is unique?[6]

Although I have already suggested a compatibility between the language use position and C/CT, the acquisition metaphor/language acquisition/*a priori* position can be accommodated as well. Recall that there is a sensitivity to initial conditions (perhaps a UG?) in such systems. Further, the type of complex systems studied in C/CT exhibit not only dynamic paths, but also systemic patterns. The pattern and path occur together, in the same way that an eddy in a stream is only visible in the flow of water. Furthermore, as I have proposed before (Larsen-Freeman 1997), the pattern that language exhibits is the same fractal pattern as other complex, dynamic, nonlinear systems. It is the nested pattern that allows languages to compress a significant amount of information into a small space. It is the pattern that is at least relatively stable from context to context and from time to time. It is the pattern that provides the "rigidity" or stability of language, which Givón believes must offset its flexibility.

In conclusion, a C/CT perspective clearly supports a social participation view of SLA; however, it does not do so to the exclusion of the psychological acquisitionist perspective. Thus, C/CT offers the wider perspective that has served SLA in the past. Importantly, in addition to affording us a wider perspective, the contribution of C/CT is that it encourages us to think in relational terms. It is not merely a question of making room for stability and flux, pattern and dynamism, acquisition and use. Rather, I am led to conclude that members of dichotomous pairs such as these can only be understood in relation to each other.

Notes

1. In this section, I draw on the exchange that was featured over two issues of *The Modern Language Journal*. However, the criticisms and responses have extended beyond this exchange (see, e.g. Larsen-Freeman 2000).
2. I am grateful to Rick Donato for calling my attention to this article.
3. For this reason, Liddicoat (1997) points out that simply rebalancing the field of SLA in light of criticisms is insufficient. It would take a reconceptualization, including a concomitant reanalysis of research methods.
4. At the workshop, I learned that one of the participants, Ronald Scollon, made a claim like this for language many years earlier in a working paper (Scollon 1977).
5. Givón proffers prototype constructions as offering a compromise between the two extremes. Most recently, however, Hopper (2000) has countered this by rejecting the compromise. Hopper notes a need to reverse the "prototype" picture of grammatical constructions. Since in natural, flowing discourse, the visible parts of the canonical construction type appear as fragments, "to view the canonical construction as a prototype and as the source of fragmentary instantiations in discourse is to put the cart before the horse" (2000:12).
6. Indeed, how the participation metaphor deals with "transfer" is a crucial question. Although the concept of "transfer" is not sufficiently process-evoking to fit the participation metaphor, Greeno (1997) does discuss it from such a perspective. Defining learning as "improved participation in interactive systems," he proceeds to account "for transfer in terms of transformations of constraints, affordances, and attunements" (1997:12). We need more such discussion from the participationist perspective.

References

Firth, A. and Wagner, J. (1997) On discourse, communication, and (some) fundamental concepts in SLA research. *Modern Language Journal* 81(iii) 285–300.

Firth, A. and Wagner, J. (1998) SLA property: No trespassing! *Modern Language Journal* 82(i) 91–4.

Gass, S. (1997) *Input, Interaction and the Second Language Learner.* Mahwah: Lawrence Erlbaum.

Gass, S. (1998) Apples and oranges, or, why apples are not oranges and don't need to be: a response to Firth and Wagner. *Modern Language Journal* 82(i) 81–90.

Givón, T. (1999) Generativity and variation: the notion "rule of grammar" revisited. In B. MacWhinney (ed.), *The Emergence of Language*. Mahwah: Lawrence Erlbaum, pp. 81–114.

Gleick, J. (1987) *Chaos: Making a New Science*. New York: Penguin Books.

Greeno, J. (1997) On claims that answer the wrong question. *Educational Researcher* 26(1) 6–17.

Haken, H. (1977/1983) *Synergetics, an Introduction: Non-equilibrium Phase Transitions and Self-organization in Physics, Chemistry and Biology*. Berlin: Springer-Verlag.

Hall, N. (ed.) (1993) *Exploring Chaos: A Guide to the New Science of Disorder*. New York: Norton.

Hopper, P. (1988) Emergent grammar and the *a priori* grammar postulate. In D. Tannen, *Linguistics in Context*. Norwood: Ablex, pp. 117–34.

Hopper, P. (1998) Emergent grammar. In M. Tomasello, *The New Psychology of Language*. Mahwah: Lawrence Erlbaum, pp. 155–75.

Hopper, P. (2000) Grammatical constructions and their discourse origins: prototype or family resemblance. General and Theoretical Paper No. 508, LAUD: Linguistic Agency, Universitat Gesamthochschule Essen.

Kasper, G. (1997) "A" stands for acquisition. *Modern Language Journal* 81(iii) 307–12.

Kirschner, D. and Whitson, J. (eds) (1997) *Situated Cognition: Social, Semiotic, and Psychological Perspectives*. Mahwah: Lawrence Erlbaum.

Lantolf, J. (1996) SLA theory building: "Letting all the flowers bloom". *Language Learning* 46(4) 713–49.

Larsen-Freeman, D. (1997) Chaos/complexity science and second language acquisition. *Applied Linguistics* 18, 141–65.

Larsen-Freeman, D. (1999) Chaos/complexity theory: blurring the boundaries. Paper presented at the Chaos/Complexity Perspective on Applied Linguistics Colloquium, American Association for Applied Linguistics Conference, Stamford, CT, March.

Larsen-Freeman, D. (2000) Second language acquisition and applied linguistics. In W. Grabe (ed.), *Applied Linguistics as an Emerging Discipline, Annual Review of Applied Linguistics*, Volume 20, pp. 165–81.

Larsen-Freeman, D. and Long, M. (1991) *An Introduction to Second Language Acquisition Research*. London: Longman.

Lemke, J. (2000) Across the scales of time: artifacts, activities, and meanings in ecosocial systems. *Mind, Culture and Activity* 7(4), 273–90.

Liddicoat, A. (1997) Interaction, social structure, and second language use: a response to Firth and Wagner. *Modern Language Journal* 81(iii) 313–17.

Long, M. (1997) Construct validity in SLA research. *Modern Language Journal* 81(iii) 318–23.

Odlum, H. (1983) *Systems Ecology*. New York: John Wiley.

Poulisse, N. (1997) Some words in defense of the psycholinguistic approach. *Modern Language Journal* 81(iii) 324–8.

Prigogine, I. and Stengers, I. (1984) *From Being to Becoming: Time and Complexity in the Physical Sciences*. New York: W.H. Freeman.

Rampton, B. (1997) Second language research in late modernity: a response to Firth and Wagner. *Modern Language Journal* 81(iii) 329–33.

Salthe, S. (1989) Self-organization in hierarchically structured systems. *Systems Research* 6, 199–208.

Scollon, R. (1977) Dissipative structures: Chipewyan consonants and the modern consciousness. *Working Papers in Linguistics*, University of Hawaii, 9(3), October–December.

Sfard, A. (1998) On two metaphors for learning and the dangers of choosing just one. *Educational Researcher*, March, 4–13.

Stewart, I. (1989) *Does God Play Dice? The Mathematics of Chaos*. Oxford: Basil Blackwell.

Tarone, E. (2000) Still wrestling with "context" in interlanguage theory. In W. Grabe (ed.), *Applied Linguistics as an Emerging Discipline, Annual Review of Applied Linguistics*, Volume 20, pp. 182–98.

Waldrop, M. (1992) *Complexity: The Emerging Science at the Edge of Order and Chaos*. New York: Simon & Schuster.

Modeling the acquisition of speech in a 'multilingual' society: An ecological approach

2

Jonathan Leather

Introduction

Perhaps inevitably, language acquisition research has tended to reflect the Western, essentially monolingual view of society and socialization pointed up by Phillipson and Skutnabb-Kangas (1996) and Nayar (1994). Most acquisition studies implicitly assume a large measure of isomorphy between linguistic, political, and cultural communities, and distinguish categorically between languages that are sequentially learned: L1, L2 (... Ln). In such a conceptualization the complexities of multilinguals' language behavior are marginalized (Kachru 1996). The 'L1' or *mother tongue* is seen as the object of 'normal' acquisition, and any other language in an acquirer's life is considered potentially problematic. The multiple language development of the many whose lives belie the 'monolingual' model would usually be considered the *final* test for a theory of acquisition. Yet the apparent complexity of 'multilingual' development can also be seen as an invitation to theoretical reappraisal and as the default case which we should address *first*.

In this chapter I first present some acquisition data which cannot be done justice by closed-system modeling of linguistic form. I go on to review some problems in the study of multilingual phonological acquisition. Finally, I discuss some alternative approaches which I suggest can be combined in a hybrid modeling framework to account better for acquisition phenomena.

A vowel in Dominica

Alvin is a six-year-old born and brought up in the Commonwealth of Dominica, the Eastern Caribbean island state. He is growing up in a linguistic situation that would often be described as bilingual *and* diglossic. The official and educational language of Dominica is English (the Caribbean *de facto* standard with some remaining limited influence from the ex-colonizer: Britain). Co-existing with English for perhaps 90 percent of the population is Kwéyòl (the French-based Creole vernacular shared with the neighboring French islands, Haiti and La Guyane). As in all of the Eastern Caribbean, there is some interpenetration of other languages spoken in the region, most notably the standard French of neighboring Martinique and Guadeloupe (which is also a school subject in Dominica).

For a minimal interpretation of the following utterances of Alvin's it is necessary to know that (a) half of Alvin's family are of indigenous Carib (rather than African) descent; (b) the Kwéyòl vowel system has no extreme front or back open vowels, so *Carib* is [ke:ɹëb] as compared to the standard British [kæɹɪb] – the vowel in 'car' would similarly be [ɐ] in contrast to a (conservative) British [ɑː]; and (c) Kwéyòl in Dominica – as in the comparable nearby St Lucia – is undergoing some relexification through its contact with English (see Allen 1994). One possible relexification in progress is the replacement of the Kwéyòl *vwati* by the English-derived *motoka* – this change is probably being led by socially mobile speakers leading more 'urban' lives.

In the first exchange below, Alvin is at home with his mother:

Alvin:	Poochi nou pa ni vwati?
	[pu̧çi nu̧ pɐ ni vwɐti]
	[Why haven't we got a car?]

A's mother:	Vwati chè kon chè chè!!
	[vwɐti çɛ kɔ̃ çɛ çɛ]
	[Cars are so very expensive!]

The following exchange took place later that day between Alvin and his 13-year-old brother Gregory (who had overheard the earlier exchange between Alvin and his mother):

Gregory:	Si mwen vini wich mwen ké achté motoka bèl, bèl, bèl!
	[si̧ mwẽ veni wiç mwẽ ke ɐçte motokɐ:: bɛl bɛl bɛl]
	[If I get rich I'm going to buy the most beautiful car!]

Alvin:	Mwen vlé nou ni vwati wich konsa ...
	[mwẽ vle nu ni vwɐti wiç kɔ̃sɐ ...]
	[I wish we could have an expensive car like that ...]

Two days later Alvin was playing with his friend Antony and Antony's toy car, which he was admiring. He said to Antony:

| Alvin: | Vwati sila i *car for Carib.* Vwati bèl ... |
| | [vwɐti silɐ ɪ *ka: fɔ ke:ɹëb* vwɐ::ti bɛl ...] |

[This car is a [motor-] *car for a Carib.* It's a beautiful
"car" . . .]

At two levels, linguistic and social factors interact here in Alvin's
phonological acquisition. First, from Gregory's speech Alvin can infer
that *motoka* is a lexical alternative to *vwati*, with an implicit distinction
according to prestige (a *motoka* being grander than a *vwati*).
Subsequently, Alvin selects the English *car* – perhaps partly because
of its formal resemblance to *motoka* – and implicitly contrasts it with
vwati. Alvin can thus locate himself through his lexical choice in a
multidimensional social space. Second, Gregory makes use of an
exaggeratedly 'British' vowel (very low, very retracted, and exaggeratedly long) to allude to car ownership as an upper-class thing – the
prerogative of those educated (or earning well) abroad, perhaps in
Britain. His vowel is halfway to being a Caribbean English parody of a
British English stereotype of a 'class' vowel. From Gregory's 'demonstration', Alvin infers and adds to his phonological resources a
sociophonetic marker realized as a combination of vowel quality and
duration. Picking up on this marker, he extrapolates it to the properly
Kwéyòl *vwati* in the trial example above.

I suggest that if we are to give a plausible account of these
conversational fragments in terms of Alvin's phonological development, we need at the very least to be able to address:

1. The formant structures and durations of vowels in the
   regional standard English and Kwéyòl;
2. Sociolinguistic dimensions of vowel variation in at least one
   of the languages (English);
3. Sociolinguistic dimensions of lexical variation in Kwéyòl;
4. The symbolic value of English to Dominican Kwéyòl speakers,
   and more specifically to Caribs;
5. Alvin's evolving vowel repertoires in Kwéyòl and English
   (which at the time when these fragments were collected were
   evidently diverging).

Research on multilingual phonological acquisition

The standard approaches to modeling phonological acquisition cannot
do justice to data like Alvin's because (a) they address single languages
as closed systems, and (b) they exclude from consideration nonphon-
etic factors – lexical and pragmatic, for instance – that may be relevant
to the acquisition process. Perhaps because of the limitations of current
models, there have been very few longitudinal investigations of
multilingual phonological development, whether in childhood (Holm

and Dodd 1999) or after puberty (see Leather and James 1996, Leather 1999). From these few studies, the following points can be made.

The 'system'

Considering the fully developed languages of the acquirer in 'product' terms, the phonological resources of bilinguals (and multilinguals) have been categorized as *coexistent, merged,* or *super-subordinate* systems (Laeufer 1997). There is evidence (though nearly all in the form of production data) that if the systems are *co-existent,* each system may differ in some ways from that of a monolingual: so long as the several systems can implement all the necessary linguistic contrasts, a bilingual may 'economize' in production routines, with some processing common to both of the languages (Watson 1991).

In the 'process' of multiple acquisition the languages apparently interact, so that the acquisition of each individual language is qualitatively different from that of a monolingual (Holm and Dodd 1999). Furthermore, in 'process' terms, it is less clear in multiple acquisition that what we are dealing with is transitional *systems* on the way to a fully elaborated phonology for each of the respective languages. Systematicity is, to be sure, one of the cornerstones of Western linguistic theory, with *system* most often equated to *mental representation or mechanism.* Yet the 'system' that we *project upon* acquirers' abilities may not always correspond to a particular inherent coherence in their phonological resources, but only describe a certain constellation of difficulties that make some sounds easier for them to produce than others (see Schnitzer 1990; Schnitzer and Krasinski 1994). Schnitzer and Krasinski (1996), for instance, found no evidence of any particular 'stage' on the way to their child informant achieving target values, but could discern only the development of a segmental repertoire. Moreover, the very notion of a determinate target system against which transitional forms can be evaluated, though central to most acquisition studies, may not withstand close scrutiny. As Charles Ferguson put it in 1979: "THE phonology of a language variety ... is a *composite* of individual phonologies in which the shared structure inevitably has indeterminacies, fuzzy boundaries, and both dialectal and idiosyncratic variation" (Ferguson 1979:198).

Individual differences

There have been too few studies of multilingual phonological acquisition to infer universal patterns from the data provided by individual acquirers (Gierut *et al.* 1994; Leather and James 1991;

Leather 1999). It is clear, however, that there is considerable individual variation. The two children studied by Schnitzer and Krasinski (1994, 1996) plainly differed in their acquisition strategies: although their social circumstances were comparable, one child was less imitative and venturesome than the other – what Ferguson (1979) has called a 'cautious system-builder.' Individual acquirers appear to have their *favorite* sounds or 'preference strategies' (Ferguson 1979), and to follow alternative routes in their acquisition of particular sounds and their elaboration of phonological resources as a whole (Ferguson 1979; Gierut *et al.* 1994). Individuals also differ in the degrees to which the linguistic input and their own linguistic knowledge influence their category judgments (Gierut 1996). There is strategic variation, too, in the degrees to which individuals focus on (a) the 'code,' and (b) the 'message' (Saville-Troike 1988).

Socialization

In terms of acquirers' implicit *goals*, socialization can be seen as progressive alignment of their individual speech with the phonological profile of a community. In terms of the acquisition *process*, socialization is the experience and activity that provides them with incentives, models, data, trials, and feedback. To explain a speaker's competence in sociolinguistic marking (Scherer and Giles 1979) or speech accommodation (Giles and Smith 1979) we must examine the interaction of their socialization and language development – an interaction that longitudinal studies of phonological acquisition have generally overlooked or ignored.

Data reduction

Most of the research on phonological acquisition – whether mono-lingual or multilingual – has based all analyses on *transcriptions* of acquirers' speech. Transcription, however, introduces a particular risk of prejudging outcomes, since in the transcribing process the researcher projects *phonemes, features,* or other categories upon the acquirer's speech output. As the acoustic signal of speech is analog in nature, transcriptions will reflect the researcher's – not the acquirer's – acoustic–phonetic perceptual category thresholds. That these may markedly differ is evident from Figure 2.1, which shows functions for the identification of synthesized speech stimuli that span a continuum of time-varying fundamental frequency (and are heard as differing in voice pitch patterning). Listeners with Standard Chinese mother tongue identified the stimuli as words (glossable as *muddy* and *fish*

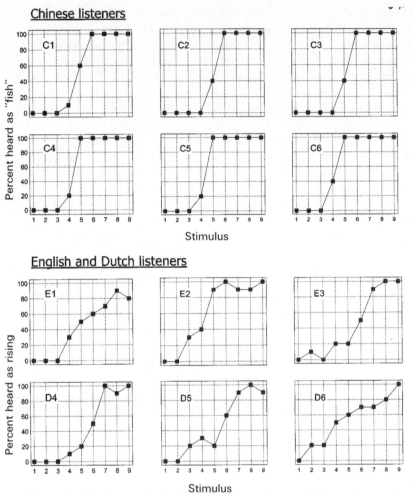

Figure 2.1 *Categorizations by Chinese (upper panel) and English and Dutch (lower panel) listeners of randomized tokens of nine synthesized speech stimuli spanning an acoustic continuum between the Standard Chinese words /ȳ/ (="muddy') and /ý/ (="fish'). The Chinese listeners judged the stimuli as one or the other of these two Chinese words; the English and Dutch listeners judged them as "level' or "rising' in pitch.*

respectively), while English- and Dutch-speaking listeners identified them as 'level' or 'rising' pitch patterns – with markedly less sharp and less consistent category crossovers.

Studies which seek to chart developmental patterning based on auditory transcriptions thus exclude from the database the *gradient* changes in an acquirer's acoustic output, some of which – whatever the 'evidence' of the researchers' ears – may be developmentally crucial. Moreover, while some fine phonetic ('subphonemic') differences may not be critical to the elaboration of a speech sound system or repertoire, they do contribute to characterizing an individual's mature speech in all its varieties (see the review by Edwards *et al.* 1999).

Analytic framework

As far as a phonological 'system' is concerned, multilingual acquisition is obviously complex. As Watson (1991) reminds us, additional languages do not just add to but potentially *multiply* the modeling difficulty. In the absence of detailed proposals for addressing multi-lingual speech development, it is not surprising that phonological acquisition research should look for its underpinnings to the models of theoretical phonology. These have predominantly claimed to account for linguistic performance in terms of the operation of linguistic *rules* upon mental *symbols*, and have constituted the dominant theoretical paradigm since the early 'generative' phonology of Chomsky and Halle (1968). The rules, it is usually implied, are internally represented in the brain and are involved in the neurophysiological processing that culminates in the production of speech. Phonological ability is thus modeled in terms of processes which operate computationally on the *formal properties of representations* – not in terms of processes which relate forms to possible *meanings* in particular human *contexts*.

The theoretical elegance pursued in mainstream phonological models may satisfy philosophical criteria, but does not by that token alone offer a better account of acquisition. Neuroscience research (see, for example, Jeannerod 1994) allows for at least the possibility that representations in the brain which underlie motor action may be of different and co-existent modes. Only in the last few years has it been suggested that linguistic rules can be thought of as simply a convenient way of describing observed behavior. The linguistic activity which we observe as apparently rule-governed may be the result of a mechanism which processes information in an entirely different way than is envisaged in the rules-and-symbols paradigm – information that could be modeled equally well, or better, by quite different means.

A hybrid syncretic approach

General principles and particular mechanisms

The balance of evidence suggests that in their acquisition of speech the auditory capacities humans make use of are *general* rather than species-specific (see Jusczyk 1997). In modeling the acquisition process a further fruitful distinction can be made between *general principles* of development and the *precise mechanisms* that are involved. Under general principles would be understood such notions as (a) acquisition proceeds in tandem with socialization; (b) goals are functional not formal. Under precise mechanisms we would aim to specify such details as (a) how prototypical settings for phonetic parameters are learned from exposure to exemplars; or (b) how an acquirer determines which potential assimilations are lawful in an environmental language. Klahr (1992) points out that the attempt at *simulating* development in the form of computer programs leads to insights about the mechanisms underlying developmental change, whereas verbal descriptions usually underspecify such mechanisms. Here, language acquisition research can profit from the findings and insights of Artificial Intelligence (AI) (see e.g. Powers, forthcoming).

Data preservation

The loss of gradient information through the auditory transcription of informants' speech need not be considered inevitable, because there are standard mathematical devices which can preserve analog information in speech data before it is input to 'front-end' learning analyses. Thus, a number of the descriptive and theoretical notions of phonology have proved amenable to modeling in terms of vector spaces constructed through quantitative dimensional analysis (Hubey 1999), and gradient changes in the acquirer's speech can be captured by the same means.

Optimality theory

Consistent with the recent trend toward a more phonetically driven phonology (e.g. Archangeli and Pulleyblank 1994), the influential linguistic framework known as *optimality theory* (OT) is based on *constraints* rather than rules (for an overview see Barlow and Gierut 1999). In OT, the set of constraints in an individual's grammar do not change over the course of acquisition, but are *reranked*. Variation between individuals is explained in terms of differential ranking of constraints at particular stages of their respective development. The name of the OT framework comes from the premise that – unlike rules – constraints are *violable*, and the candidate form that violates the *fewest* high-ranked constraints is the one that is chosen. In other words, you do the best you can in the circumstances. What in OT is conceptualized as 'the emergence of the unmarked' compares to the settling of a system into an equilibrium.

Phenomenological phonology

Whether the *constraints* of OT can wholly replace rules as a formal mechanism remains controversial (McMahon 2000). Contrasting at a different level with the rules-and-representations model of phonological development, a *phenomenological* approach contends that 'there is no adequate analogy or model of a human being when it comes to language use' (Fraser 1997), so the language user is conceived of as a human being with consciousness, 'engaged in feeling, thinking, and interpreting in a way which is always meaning-oriented and context-based.' Phenomenological phonology considers representations not as the *basis* of mental processes but as their *product* (so they may be more felicitously termed 'descriptions'). A *description*, then, is the product of an interaction between a 'phonetic Something,' a context, and a 'Subjective viewpoint' (Fraser 1997). Such an approach factors the situated, real-world experience of the acquirer into modeling of the acquisition process.

Connectionism

The connectionist modeling of AI aligns promisingly with the constraint-based framework of OT, and has already yielded encouraging results in phonology (e.g. Plaut and Kello 1999; Gupta and Touretzky 1994). Through connectionist models, high-level 'emergent' properties can be systematically derived from lower-level data (Churchland and Sejnowski 1992), through the 'gradual, experience-driven adjustment of connection weights between levels of distributed processing' (Gupta and Dell 1999). The strength of the connectionist approach is that, in their adaptive responses to changing inputs, connectionist models that do not embody any explicit rules are capable of manifesting linguistic behavior that nevertheless appears to be rule-governed.

Connectionist models of human learning have proved successful in many basic forms of inductive generalization, extracting new knowledge from the (statistical) properties of long series of exemplars. This is one aspect of the discovery (by the acquirer) of phonological form through repeated exposure to phones, syllables, words, and so on; and it could be modeled through the operation of connectionist designs on the vector spaces mentioned above. The connectionist architecture offered by certain kinds of neural networks (see Anderson

1999) has a high fault tolerance and is therefore well suited to processing the 'imperfect' exemplars of speech in the 'noisy' conditions of real life.

However, the connectionist learning that a neural network can perform is at a relatively low level of abstraction; such a network is not equipped to carry through the logical reasoning that *grammatical* decisions on sound patterning may entail. Furthermore, such systematic decision-making is not necessarily based on 'either/or' conditions in the inputs, and so may be better addressed in terms of fuzzy sets and fuzzy logic.

Fuzzy logic

Fuzzy logic was introduced with the specific aim of handling the propositional uncertainty of much natural language, which it does by extending conventional (binary) logic so as to handle the concept of partial truth – that is, truth values which lie *between* 'true' and 'false.' In synthetic combined designs like that of Lin and Lee (1994), neural networks provide a connectionist structure and learning abilities to fuzzy logic systems, while the fuzzy logic systems provide a structural framework with higher-level IF-THEN thinking and reasoning to the neural networks.

Representational redescription

The core problem of 'traditional' behavior-based AI is how to map from a perception model to an action model – in phonological acquisition, how to get from auditory speech perception to speech production. In connectionist models, the neural network is for this purpose the agent of action. But the study of natural language raises the further problem of accounting for *metalinguistic* ability, which must include at least the ability to make implicit linguistic knowledge in some way *explicit*. Since the nature of metalinguistic knowledge seems to be related to a person's individual language background (Liouw and Poon 1998), we may imagine it is produced as a function of acquisition. *Representational redescription* (RepRed) is one solution that has been proposed to map between action and perception, and should therefore be capable of addressing metalinguistic ability. RepRed is 'the hypothesized process by which information that is *in* a cognitive system becomes progressively explicit knowledge *to* that system' (Karmiloff-Smith 1992). RepRed aims to offer a means of modeling how acquirers capitalize heuristically on their experience, reviewing an *activity* and recasting it in the form of a *mental schema* which can be put to use in further learning. RepRed can thus establish links in acquisition between speech perception, speech production, and phonological knowledge.

Reactive reasoning

It is by no means clear that all acquisition needs to be modeled in terms of representations and/or variable-based logic. The approach known as *reactive reasoning* (ReaRea) focuses instead on units of directly coupled perceptions and actions (Brooks 1991). ReaRea models action without planning – that is, action directly triggered by the environment rather than resulting from deliberation. In a ReaRea system the complex representation processing of traditional AI systems is, as it were, precompiled as a specialized program structure. The finding that it can result in computational savings (Bryson and Lowe 1997) makes such direct couplings cognitively plausible as well. Such a (sub-)system would be capable of handling what have been called 'phonological idioms' (Moskowitz 1980) – the one-off *ad hoc* wholes or prefabs that apparently get learned largely independently of mainline phonological development.

Evolutionary change

While there are reasons for considering language as something other than simply a *culturally invented* tool (Bickerton 1996), its acquisition and transmission clearly involve social and cultural interaction. From an activity-theoretic perspective all forms of human praxis are developmental processes, with the activity of the individual in everyday life *situated* and *symbiotic* within a larger cultural/historical context (Engestrom 1987). Like other forms of human activity, learning is seen in activity theory as being mediated by *tools* in a broad sense of the term. These *tools* are created and transformed during the progression of an activity, and carry with them residues of a particular culture which is thereby transmitted (Nardi 1996). Language, then, is a tool that the acquirer constructs and reconstructs together with something of the environmental culture. There is some evidence that, in language acquisition, learning as 'tool construction' may take place during silent periods (Saville-Troike 1988), while (at a fairly late stage of acquisition) participation in a range of discourses, and some success in controlling topic and turn-taking, may be preconditions for further progress (Damhuis 1995).

It has been shown that in sociocultural interaction, information patterns (e.g. ideas, attitudes, mannerisms, language features) adapt to environmental constraints through variation, selection, and replication (Gabora 2000). Evolutionary theory would consider the language acquirer as a *complex adaptive system* (comparable in the nonhuman world to a cell or an ant colony, and at the social level to a political party or a scholarly community). The phonology that older children acquire tends to be that of their peer group rather than that of their parents (Baron-Cohen and Staunton 1994). Yet the phonology of the peer group is itself indeterminate and in a natural state of flux, conditioned by the phonological behaviors of its various members. The agents of language evolution are individual speakers, since the variation that contributes to evolution starts at the interidiolectal level. As in population genetics, linguistic changes are brought about through selection at the level of individual speakers who, while interacting with each other, bring the varying features of their idiolects into competition (Mufwene 1998). Such evolutionary change, Mufwene points out, can be well reconciled with the model of language change proposed by the Milroys' sociolinguistic network theory (Milroy 1992; Milroy and Milroy 1985), and with the short-term adaptations modeled by Giles as speech accommodation (Giles and Smith 1979).

More particularly (and broadly following Brown 1995:14), we may see an idiolectal phonology as a complex adaptive system, in that:

1. It consists of numerous *components of different kinds* which interface with each other – psychoacoustic thresholds, combinatorial constraints, hierarchical structural relations, etc.;
2. Its *components interact nonlinearly* and on different temporal and spatial scales; in terms of current phonological theory, according to their *tiering* and *feature geometries*;
3. It '*organizes itself*' to produce complex coding and control structures and (in speech production) neurophysiological behaviors;
4. It *responds adaptively to environmental change* – for instance as speech accommodation on a minute-to-minute basis, and as society-wide accent shift in the long term.

Speaker–hearers/acquirers find themselves in an environment that is continuously changed by their own reactions to, and interactions with, other agents in the system. With the acquirers' only source of data in this sense in a state of flux, it is clear that their progress can be only partially predicted or determined: an acquirer's linguistic ecosystem is not – *pace* Newton – directed, mechanistic, or linear.

Nonlinearity

Language acquisition research, like much else in the human sciences, has tended to expect – and even assume – linear progressions based on equilibrium and stability. Yet as Courtney Brown points out, human behavior can be as nonlinear as other processes in the universe (Brown 2000). Some of those aspects of the acquirer's transitional language which evolve continuously can be modeled as a *dynamic system* – i.e. a set of functions (rules, equations) that specify how variables change over time (see e.g. Thelen and Smith 1994). But since some of the longitudinal changes observable in language acquisition data are *discontinuous*, any transitional language should be approached as a *nonlinear* system. Nonlinear dynamic systems theory gives a particular meaning to the concept of 'variability' and the term 'unpredictable;' and it provides new tools for exploring time series (longitudinal) data. Statistical analyses have most often treated language as a *fixed* effect, with time as an independent variable. Statistical analysis based on *survival analysis* treats time as the *outcome* and can thus empirically estimate the probability that an individual will experience a qualitative change of state *at a given time* (Gruber 1999).

While the gradual and cumulative type of learning performed by neural networks can simulate the mapping of acoustic–phonetic continua onto discrete categories of phonological representation, not all phonological acquisition can be modeled as gradual. Phonological knowledge may be the sudden result of a single event – such as a first exposure to a minimal lexical pair, or hearing a word hyperarticulated for comic effect. Epiphanies of this kind call for nonlinear modeling.

Chaos, complexity and catastrophe

The development of acquirers' linguistic ability is deterministic, yet in some respects also unpredictable, and the language acquirer may to this extent be viewed as a *chaotic system*. Chaotic systems are not simply *random*. They can change in any of a number of different directions, depending on tiny differences in the starting conditions. For specific initial conditions, the system will evolve in a specific way. But knowledge of initial conditions is never perfect, so that the behavior of the system tends to be much less predictable than might be expected as over time 'errors' multiply exponentially (Gleick 1987). The chaos–theoretic perspective underlines the importance of details in acquisition research: as Larsen-Freeman (1997) has pointed out, it may be the 'small things' in acquisition that matter the most.

Cambel (1993) specifies three properties of a chaotic system:

1. The system is neither completely deterministic nor completely random, and exhibits both characteristics.
2. The causes and effects of the events that the system experiences are not proportional.
3. The different parts of the (complex) system are linked and interact with one another. These properties describe important characteristics of an acquirer's developing phonological ability.

The 'edge' of chaos (Holland 1998) is the point at which the system performs at its greatest potential and is able to carry out maximally complex processing. This area of equipoise between stability and instability is where creative reorganization is evinced. It is such reorganization that seems to inform the sudden rather than incremental emergence of syntax observed by Bickerton (1996). In phonological development it was observed in an experiment on computer-managed lexical tone training of nontonal speakers (Leather 1997). Figure 2.2 shows how acquirers learning to identify random sequences of tone stimuli at particular moments radically reconstructed their (transitional) system for tone identification. Thus, in the first column, listener D1 can be seen after trial #71 to have formed a good prototype for tone 4, with apparently some destabilization of tone 2 which is resolved after trial #75. In the second column the same listener, confronted with interspeaker variation, appears to succeed in correctly distinguishing tones 3 and 4 by trial #46, but proves to need a further reorganization (in trials 52 through 61) to finalize the contrasts between tones 3 and 2.

Some of these radical reconstructions may be more properly termed *catastrophes* – since in each case a small change in environmental conditions apparently triggers a sudden, discontinuous jump in a system's evolution. Catastrophe theory offers a means of describing *dis*continuous changes in the acquirer's developing system along a continuous 'morphogenetic landscape' (the trajectory that elaborates the system's structure through its complex exchanges with its environment). The theory, moreover, redresses an imbalance in much contemporary acquisition research by treating the dynamic of the acquirer's acquisition 'system' not as unfolding from within but as responding to influences from outside (i.e. speech inputs).

Emergence

No single static model can do justice to the whole course of acquisition if in some respect(s), at some moment(s), the acquirer's phonological

Single speaker Listener: D1					Mixed speakers Listener: D1					Mixed speakers Listener: D2			
Tone presented:	1	2	3	4	Tone presented:	1	2	3	4	Tone presented:	1	2	3	4
trial #					trial #					trial #				
63				2	39	*				92				1
64				*	40		*			93		2		
65		*			41				3	94			4	
66			*		42			4		95			*	
67		*			43				3	96		1		
68	*				44	*				97				1
69			*		45			4		98			2	
70	*				46		4			99		2		
71				2	47				*	100			*	
72				*	48			*		101				*
73	*				49	*				102		2		
74			*		50		*			103			1	
75		1			51		*			104				*
76	*				52				3	105		*		
77			*		53			4		106			*	
78	*				54	*				107		*		
79			*		55			2		108			*	
80	*				56				*	109		*		
81		*			57	*				110				1
82	*				58		*			111		2		
83				*	59				3	112		*		
...					60		3			113		2		
...					61			2		114			*	
...					62	*				115				*
					63			*		116			*	
					64	*				117		*		
					65				*	118		4		
					66	*				119				*
					67		*			120		*		
					68				*	121			*	
					69			*		...				
					70	*				...				
					...					...				
					...									

Figure 2.2 Excerpts from the learning logs of two Dutch-speaking learners following computer-managed training in the perception of the four tonally distinguished Chinese words /ȳ/ ('muddy'), /ý/ ('fish'), /y̌/ ('rain") and /ỳ/ ('jade"). For each trial, the stimulus word is identified by the column in which the entry is located (corresponding to the word's tone). A star signifies correct identification of the stimulus; a number denotes the tone of the word otherwise heard.

behavior is *emergent*. While it is not clear that this is the case in phonological acquisition, it cannot be ruled out. The modeling problem that emergence poses can only be escaped, Heylighen has argued, by abandoning the mechanistic approach in which models are composed of invariant distinctions (Heylighen 1991). Our approach would then be to attempt first to model how distinctions – and hence

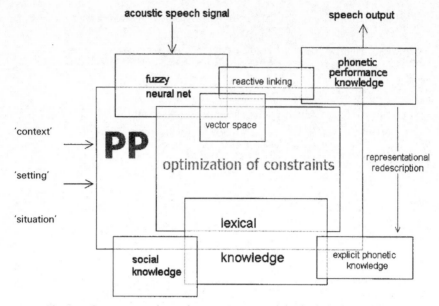

Figure 2.3 *An outline of a syncretic model of phonological acquisition grounded in phenomenological phonology (PP).*

how models themselves – change: our goal would be, in other words, a *metamodel*. This would distinguish different types of models and the different types of transitions between models.

Summary

This complex of knowledge processing and system building is represented in Figure 2.3 as a programmatic outline of a syncretic model of phonological acquisition.
    In this model:

- The acquirer is approached as a *complex adaptive system* in their social environment.
- *Phenomenological phonology* situates the acquirer as a vocal person in their world.
- *Social knowledge* mediates between the acquirer's lexicon (in the broad sense) and phonological constraints of the embodied situation.
- *Optimality theory* makes explicit the manner in which the acquirer's developing resources find structural equilibrium.
- *Vector spaces* specify phonetic details of transitional repertoires (and target 'systems').

- *Neural nets* extract patterns (types) from exemplars (tokens).
- *Fuzzy sets* and *fuzzy logic* interface connectionist networks with the 'ragged' data of real speech.
- *Reactive reasoning* captures 'phonological idioms' that bypass parse processing.
- *Representational redescription* maps the acquirers' language performance onto their knowledge, making details of language ability accessible to them as (metalinguistic) intuitions.

Further possible elements in the model would be:

- *Chaos theory* – setting empirical limits on the predictions that can be made for an individual's (nonlinear) development, and *catastrophe theory* addressing *dis*continuous changes.
- Meta-theory of *emergence* to attempt to account for any wholly unpredictable outcomes.

Conclusion

Marvin Minsky, doyen of AI research, wrote over 10 years ago that there is no one best way to represent knowledge, and that the limitations of machine intelligence stem largely from seeking 'unified theories' or from trying to repair the deficiencies of theoretically elegant but conceptually impoverished ideological positions (Minsky 1990). Any formally neat type of knowledge representation or inference needs to be complemented by some 'scruffier' kind of machinery. Combining different types of representation in a complementary architecture should lead to the best of several worlds. In any event, it should be possible to escape the hegemony of mainstream linguistic theory by thinking in hybrid (and interdisciplinary) terms, with diverse components fulfilling complementary modeling functions in an orchestrated whole.

In this chapter I have outlined elements in what might be termed an 'ecological' approach to modeling the development of speech. In future work I aim to examine how such an approach can be brought to bear upon data like Alvin's.

References

Allen, J. (1994) *Sainte-Lucie: relexification, décréolisation, recréolisation ou adlexification?* Mémoire de DEA des Sciences du Langage, Université Lumière Lyon II.

Anderson, B. (1999) Kohonen neural networks and language. *Brain and Language* 70, 86–94.

Archangeli, D. and Pulleyblank, D. (1994) *Grounded Phonology*. Cambridge: MIT Press.

Barlow, J.A. and Gierut, J.A. (1999). Optimality theory in phonological acquisition. *Journal of Speech, Language, and Hearing Research* 42, 1482–98.

Baron-Cohen, S. and Staunton, R. (1994) Do children with autism acquire the phonology of their peers? An examination of group identification through the window of bilingualism. *First Language* 14, 241–8.

Bickerton, D. (1996) *Language and Human Behaviour*. London: UCL Press.

Brooks, R.A. (1991) Intelligence without representation. *Artificial Intelligence* 47, 139–59.

Brown, C. (2000) *http://www.courtneybrown.com/socsci/cb.ss.htm*

Brown, J.H. (1995) *Macroecology*. Chicago: University of Chicago Press.

Bryson, J. and Lowe, W. (1997) Commentary on Ballard, D.H., Hayhoe, M.M., Pook, P.K. and Rao, R.P.N., Deictic codes for the embodiment of cognition. *Behavioral and Brain Science* 20, 743–4.

Cambel, A.B. (1993) *Applied Chaos Theory: A Paradigm for Complexity*. San Diego: Academic Press.

Chomsky, N. and Halle, M. (1968) *The Sound Pattern of English*. New York: Harper & Row.

Churchland, P.S. and Sejnowski, T. (1992) *The Computational Brain*. Cambridge, MIT Press.

Damhuis, R. (1995) *Interaction and Second Language Acquisition*. Amsterdam: IFOTT.

Edwards, J., Fourakis, M., Beckman, M.E. and Fox, R.A. (1999) Characterizing knowledge deficits in phonological disorders. *Journal of Speech, Language, and Hearing Research* 42, 169–86.

Engestrom, Y. (1987) *Learning by Expanding: An Activity-theoretical Approach to Developmental Research*. Helsinki: Orienta-Konsultit.

Ferguson, C.A. (1979) Phonology as an individual access system: Some data from language acquisition. In C.J. Fillmore, D. Kempler and W-S.Y. Wang (eds), *Individual Differences in Language Ability and Language Behavior*. New York: Academic Press, pp. 189–201.

Fraser, H. (1997) Phenomenological phonology and second language pronunciation. In J. Leather and A. James (eds), *New Sounds 97: Proceedings of the Third International Symposium on the Acquisition of Second-Language Speech*. Klagenfurt: University of Klagenfurt, pp. 89–95.

Gabora, L. (2000) *http://www.vub.ac.be/CLEA/liane/*

Gierut, J.A. (1996) Categorization and feature specification in phonological acquisition. *Journal of Child Language* 23, 397–415.

Gierut, J.A., Simmerman, C.L. and Neumann, H.J. (1994) Phonemic structures of delayed phonological development. *Journal of Child Language* 21, 291–316.

Giles, H. and Smith, P. (1979) Accommodation theory: optimal levels of convergence. In H. Giles and R. St Clair (eds), *Language and Social Psychology*. Oxford: Basil Blackwell, pp. 45–65.

Gleick, J. (1987) *Chaos: Making a New Science*. New York: Viking.

Gruber, F.A. (1999) Tutorial: survival analysis – a statistic for clinical, efficacy, and theoretical applications. *Journal of Speech, Language, and Hearing Research* 42, 432–47.

Gupta, P. and Dell, G.S. (1999) The emergence of language from serial order and procedural memory. In B. MacWhinney (ed.), *The Emergence of Language*. Mahwah: Erlbaum, pp. 447–81.

Gupta, P. and Touretzky, D.S. (1994) Connectionist models and linguistic theory: investigations of stress systems in language. *Cognitive Science* 18, 1–50.

Heylighen, F. (1991) Modelling Emergence. In G. Kampis (ed.), *World Futures Journal of General Evolution* (Special issue on Emergence, ed. G. Kampis) 31, 89–104.

Holland, J.H. (1998) *Emergence: From Chaos to Order*. Reading: Helix Books.

Holm, A. and Dodd, B. (1999) A longitudinal study of the phonological development of two Cantonese-English bilingual children. *Applied Psycholinguistics* 20, 349–76.

Hubey, H.M. (1999) Vector phase space for speech analysis via dimensional analysis. *Journal of Quantitative Linguistics* 6(2), 117–48.

Jeannerod, M. (1994) The representing brain: neural correlates of motor intention and imagery. *Behavioral and Brain Sciences* 17(2), 187–245.

Jusczyk, P. (1997) *The Discovery of Spoken Language*. Cambridge: MIT Press.

Kachru, B.B. (1996) The paradigms of marginality. *World Englishes* 15, 241–55.

Karmiloff-Smith, A. (1992) *Beyond Modularity: A Developmental Perspective on Cognitive Science*. Cambridge: MIT Press.

Klahr, D. (1992) Information-processing approaches to cognitive development. In M.H. Bornstein and M.E. Lamb (eds), *Developmental Psychology: An Advanced Textbook*, 3rd edn. Hillsdale: Erlbaum, pp. 273–335.

Laeufer, C. (1997) Towards a typology of bilingual phonological systems. In A. James and J. Leather (eds), *Second-language Speech: Structure and Process*. Berlin: Mouton de Gruyter, pp. 325–42.

Larsen-Freeman, D. (1997) Chaos/complexity science and second language acquisition, *Applied Linguistics*, 141–65.

Leather, J. (1997) Interrelation of perceptual and productive learning in the initial acquisition of second-language tone. In A. James and J. Leather (eds), *Second-language Speech: Structure and Process.* Berlin: Mouton de Gruyter, pp. 75–101.

Leather, J. (1999) Second-language speech research: an introduction. *Language Learning* 49(S1) 1–56.

Leather, J. and James, A. (1991) The acquisition of second-language speech. *Studies in Second Language Acquisition* 13, 305–41.

Leather, J. and James, A. (1996) Second language speech. In W.C. Ritchie and T.K. Bhatia (eds), *Handbook of Second Language Acquisition.* New York: Academic Press, pp. 269–316.

Lin, C.-T. and Lee, C.S.G. (1994) Supervised and unsupervised learning with fuzzy similarity for neural-network-based fuzzy logic control systems. In R. Yager and L.A. Zadeh (eds), *Fuzzy sets, Neural Networks, and Soft Computing.* New York: Van Nostrand Reinhold, pp. 85–125.

Liouw, S.J.R. and Poon, K.K.L. (1998) Phonological awarenesss in multilingual Chinese children. *Applied Psycholinguistics* 19, 339–62.

McMahon, A. (2000) *Change, Chance and Optimality.* Oxford: Oxford University Press.

Milroy, J. (1992) *Linguistic Variation and Change: On the Historical Sociolinguistics of English.* Oxford: Blackwell.

Milroy, J. and Milroy, L. (1985) Linguistic change, social network and speaker innovation. *Journal of Linguistics* 21, 339–84.

Minsky, M. (1990) Logical vs. analogical, or symbolic vs. connectionist, or neat vs. scruffy. In P.H. Winston (ed.), *Artificial Intelligence at MIT: Expanding frontiers*, Vol. 1. Cambridge: MIT Press.

Moskowitz, B.A. (1980) Idioms in phonological acquisition and phonological change. *Journal of Phonetics* 8, 69–83.

Mufwene, S.S. (1998) Language contact, evolution, and death: how ecology rolls the dice. In G.E. Kindell and M.P. Lewis (eds), *Assessing Ethnolinguistic Vitality.* Dallas: Summer Institute of Linguistics.

Nardi, B.A. (1996) Studying context: a comparison of activity theory, situated action models and distributed cognition. In B.A. Nardi (ed.), *Context and Consciousness: Activity Theory and Human-Computer Interaction.* Cambridge: MIT Press.

Nayar, P.B. (1994) Whose English is it? *TESL-EJ* 1(1), F1.

Phillipson, R. and Skutnabb-Kangas, T. (1996), English only worldwide or language ecology? *TESOL Quarterly* 30, 429–52.

Plaut, D.C. and Kello, C.T. (1999) The emergence of phonology from the interplay of speech comprehension and production: A distributed connectionist approach. In B. MacWhinney (ed.), *The Emergence of Language*. Mahwah: Erlbaum, pp. 381–415.

Powers, D. (forthcoming) Robot babies: what can they teach us about language acquisition? In J. Leather and J. van Dam (eds), *Ecology of Language Acquisition*. Dordrecht: Kluwer Academic.

Saville-Troike, M. (1988) Private speech: Evidence for second language learning strategies during the silent period. *Journal of Child Language* 15, 567–90.

Scherer, K.R. and Giles, H. (eds) (1979) *Social Markers in Speech*. Cambridge: Cambridge University Press.

Schnitzer, M. (1990) Critique of linguistic knowledge. *Language and Communication* 10, 95–126.

Schnitzer, M. and Krasinksi, E. (1994) The development of segmental phonological production in a bilingual child. *Journal of Child Language* 21, 585–622.

Schnitzer, M. and Krasinksi, E. (1996) The development of segmental phonological production in a bilingual child: a contrasting second case. *Journal of Child Language* 23, 547–71.

Thelen, E. and Smith, L.B. (1994) Dynamic systems: exploring paradigms for change. In their, *A Dynamic Systems Approach to the Development of Cognition and Action*. Cambridge: MIT Press, pp. 45–69.

Watson, I. (1991) Phonological processing in two languages. In E. Bialystok (ed.), *Language Processing in Bilinguals*. Cambridge: Cambridge University, pp. 25–48.

3 Language development and identity: multiple timescales in the social ecology of learning

Jay L. Lemke

Language is appropriately used in the course of social activities only when it is deployed from some recognizable social stance or identifiable social role. We have not learned to speak academic English or scientific English if we do not know how academics or scientists speak across a range of social situations. To some degree we must be able to play the part and assume the identities, attitudes, values, and dispositions for making appropriate meanings with conventional linguistic forms. Identities can be conceptualized in this context as being constituted by the orientational stances we take, toward others and toward the contents and effects of our own utterances, in enacting roles within specialized subcultures by speaking and writing in the appropriate registers and genres. Language competence in this sense is as much an ensemble of virtual identities as a language itself is an ensemble of its heteroglossic voices (Bakhtin 1935).

How do we develop appropriate identities for competently using the specialized registers of a language? How do brief encounters in classrooms and laboratories, over time, come to add up to appropriate linguistic participation in a subculture? What are the ways in which individuals in communities integrate activity and meaning-making across timescales from the events of a minute to those of a day, from those of a day to those of a lifetime? What are the corresponding scales of the social ecologies in which such integrations take place, from local conversational settings to global institutions? How does the inevitable imbedding of practices that take but a moment within longer-timescale processes condition and enable the acquisition of language-user identities?

I would like to try to more carefully define some of these issues and sketch out a theoretical framework within which they can be effectively investigated.

Identities, trajectories, and scales: ecosocial dynamics

The theoretical framework within which I would like to address questions of language and identity development is a hybrid of social semiotics and ecosystem dynamics, which I have called ecosocial dynamics (e.g. Lemke 1993, 1995; see also Halliday 1978; Hodge and Kress 1988; Gee 1992). Social semiotics is a theoretical approach deriving from the work of Michael Halliday on the role of language in society, which points to the way in which the social functions of language or other semiotic resources (e.g. visual representations, ritualized actions, etc.) help determine the variety of those resources. Ecosystem dynamics is the set of theories in biology that examines the ways in which energy and matter flow through ecological systems and maintain relatively stable patterns of organization. In ecosocial dynamics (which only claims to be one useful perspective on general issues of social dynamics), we recognize first that human social systems are more specified instances of natural ecosystems, distinguished primarily by the role of semiotic practices in co-determining the flows of matter, energy, and information which constitute the system. Semiotic practices are themselves conceptualized as material processes in which variety and variation on lower-scale levels of organization are reorganized as useful information for higher-scale levels by the dynamical emergence of new, self-organizing phenomena at inter-mediate levels (Lemke 2000a). Ecosocial systems are, to a first approximation, hierarchies of organizational levels in which each emergent level of organization is constrained by the level above it in scale, while itself being an organization of units and interactions one level below. Scale is measured here quantitatively by differences of one to two orders of magnitude (i.e. factors of tenfold to a hundredfold increase) in typical energies, masses, the spatial extent of organizational patterns, and especially in the characteristic times for typical processes to cycle or complete.

Within this general picture, human organisms constitute just one intermediate level of organization between those of physiology and cellular or molecular biochemistry below and social-ecological communities on various scales above. Each level is regarded as a metastable, dynamically emergent pattern of organization, which exists by virtue of interactions between the system and its environment, and in which order is accumulated and disorder exported to higher levels (i.e. dissipated, if we're lucky). The units of analysis at every level are, most basically, *processes*, because this aims to be a dynamical model. Structures are epiphenomena of material interaction processes taking place one level below, and they may in turn function as virtual participants in processes at the next level above. A dynamical level of the system is defined as including everything (material and artifactual, whether biological or not) which significantly participates in system dynamics at the appropriate timescale (i.e. in processes that take place at roughly the same rate within about a factor of 10).

At the level of the communities in which humans most directly participate, ecosocial systems include not only people, but artifacts, architectures, landscapes, soils, bacteria, food crops, etc. An ecosocial system consists of social processes and semiotic practices, not of organisms. (Semiotic models such as Latour's actant networks are similar in that actants, both human and nonhuman, are defined as functional units in activities, not as ontologically prior realia; Latour 1993, 1999). Semiotic practices are conceptualized as ecosocial processes, which are simply the material processes by which organisms in communities interact with one another and with other actants in ways that are adaptive in the context of higher-scale levels than that at which the material interaction itself takes place. The whole organism, for example, may respond to an interaction between a sensor membrane (in the nose) and an inhaled molecule, not only at the level of molecular and membrane chemistry, but also at a higher-scale organismic level, 'interpreting' the interaction as a tell-tale or *sign* of a food source, nearby predator, or potential mate (i.e. by sense of smell). In ecosocial systems, the interpretation of actants as signs, as well as direct material interactions with them, leads to different patterns of activity, and different distributions and flows of matter, energy, and information; actions based on meanings co-constitute the 'attractors' of the system dynamics, i.e. the dynamical states toward which a system tends when left to its own devices. They participate in shaping epigenetic trajectories of development across all scale levels. These epigenetic trajectories are the pathways of development trail-blazed for us by evolution, but recapitulated uniquely by every developing organism in interaction with its environment. ("Epigenetic" means following genetic guidance but also having input from the environment during development.)

What does this mean for human development? First, that human organisms only develop normally in the presence of environmental distributions of available matter, energy, and information which afford recapitulation of phylogenetically evolved trajectories. Second, that molecular scale information in the genome assists in the self-organization of higher scale structures, but only if the phylogenetically 'expected' environmental complements are present, and only with the result that the emergent structures will themselves be "tuned" to be selectively sensitive to particular kinds of further environmental input.

Third, that *all levels of organization* in an ecosocial system are in a continuous process of development, enabling (from below) and constraining (from above) development at each intermediate level, but with each level developing at a significantly different characteristic timescale (i.e. rate; faster at lower levels, more slowly at higher levels).

Along its developmental trajectory, an organism-in-community is both approximately recapitulating its evolutionary lineage, which is characteristic of its type (species, culture, caste habitus), and individuating uniquely, i.e. to some degree diverging from the typical pathway of its species. The unit of evolution is the whole developmental trajectory (cf. Salthe 1993), from conception to decomposition; it is the species-specific trajectory as a whole which is adaptive to environments on all relevant scales. Because developmental processes across different scale levels strongly interact with one another, there is no single linear progression in development, and no meaning to claims that later developmental stages (adults) are better adapted than earlier ones (children). It is the typical human conception-to-embryo-to-infant-to-child-to-juvenile-to-adult-to-elder-to-death trajectory that has evolved, and it is this trajectory *as a whole* that has come to be adapted to the human environment.

The shift from an organism-centered to to a multiple-timescale system view of development has profound implications for our views of education, language learning, and indeed the social order of relations among humans at different ages. Serious moral and political questions are raised by this change in perspective; views often taken as commonsensical or scientific become suspect as ideologically motivated by the power interests of dominant age groups, just as formerly gender domination and ethnic-racial dominations have had to be questioned as the intellectual paradigms supporting them have been superseded. I will return to these issues later in this discussion.

Identity and semiotic practice

Let us narrow our focus now, toward language and the concept of identity. As an organism develops in an ecosocial community (and this is not a development that is strictly and predictably controlled from within, but a result of system–environment interactions, in many ways contingent and variable), among the emergent organizational patterns in its interactions with others is its coming-to-use-language. But not just language; indeed, in early stages it seems clear that there are proto-semiotics which are precursors to what we later analytically distinguish as language, gesture, mime, and all the forms of motor-based communication (for more discussion, see Lemke, in press. Speaking is a specialization within vocal gesturing, integrated in behavior with other fine and gross motor communicative behavior patterns. Language is a formal sign system that arises for most (but not all) of us within the context of speaking-within-vocalizing-within-action. What linguistics calls "language" is not, taken in isolation, an appropriate unit of analysis for developmental research; such units need to be defined more functionally, out of the flow and patternings of communicative-interactive-motor behavior. Only the temporary prestige of linguistics as an academic discipline has distracted research from this obvious principle (which is of course observed in practice, if not always made explicit in theory, by many researchers). You cannot, neither materially nor physiologically nor culturally, make meaning *only* with the formal linguistic sign system; other modes of meaning-making are always functionally coupled with language use in real activity.

Language in use is always language-within-activity: socially and culturally meaningful, directly observable behavior – equally social in its meanings whether interactional or solo in its production. Language is always "addressed" and "dialogical" (Bakhtin 1929, 1935); it always constructs an orientational stance toward real or potential interlocutors, and toward the content of what is said. You cannot speak without offering or requesting information or action, without implicitly or explicitly evaluating the likelihood, usuality, desirability, appropriateness, or importance of what you or others say, or without taking up a position within the system of possible social viewpoints on any topic, or without providing indexical information by which you are viewed by others as occupying a position in the system of social statuses. Speaking is not possible without the constitution and construal of what we believe, what we value, and where we find ourselves in the systems of social classification.

What else is an *identity* but the performance, verbally and nonverbally, of a possible constellation of attitudes, beliefs, and values that has a recognizable coherence by the criteria of some community? Of course identity is complex; we define it on many timescales of behavioral coherence. There are the identities we assume in each particular activity type in which we engage: the identities we perform in the conference room, in the playroom, and in the bedroom. There are also the identities we maintain, or construct, for ourselves and ask others to uphold for us, across settings: our gender identities, our social class identities, our age group identities.

It is particularly important that we are not deluded by the normative ideal of a consistent, fixed, stereotypical identity. This "ideal" is the product of our highly regulative, institution-dominated, modernist culture. Modernist institutions (families, schools, corporations, etc.) and the values they support tend to coerce us towards fixed and predictable, role-adapted identities, but most people in fact mobilize and strategically deploy, on various timescales, identity performances and identity claims that contradict the standpoint of modernist identity standardization. Many of us successfully play with identity performances and claims that are in turn both macho and gentle, feminine and assertive, African and Latino, middle- and working-class, secular and spiritual, juvenile and elder, conformist and rebellious, rational and poetic, straight and gay, anglophone and francophone. We surf across the identity possibilities of our cultures, taking them as semiotic resources to play with rather than as essentialist necessities of our being. Generation by generation, and especially among those most free from or most ignored by dominant institutions, identity has become a work-in-progress, more stabilized by boredom, habit, and social routine than by institutionalized conformity.

Individual developmental trajectories on longer timescales may be envisioned as "envelopes" of the shorter timescale trajectories. Lifelong development is a vague trending summation, usually retrospective, over many specific kinds of changes in our patterns of behavior, each of which accumulated from many specific incidents or periods of engagement in some activity. Seen from the short-term scale, this moment's performance may or may not ever again recur; some culturally significant aspects of it may be enacted again, soon or much later; there may be other kinds of continuity constructed among these events or none. What ties together the learning of minutes to make the learning of a day? Or of a lifetime? The most basic answer is the physiological continuity (such as it is) of the body itself, and along with it, of the many signifying artifacts and animate others that mediate and afford our momentary performances and our efforts to construct long-timescale continuities and trends (*via* our skimpy diaries and full closets, our libraries and back yards, friends and children, pets and cars).

A multiscale model of development: becoming the village

A traditional saying has it that "it takes a village to raise a child." Why? In the ecosocial model, the answer is that normal development is the process of "becoming the village" (Lemke 2002). By this I mean that to live successfully in a community we have to learn to interact across the inevitable and substantial differences that constitute the diversity of a community. Communities, like other ecosystems, are not defined by what their participants have in common, but by how their inter-dependence on one another articulates across differences of viewpoint, beliefs, values, and practices (cf. Wallace 1970 on "ordered hetero-geneity"). At every age we normally live in communities containing those both younger and older than ourselves, and those similar and different, along all the dimensions that are used to constitute social castes by age, gender, sexuality, class, occupation, religion, ethnicity, "race" or whatever other arbitrary reductions of the high-dimensional variety of human behaviors come to count in a community. We have to learn how to interact successfully with the whole range of diversity in our "village;" we have to be able to shift our own patterns of behavior responsively, and so to "mirror" in ourselves (not by replication but by functional responsiveness) this diversity. If we could watch any villager, at any age, seeing only their body and actions and hearing only their speech and vocalizations, as they went about a day of living and doing, but blanking out all else, we would still learn a great deal about the whole village: its terrain and its artifacts, its human diversity, activity types, and much else.

What we call our identities are our modes of response to the diversity of our villages. Identities are fractal, as ecosocial systems themselves are fractal mosaics. On each scale of space and time, of project activities and interactions, there are more localized and more globally relevant identities. We have a specialized identity for every person we meet, for every activity we engage in, but each of these grows in part out of our prior patterns of interaction with others, as well as the uniqueness of the moment. Mediating all of these is the continuity of material objects, of our own body and all that surrounds us, as participants to varying degrees in our activities, by which we link across time from moment to moment and event to event, person to person, activity to activity, on many timescales. From body hexis to every cultural habitus (Bourdieu 1990), our physiologies are also our diaries, along with what is written on paper or cut into cloth or wood. All these material mediators not only remind us of our past, but are taken up again and again as partners in activity, aiding our continuity by extending the body through persistent tools and material signs.

We are what we eat, how we dress, where we walk, what we read and write, hear and say, to this other and to that, in this repeated activity type and that. But increasingly we are not so bound to the habitus of class, gender, sexuality, or culture as Bourdieu's idealized model of modernist identity presumes. Many of us simply do not live our lives entirely within the institutions and milieux of a single culture or social class and, even when we do, the forces of social control they exert to deny us wider latitude in our behavior grow weaker as we are presented with more alternatives by larger society. We do not have to obey or believe parents, clergy, teachers, bosses, governments, or media to the extent that we have other feasible options. Moreover, few communities today insulate their members effectively from the subversive texts and values of other communities. Barriers between cultures and languages are weaker today; our loyalties to them are moderated by our multiple lives and lifestyles.

Identity in education: extending behavioral repertory to longer timescales

Let's specify again, toward the case of classroom learning as an example of the general process of ecosocially-mediated development. Schooling is supposed to facilitate certain long-term changes in the behavior patterns of students. Both educators and their critics wonder how lasting these changes are and how far they carry beyond the walls of the school. Do lasting changes occur in the course of a 40-minute lesson? Even if we imagined that some apparently fundamental change did take place in a "breakthrough" moment, would it still count if it disappeared the next day? Or the next week? Fundamental change in attitudes or habits of reasoning cannot take place on short timescales. Even if short-term events *contribute toward* such changes, it is only the fact that they are *not* soon erased, do *not* quickly fade, and are reinforced by subsequent events which makes for the kind of persistent change we really mean by "learning." It is the longer-term process, including the effects of subsequent events, which determines for us the reality of basic human social development.

So how could events on the timescale of a conversation or an experiment or reading a story ever contribute to identity development in this sense? The classroom is no different from anywhere else in our world of social artifacts. Its developmental input is there not only on the walls but in the very fact that there are walls; not just in the words in the textbook, but in the existence and use of textbooks. But it is first and foremost in those respects in which the classroom is exactly like the rest of the social world that it contributes to the formation of identities and habits of action that are formed across the longer timescales we also spend in other places. It is not what is unique about classrooms that contributes to our identity development, but what is the same about them compared to many other sites in our culture. Identities develop over intermediate timescales, during which the trajectory of the developing social person takes him and her from classroom to classroom, from school to schoolyard, to street corner, home, shopping mall, Web and TV worlds. The timescale that is relevant to identity development for sampling all these worlds is the timescale on which we move from world to world and create ways of mobilizing consistent identity features across multiple venues.

There is a second key factor in the role of momentary experience in the development of longer-term patterns of behavior. It is not just when or how often do we have occasion to repeat (always with variation) some learned practice or way of interacting with a person or an artifact (or a natural place), but how intensely do these experiences matter to us? The person we become for a moment with a stranger for whom we have no strong feelings and whom we never see or remember again may be transient indeed. The person we feel ourselves to be when interacting with someone we feel strongly about, again and again over the course of a lifetime, becomes an essential part of who we are. The self I am when I am writing, or teaching, or doing those things that mean something fundamental to me, and that I can do over many years, is basic to my identity. Even the self I am whenever I read a particular book, hear a particular kind of music, play or sing or dance to that music, if I feel strongly enough about it, can become basic to my identity. When I teach, or write, or have conversations with colleagues, I am often working to recreate activities and senses of self that are basic to my identity repertory. I am seeking to keep identity-constituting processes going on longer timescales and across a wider range of settings and participants. To some extent, whatever I am doing, I am also doing "identity work," and what I choose to do more often and with greater affective engagement may well be what works best for me in confirming elements of my identity repertory about which I have the strongest concerns (e.g. gender identity, class identity, and other more specific culturally salient aspects of identity resources).

It is somewhat ironic that classroom education and formal curricula, which are supposed to create longer-term continuity from lesson to lesson and unit to unit (though not, after the earliest years, from hour to hour across the school day or from year to year even in the same subject), are narrowly focused on informational content which is more or less unique to school experience, while the major developmental processes of these years appear to be about the accumulation of identity resources that can instantiate larger-scale social stereotypes for gender-, class-, age-, and culture-specific identities. Students are mainly going about the business of learning to act like six-year-olds or 12-year-olds, to act masculine or feminine, gay or heterosexual, middle-class or working-class, Jewish or Catholic, Irish-American or Jamaican-American, or any of the many dozens of sociotypical identities for which there are identity kits available in a particular community (cf. Gee 1992). Many are, of course, also learning to mobilize and hybridize multiple identities that modernist institutions have traditionally seen as incompatible. Whatever we offer up in the classroom becomes an opportunity to pursue longer-term agendas of building identity repertories and resources. Our primary affective engagement is with this agenda, with becoming all the selves we want to be, and not with learning this or that bit of curriculum, except insofar as it fits our particular agenda or insofar as "being a good student" or "not falling for that bullshit" belongs to our repertory. Perhaps later in schooling, a few of us are also working to acquire, within these larger identity repertories, specific resources for identities as "future scientists" or "future teachers."

Language and identity: categorial semantics and meaning-by-degree

No one seems to doubt that language, both in its communicative functions and in its systems of semantic classification, plays a major role in identity development. I have mainly spoken so far about the communicative-interactional function, but what is most specific about the contribution of language arises from its categorial semantics. Natural language construes relations among types and between types and instances of types. It makes meaning by creating differences of kind, far more than by creating differences of degree. Yet we also know that material phenomena of all kinds differ significantly by degree, and that differences of degree may become resources for the emergence of new kinds or types. Mathematics begins and develops over much of its history as an extension of the semantics of natural language toward more precise description of differences of degree (Lemke 1999, in press).

The semantics of natural language is complemented by resources for meaning-by-degree such as vocal intensity and coloring, bodily and facial gesture and posture, the pacing of speech and activity, and drawing and visual representations of many kinds, with their resources for variations of degree in color, shape, shading, etc. Identities may be constituted and expressed as much in how we draw as in what we write, and as much by our movement and vocal styles as by the semantic content of our talk. But natural language semantics lends itself far better to categorical distinction than to subtleties of degree. It is language that allows us to dichotomously contrast male and female, straight and gay, child and adult, black and white, Dutch and Deutsch, when we really know that none of these are singular categories; all are constructed from variation along many potentially independent dimensions, and most variation along each of these is far more nearly quasicontinuous than categorial. Logocentric cultures and modes of academic analysis bias us to classify identity options too categorically, to marginalize the normal hybridity of identities across our artificial categories, and to pay too much attention to the verbal-typological construction and performance of identity, and not enough to the integral nonverbal-continuous modes by which we make meaning and meaningful identity.

Do we construct different identities for ourselves when speaking different languages or different dialects of "the same" language? In the ways I have defined identity we surely do, the more so as we consistently distribute our use of language varieties and languages among different activity types and typical settings (cf. code-switching, diglossia). Also, in speaking, we perform differences in styles of vocalization, in speech rhythms, and intonation patterns, and in facial, gestural, and movement styles. Identity differences will also be greater insofar as we come to speak different registers and use different genres in the two languages, as we come to use different registers of politeness and constructions that index and constitute different modes of interpersonal relationships (formality, intimacy, aggression, concilia-tion, affiliation, empathy), and as we come to enact different social roles and take up different social statuses and positions. At the same time, given the patterns of redundancy that make culture, we are also likely to express different beliefs, attitudes, and values, even if only to the degree that such matters are untranslatable between the semantic systems of different languages and dialects.

At the later stages of socialization, particularly in academic contexts, we use language to put on professional or preprofessional identities. There are substantial differences in values, attitudes, and semantic orientations (Hasan 1996), indexed and constituted in part through language use, not only between differently gendered speakers, or those with different class-habitus repertoires, but also among historians, literary critics, biologists, and mathematicians (not to mention lawyers, librarians, and administrators!). Professional sub-communities regulate the range and types of identities that are considered acceptable or "promising" and may well do so with evident class and gender biases, but also with subtler distinctions that make them seem more compatible with acceptable identities in various ethnic and cultural traditions as well. Much of this, in logocentric academia, is regulated by specifying the pragmatics of register use. It is not enough to master the vocabulary, the preferred grammatical constructions, the semantic systems of classification and collocation; you have to learn how and when to make which kinds of jokes, how to mix the formal register with informal talk, to appear to "think" and "come from" the preferred attitudinal stance of physicists or economists or computer programmers.

It is a wonderful mystery how language socialization and specialist enculturation take place in their normal contexts. But it is a more poignant and humanly crucial question how they so often fail to occur in educational settings. Modern democratic systems of mass education seek, in their own eyes, to make the opportunities of middle-class lifestyles available to all. More cynically, we may say that they seek to produce as many well-trained workers for middle-class occupations as the employment economy needs, and that unwittingly (for the most part) they also serve to justify the lesser life chances of all the rest in terms of individual lack of talent or willingness to study. A few supporters of critical educational models seek to empower all students to understand social inequities and the belief and attitude systems that sustain them. On a larger scale, however, the very structural artifacts of our educational system may well serve to maximize the disparity in achievement between those who come to school most ready to learn what and how the school teaches, and all the rest.

Heterochrony, heterogeneity, and development

I want to conclude this theoretical discussion by contrasting my description of the normal course of "becoming the village" with the artificial educational arrangements in modern societies that claim to facilitate this process. At the same time I will raise some troubling questions about the ideological dimensions of our supposedly scientific theories of human development, including language development and language learning.

Schooling segregates students by age; natural communities insure interactions across all age groups. The model of multiscale, ecosocially-mediated development I have presented here is a sort of grand generalization of the social learning theories of Vygotsky, not unlike many more directly neo-Vygotskyan models (e.g. Lave 1988; Lave and Wenger 1991; Rogoff 1990; Cole 1996). But it implies a more radical educational critique. If natural intellectual and social development is supported by participation in communities with all their diversity intact, particularly their age diversity, then every homogenization of schooling environments, especially age-grading, is likely to block many natural and necessary processes of developmental input.

On its face, our society is one in which a particular culturally self-defined age group (broadly from age 30–70, more narrowly 40–60, and most dominantly 50–60) has so ordered our institutions as to enable it to allocate to itself disproportiate social resources and opportunities at the expense of all those of younger and older ages. I see this as no different from social-class inequity and exploitation, gender/sexuality domination, or the politics of racism and ethnocentrism. Women, workers, serfs, gays, and people of color have all been compared to "children" in efforts to rationalize their exploitation and lack of access to institutional power. To these disempowered castes one can add "senior citizens" and younger adults, not to mention the youngest age groups themselves. Developmental theory is often used today to justify the disempowerment of nondominant age groups just as many other once-accepted scientific doctrines have played this role in the past, justifying racism, sexism, and class oppression.

The logic of biology and dynamical systems theory implies that it is the whole dynamical-developmental life-trajectory which is the unit of adaptive evolution, and not, certainly, the adult phase alone. As a species we are equally well (or poorly) adapted to our natural and social environments at all ages from womb to tomb. Ideologically, however, it is not in the interests of the dominant age group to recognize too visibly the many ways in which younger humans are superior to mature adults. We originally separated age groups in schools out of eighteenth-century fears that older students would morally corrupt younger ones, but we continue today to rationalize this separation by the doctrine that there must be some ideal method of teaching that is specific to each small range of ages and radically distinct from those appropriate to other age groups. We ground this notion of linear developmental change in a highly implausible model that maps linear notions of clock time onto complex, multiple timescale, developmental processes.

Biology and dynamical systems theory afford a critique of the application of linear notions of time to complex multiscale systems. This critique replaces the notion of a single dynamical time with a hierarchy of overlapping characteristic times of processes on the many different scales of dynamical organization of the system. A particular event on some local timescale may simultaneously also be part of many other processes on longer timescales, where the minimal functionally meaningful time-steps will span some distance into the event's past and its future as measured on its own timescale. Thus, from the viewpoint of "linear time" for such systems, the dominant temporal regime is one of *heterochrony*: certain events widely separated in linear time may be more relevant to meaningful behavior now than other events which are closer in linear time.

In ecosocial systems, I believe, it is particularly the circulation of material artifacts that function as signs (e.g. texts, but also inscribed bodies and other semiotic artifacts; Lemke 2000b) which serves to integrate social processes across timescales from the interactional to the institutional, from the local to the global. A book written hundreds of years ago, kept in print and circulation by the actions of persons and institutions functioning across many intermediate timescales (critics, educators, publishers, bankers, foresters, makers of presses, truck drivers, etc. etc.), made more likely to fall into our hands at this moment by customary linkages among social practices and settings, now mediates our present, short-term conversation. Our conversation in turn, our buying the book, or borrowing it from a library, participates in and sustains many social-institutional processes on many inter-mediate timescales. Architectural plans, scale models, and paintings made decades ago for a modern cathedral, copied and transformed and in the hands of builders, alter the builders' interactions with stone and steel now.

What then of development? It certainly does not run by clock time, but by its own internally generated timeclocks, many of them, on many different timescales, cycling at vastly different rates (molecular, cellular, organismic, ecological), and "synchronized" not by the calibrations of some Bureau of Standards clock, but by actual dynamical interdependences and the transfer of information across levels of organization. Which past events are most relevant to the *now* of learning? Not, in general, those which most immediately precede it by clock time. What larger-scale, longer-term developmental processes, such as identity development, play a role in learning now? What sign-carriers, themselves the products of larger-scale longer-time institu-tional or social and cultural developments, intervene in the *now* and entrain it as part of their own dynamics?

If you face a 12-year-old in the classroom, do you not also face elements of his behavioral repertory that were formed at age 10, or age six, and still remain active or dormant and waiting to be recalled? Do you not also face a human being who has been learning to interact with a six-year-old sibling and a 10-year-old friend, a 15-year-old nemesis, and a 30-year-old parent? Do we imagine that this 12-year-old does not have responsive repertories that mirror the behavioral patterns, beliefs, attitudes, and values of these different-age others? And how can this person not have also formed anticipations and expectations about the behavior of people, and of himself, at still later ages? He may be 12 by the calibrations of calendars, but as a member of the community he is dynamically heterochronous, some mix of every age he's already been, and every age he's learned to cope with, and many ages he's begun to understand and imagine and model. The age we see is to a large degree the age-identity we know how to call forth; it is itself always an age-identity mix, with which he responds to us and to this situation.

If you face a second 12-year-old, she will almost certainly present a different age-mixing profile in response to the activity of the moment. She has, after all, lived a different life, mixed with a different combination of people of different ages, interacted with them to different degrees, and formed different ways of doing so. We should not think of someone's developmental stage as specific to their chronological age, but rather, at each chronological age as a distribution across their acquired repertory of age-typical behaviors and ways of responding. As we become the village, we come to embody something of all the ages we encounter in the village. We are, at every age, a unique mix of our younger selves, our ways of being with those who are younger, those who are close to us in age, and also those who are much older. By the calendar we may have a single age, but developmentally, in a community, we are best characterized by a distribution of age-typical behaviors and responses. Development of this kind is clearly inhibited by educational practices such as age-grading that artificially reduce the opportunity of students to interact with those both much younger and much older than themselves across a wide range of normal social situations.

Language socialization and academic language study

Among the questions which preoccupy language students, language teachers, and researchers today, there are three which I would like to address from the viewpoint of the multiple timescales approach to ecosocial systems.

What constitutes the highest level of success in language learning?

The traditional answer to this question is some notion of "fluency," which for me presents a very impoverished view of what people use language to do. It is a merely instrumental notion: that we should be ready to speak and comprehend as fast as a native speaker, that our use of the language should have become relatively automatic and transparent as a medium, so that our thoughts become words and their words become meanings almost as if language played no part, completely unproblematically. This seems to me a robotic notion, a survival from the twentieth century, before we understood that there is no meaning (and no mind) apart from semiotic systems and strategies through which meaning is constructed. It also seems to be a view specifically oriented to industrial notions of efficiency as maximum work product per unit time.

Let me propose some alternatives. At the shortest timescale, of conversational interaction and repartee, the most sophisticated things we do with language are our manipulations of social situations in culturally acceptable and favored ways: humour and wit, sincerity and authenticity of emotion, the power to mesmerize our interlocutors and bring them to laughter or tears. It is, in short, the *affective sensibility* of language use that we must better articulate in order to orient language learners to what language, first or second, is fully capable of. Formal linguistics, allied with an over-rationalized cognitive psychology, has effectively dehumanized the dominant conception of language as much as it has unsocialized it. We can learn to write mathematical theorems, engineering specifications, or computer program help files with very little sophistication in a second language, and for competent readers our errors or infelicities will have very few functional consequences. Even the skills of integrating language with visual representations in technical writing (e.g. Lemke 1998; Lynch and Woolgar 1988; Ochs *et al.* 1996), while important, are not particularly sophisticated as modes of language use. Machine translation is already almost good enough for these purposes in specialized domains; there is hardly much point today to teaching or learning a language if this is all we wish to achieve. We need to articulate how much more there is to the human uses of language, and begin to think about how they are taught and learned.

The next relevant timescale, I think, is that of longer-term activities, those that stretch over days and weeks, in which texts integrate the work of a group. Here it is the social-collaborative uses of language that matter most, and if a second language is relevant it can only be because the group is collectively bi- or multilingual. In that case collaborative activity is most efficient when members use their multiple languages (including multiple dialects) in communicating and co-ordinating over time. The corresponding language skills are again ones that are almost totally ignored by modernist notions of the autonomy of Languages, namely the skills of code-shifting and code-mixing. Language in use in the multilingual situation, which has been common enough in the past and is likely to become almost universal in the future, is not a matter of translation between discrete and distinct language systems. It is rather a matter of their *functional integration*. Students should learn to construct bilingual dialogues and texts which break every traditional rule of the separateness and autonomy of distinct languages, for those rules serve the interests of nineteenth-century nationalism and are anachronistic in the twenty-first-century world of global networks and communities. If we do stay with a single language tradition throughout an extended text, then that should be recognized as itself a meaningful *choice* we have learned to make within our multilingual repertoire.

The longest timescale I will consider here is that of the years over which we achieve *subtlety* in our use of a language. For the individual, this means acquiring a *feel* for a language, in a bodily sense. There are changes over time and development with another language in how we "hold ourselves," not just our vocal apparatus, but our whole face, our posture and stance, our body hexis. There are changes in how we move and how we feel, in the rhythms and musicality of our speech, the timbre and "grain" of our voice. We add new dimensions to our Selves; we expand, through use of the language, our repertory of possible identities and ways of being human. And this implies also a change in the communities we participate in. We should not imagine that individuals come to speak second and third languages apart from the norms and values of their communities. In a community that prizes monolingualism, learning another language is often an empty exercise: merely academic, merely instrumental, merely a status marker. The long-term goal of language teaching and learning must be to create a society that values multilingualism and practices multilingualism. That goal does not have to be achieved in every local geographical community in which we participate. It is sufficient if enough of our lives, enough of what matters to us in life, takes place in some community, perhaps a distributed and global one, where we can be free to assemble more complex humanities for ourselves and our friends than those that are permitted in communities that actively repress human diversity.

How should we gauge success in language learning?

Not, certainly, by any means that looks only at a single timescale of language use. No test or task that lasts but a few minutes or an hour gauges what we can do with language across the full range of human timescales. Nor can any test or task separate language skills from the social skills and cultural knowledge needed for every task. Why do we not gauge language skills *comparatively* in each of two languages (say, the L1 and L2) and in the free intermixture of those languages to see how people accomplish a task similarly and differently in each of these three natural conditions? Why do we not gauge language development in an L2 (and with the L1–L2 mix) *longitudinally* over months and years, looking not only at the current "final state" but at patterns of development: the invariances and changes, the habits won and lost, the emergence of styles and preferences? There is no "final state" for processes that are always still ongoing in language learning and development. It is those processes themselves that are the phenomenon, not what someone does on any given day in some relatively short period of time. We cannot in principle observe developmental processes with short-term tasks. There is also no relevant "final state" in the sense that the whole point of gauging language development is to act with respect to the future: to recommend what to do next, to set a course of learning for a longer future period, to develop expectations of what we can do with the language in various possible futures.

What should be our research agendas for studying language development in the coming decades?

It should be made clear that I am deliberately using the phrase "language development" here against the grain of the learning/ acquisition/development and L1/L2 distinctions. The phenomenon that occurs is that people add elements of a new linguistic resource system to their communicative and semantic repertoires. Language use is integral to personal and social development, part of the short- and long-term developmental processes of both persons and communities. Personal and community development continues through the medium of additional languages as well as the first language, and, I believe, occurs most naturally and basically by the functional integration of what nation states and formal linguists demand be kept strictly separated. It might be a salutary inversion of traditional research perspectives to begin by looking at the role of multilingual activity (or its suppression) in a community, and then taking this as the context in relation to which individuals develop (in part) by using more than one "language."

I also think we need to welcome into our research a renewed skepticism regarding the autonomy and coherence of "languages." The notion of "a language" seems to me little more than a Platonist relic. I cannot see it as a cogent unit of analysis, neither behaviorally nor socially. Its unity is a purely formal construction of our current ways of describing verbal behavior in the aggregate, rather than on the actual occasions of its occurrence as a material–semiotic phenomenon. It is not at all obvious that if they were not politically prevented from doing so, "languages" would not mix and dissolve into one another, but we understand almost nothing of such a process, and so almost nothing of the functional units where this mixing might take place. We have theories of the artificially maintained formal structural systems of "Languages," but not of the dynamic social processes of multilingual communication and activity not tightly constrained by institutional norms. Could it be that all our current pedagogical methods in fact make multilingual development more difficult than it need be, simply because we bow to dominant political and ideological pressures to keep "languages" pure and separate? How would we know? We have at this point so "naturalized" the process of (especially second-)

"language acquisition," as if it took place in an imaginary parallel universe of mind, that we are left with almost no understanding of how it occurs in the real social ecology of persons, artifacts, sounds, and material activities. We have a vast research literature on what happens under the artificial conditions of academic language learning, but very little on what people might actually do socially under conditions of partial multilingualism outside stable multilingual communities. What do we know about how *communities* "acquire" additional languages? In the model of ecosocial system dynamics that I have partially sketched here, that knowledge is a prerequisite for better understanding of multiple language development in individuals.

References

Bakhtin, M. (1929) *Problems of Dostoevsky's Poetics*. Trans by R.W. Rostel (1973) Ann Arbor: Ardis.

Bakhtin, M. (1935) Discourse in the novel. In M. Holquist (ed.), *The Dialogic Imagination* (1981). Austin: University of Texas Press.

Bourdieu, P. (1990) *The Logic of Practice*. Stanford: Stanford University Press.

Cole, M. (1996) *Cultural Psychology*. Cambridge, MA: Harvard University Press.

Gee, J.P. (1992) *The Social Mind*. New York: Bergin and Garvey.

Halliday, M.A.K. (1978) *Language as Social Semiotic*. London: Edward Arnold.

Hasan, R. (1996) *Ways of Saying, Ways of Meaning*. London: Cassell.

Hodge, R. and Kress, G. (1988) *Social Semiotics*. Ithaca, NY: Cornell University Press.

Latour, B. (1993) *We Have Never Been Modern*. Cambridge, MA: Harvard University Press.

Latour, B. (1999) *Pandora's Hope*. Cambridge, MA: Harvard University Press.

Lave, J. (1988) *Cognition in Practice*. Cambridge: Cambridge University Press.

Lave, J. and Wenger, E. (1991) *Situated Learning: Legitimate Peripheral Participation*. Cambridge: Cambridge University Press.

Lemke, J.L. (1993) Discourse, dynamics, and social change. *Cultural Dynamics* 6(1), 243–75.

Lemke, J.L. (1995) *Textual Politics: Discourse and Social Dynamics*. London: Taylor & Francis.

Lemke, J.L. (1998) Multiplying meaning: Visual and verbal semiotics in scientific text. In J.R. Martin and R. Veel (eds), *Reading Science*. London: Routledge, pp. 87–113.

Lemke, J.L. (1999) Typological and topological meaning in diagnostic discourse. *Discourse Processes* 27(2), 173–185.

Lemke, J.L. (2000a) Opening up closures: semiotics across scales. In J. Chandler and G. van de Vijver (eds), *Closure: Emergent Organizations and Their Dynamics*. New York: Annals of the New York Academy of Sciences, pp. 100–11.

Lemke, J.L. (2000b) Across the scales of time: artifacts, activities, and meanings in ecosocial systems. *Mind, Culture, and Activity* 7(4), 273–90.

Lemke, J.L. (2002) Becoming the village: education across lives. To appear in G. Wells and G. Claxton (eds), *Learning for Life in the 21st Century: Sociocultural Perspectives on the Future of Education*. Oxford: Blackwell.

Lemke, J.L. (in press) Mathematics in the middle: measure, picture, gesture, sign, and word. In M. Anderson, A. Saenz-Ludlow, S. Zellweger, and V. Cifarelli, (eds), *Educational Perspectives on Mathematics as Semiosis: From Thinking to Interpreting to Knowing*. Ottawa: Legas Publishing, pp. 215–34.

Lynch, M. and Woolgar, S. (1988) *Representation in Scientific Practice*. Cambridge, MA: MIT Press.

Ochs, E., Gonzales, P. and Jacoby, S. (1996), When I come down I'm in the domain state . . .: grammar and graphic representation in the interpretive activity of physicists. In E. Ochs, E. Schegloff and S. Thompson (eds), *Interaction and Grammar*. New York: Cambridge University Press.

Rogoff, B. (1990) *Apprenticeship in Thinking: Cognitive Development in Social Context*. New York: Oxford University Press.

Salthe, S.N. (1993) *Development and Evolution*. Cambridge, MA: MIT Press.

Wallace, A.F.C. (1970) *Culture and Personality*, 2nd edn. New York: Random House.

Commentaries

Editors: Edward Bodine and Claire Kramsch

Language development as spatial and temporal positioning

These and the other *Commentaries* are meant to reflect the discussion that took place among the participants at the UC Berkeley workshop. They are not a transcription of the actual discussion, but, rather, a reconstruction of the various lines of argument advanced during the discussion period. We have structured these commentaries around key questions or issues that the participants addressed during the workshop.

Where precisely does an ecological approach to the study of language development depart from more traditional models and theories? What metaphors seem to be orienting new thinking in this area?

CANDLIN   An ecological perspective on language development may not be as new as we would expect. Already in the mid-1980s, we can see William Rutherford's work on the acquisition of grammar being driven by an organic type of metaphor derived from biological science.[1] Of course, at the time, the mainstream of the field was not ready for this direction. This resistance to new metaphors, to new ways of conceptualizing social and linguistic phenomena, is something that continues to plague us, not just in terms of research theory but educational practice as well. The notion of stage is imbedded in the day-to-day work of speech pathologists as well as language instructors, not to mention the populations who are served through educational and interventional programs. I personally believe we finally have the seeds and ground for a truly ecological perspective in the study of language development. Yet there remain formidable obstacles beyond the kind of intellectual or professional strife Diane Larsen-Freeman has pointed out. These have to do with persistent "commonsense" notions about how language is learned and used.

LARSEN-FREEMAN   Perhaps the greatest challenge to an ecological understanding of language is the widespread view that it is essentially *atomistic*; that is, it can be dissected and treated in bits and pieces. Yet before we talk about resistance to new metaphors, I would like to draw our attention to the dilemma of the practitioner. Rutherford was describing some fairly general and abstract dynamics of development. Where does this leave the language teacher, for example? How does the educator operationalize Rutherford's ecological metaphor in a way that makes practical sense? This has to do with the day-by-day, week-by-week decision-making and planning that comprises so much of teachers' work. So, the critical question is not just one of "stage" but also one of operational unit. You can't teach "The Language" all on the first day. The educator must make instructional choices based on pedagogical units of measurements of progress. I think the field of second-language acquisition continues to struggle with this dilemma. We have task-based methods, content-based methods, and many other integrative approaches that are essentially attempts to get at language more holistically. At the same time, there is a real penchant among practitioners and researchers alike for looking at language atomistically – and even among people who promote these particular pedagogical approaches.

To what extent can acquisitional and participatory modes of learning be seen as ecologically distinct but codependent?

WEINBERG   I believe that looking at deaf education forces us to take a middle ground, or perhaps more accurately, a holistic view that encompasses aspects of both participation and acquisition. Almost all deaf students end up acquiring a basic knowledge of the English language. At the same time, they also learn to participate in a variety of different communities. Residential students learn to be part of a deaf community that uses English primarily in its written form to interact with hearing people. Mainstreamed students, on the other hand, learn to function as members of the hearing community in which spoken English is the primary mode of communication. Of course, for both groups the context in which English is learned affects acquisition, illustrating the complex relationship between acquisition and participation. Indeed, as Jonathan Leather has pointed out, acquisition is perhaps best modeled not through a single theoretical perspective but by the integration of multiple perspectives, leading to an all-encompassing account of learner behavior that takes into consideration the relationship between learner and context on a number of different levels.

CANDLIN   I think that I would recast slightly your description of the coming together of the acquisitional and participatory. Groups of learners can be both acquisitional and participatory, but each modality should also be understood *according to its own terms*. I think we have to be a little bit careful here and appreciate the subtlety of the interlink between the acquisitional and participatory. These two metaphors for development are closely intertwined. Yet the internal chemistry of each is quite distinct. Of course, society has foisted upon us this extremely polarized way of looking at development, which in an institutional context makes approaching the question of educational success rather complicated.

WEINBERG This whole process–product separation can be very counterproductive in my experience in deaf education. Certain approaches to deaf education have this very particular product in mind for enabling students to gain better communicative access. However, different groups and different individuals go about solving communication problems from their own distinctive points of view. The ultimate question for deaf education may not be which specific path to take but, rather, how to offer a diversity of paths to accommodate diverse modalities of learning.

"How can we tell the dancer from the dance?" What are the methodological implications of an ecological framework for researching language in educational settings?

OCHS   An important issue – one I have been struggling to connect to the discussion – has to do with levels of scale. Comprehending all these levels is a daunting task: there is interaction on so many levels at once! The real challenge for the researcher is moving from understanding these configurations of actors in relative stasis on the ground to higher levels of interaction. I have to say that I really like what the chaos/complexity model has to offer on a conceptual level. But when I look at a transcript, I start wondering how I am going to get from theory to practice. How are we going to move from these highly conceptual spaces to the actual classroom? And this is not just a methodological challenge; it is also ideological.

How does all this connect together? I've been struggling to find a way of expressing this larger sense of interconnection. I especially liked Jonathan Leather's notion of a phenomenological phonology. And Jay Lemke's discussion of the experience of nearness not as something that has to do necessarily with physical or temporal proximity seems to get at this principle of unity. We might call this a phenomenology of nearness. I am wondering if and how we can put all this clearly.

CANDLIN   In considering how the ecological models we've talked about come together as in a coherent system, I think it's important to ask what are the kinds of empirical directives coming out of a complexity approach that do not come out of any other kind of theory? In other words, what extra purchase does this perspective give us? An ethnographic injunction to be holistic, for example?

LARSEN-FREEMAN   I'm not entirely sure what the methodological implications of an ecological approach might be. What it does do, I think, is prevent premature closure. I think it says we should not be reductionistic. All along, I've been chanting "look up, look down, look inside, look outside, look back, look forth," the point being that I think we can no longer just say that "we've got it!" And I am not necessarily talking about the part we all do at the end and say further research is needed on this. This new perspective really forces us into a position of humility with regards to what we are looking at. It encourages us to recognize just how limited our current tools of analysis are and how much more there is to be seen. As researchers, it means that we've got to remind ourselves that we can't just isolate and examine one part and assume that this will tell us anything substantive about the whole. That being said, I am also human, and the scope at which I can take it all in obviously is limited. So this new theoretical orientation seems to me to ask us to look at the *in between,* to look in relational terms. It may turn out that it has more power for us as researchers in shaping attitude than in actual methodological intervention.

BODINE   For me, our discussion of such themes as ecological interrelationality and synthesis brings to mind the last lines of "Among School Children" by W.B. Yeats, who was in his own way struggling to come to terms with processes of growth and change.[2] The poem ends with the following two questions:

> O chestnut-tree, great-rooted blossomer,
> Are you the leaf, the blossom or the bole?
> O body swayed to music, O brightening glance,
> How can we tell the dancer from the dance?

The first speaks to our perception of what defines the chestnut tree. Is it any one of its constituent parts, or the unity of all these – "great-rooted blossomer"? This question, interestingly, is addressed directly to the chestnut tree itself. If we take the tree as an archetype, or more precisely, an *embodiment* of natural synthesis, the answer to this question is best sought through dialog with the natural world. The second question speaks to our perception of what constitutes the dance. Can we experience the dancer apart from the dance? Taking the dancer/dance as an embodiment of social synthesis, the answer to the question, addressed to us, may only be explored through dialog among ourselves. In this passage, I believe, Yeats is questioning our very habits of apprehension. Can we separate perception from the esthetic experience through which it is received without a certain loss of knowledge? Of course, this question is not answered for us. The poem delights by leaving us at the end of a question mark; it does not claim the last word. Rather, I think, the internal dialogism that is the poem opens up at the end to include us in a special conversation about growth, aging, and change. "How can we tell the dancer from the dance?" We have been addressed in the deepest Bakhtinian sense.

How do we assess the value of the "ecology metaphor" in modeling complex processes of language development? What are its advantages and disadvantages?

LEMKE   The model that I have been trying to construct is material on all levels. Semiosis is a process grounded in material bodies and artifacts. But it occurs only in social systems with a high degree of complexity to them. What is the dynamical nature of such systems? Answering this question means reconceptualizing a number of things we're used to thinking of as outside the framework of material processes. To do this, we must start first by recognizing our analytical constructions and seeing them for the metadiscursive practices that they are. If you look at the set of levels in my model, there is no cognitive level as such. You go directly from neurological-level processes to motor-level processes. These motor processes – at least some of them – become specialized into various kinds of semiotic processes, e.g. vocalizing into speaking. So, I would characterize this model as radically materialist. Semiosis emerges from behavioral interaction on multiple levels of the material system.

VAN LIER   It seems this model comes rather close to the kind of materialist reductionism found in traditional behaviorist theories. In mapping out an ecological theory based entirely on a material system of scales, it would seem particularly difficult to avoid lapsing into that kind of reductionism.

LEMKE   The model does not – as complex system theory models generally do not – permit causality to cross scales. A fundamental question is why would the system of interpretance exist at a higher scale level than the phenomenon being interpreted? The answer is that semiotic processes essentially require taking context into account, i.e. no sign points to its referent. The connection between sign and referent, which is Peirce's great contribution, must be made by a third element. This model indicates that this third element must be a system at a higher level of scale; that is, high enough to take into account relative contextualizations. There is no meaning without contextualization, and there is no contextualization unless the contextualizing system is at a higher scale level than that which is being contextualized.

VAN LIER   Ah, but how can that level be *both* material and interpretative?

LEMKE   How can it *not* be both? We're talking about the organism engaging in a system of social practices, be they discursive or ritualistic. The system of interpretance is again precisely the material system. The molecules themselves do not cause the interpretation. They can be interpreted in any number of different ways. You have to look higher up the scale system in order to decide how they will be interpreted. Now, there may be an issue of reductionism insofar as the source of the interpretation is concerned. But let me say first that I am reluctant, given the platonic leanings of mainstream cognitive science, to assign a separate, purely cognitive level in my model. Let me make clear that this model is not reductionistic in the sense that material–behavioral processes at the lowest scales get replaced with neurological processes. Rather, mechanisms previously called "cognitive" are now reconceptualized as "social-semiotic." In terms of analysis, this means understanding language use as sandwiched between two systems: the semiotic system of social interaction and the system of afforded neurological processes.

BODINE   In many ways, these ecological models borrow most ostensibly from biological theories. We talk about organism, emergence, trajectory, adaptation, affordance, etc. What might be the implications of working so intimately within this metaphor for our research? Should we examine the ways we are thinking about and applying the word "ecological" in our research?

LARSEN-FREEMAN   Absolutely. This is the century of biology, we are told, so it is not surprising that we borrow our metaphor from biology. Metaphors can be very powerful in shaping the way that we think. Therefore, it's important for us to call attention to the fact that the mainstream of the field is operating according to a different metaphor or set of metaphors. The ecological metaphor is undoubtedly nonmainstream at this point, and therefore one of its contributions is that it enables us to see the assumptions underlying more traditional paradigms. This is not to say that we should leave our own metaphors and their implications unexamined. We have to keep on looking at our own ways of conceptualizing, both creatively and critically. This attitude is, I believe, part of the complexity-theoretic perspective. It encourages us to take a stance of humility. What this means for the researcher is a certain imperative: *to keep looking at the phenomenon from different angles because it is essentially dynamic and constantly transformative.*

LEMKE   What concerns me most about mainstream paradigms is their drive toward hegemony itself. As social scientists, we have inherited a very shaky system of social analysis. The ways we have traditionally conceptualized the organization of human communities has often unwittingly played into the existing relations of domination. It seems to me that one of the most important elements to come out of a complexity-theoretic model is a political agenda. What are the alternative social technologies of organization at a higher scale that don't force us into our historical role?

LANTOLF   I think this is well said. But it seems to me that in a field like physics, for example, where one has a plurality of rules, say in relativity theory and Newtonian mechanics, you run into incommensurability. In the end, though, it turns out that both of those theories can be useful at the practical level.

LEMKE   I wish it were true. However, the ideology and the culture of physics, and the natural sciences in general, are very hegemonic in nature. From this perspective, there may be a special case of this or that, but ultimately, all incompatibility must be resolved under a unitary theory, *the* unitary theory. There can be only one master in this universe.

WILIARTY   Are we suggesting that hegemonic forces come from outside the system? Are they themselves not emergent in various social systems? I think an ecological model must account for this aspect of emergence as well.

LANTOLF   You're quite right. It is the danger of *naturalizing* our metaphors that we have to be most aware of. The field of second-language acquisition research inherited the computational metaphor, that is, "the mind as machine," from theoretical linguistics and cognitive science. Today, this is understood as foundational; it goes unquestioned. Interestingly, even Chomsky, once so deeply invested in this metaphor, now argues that the computational metaphor is dangerous in that the mind may not really be a computer at all, as we understand it; yet he continues to talk about computations.[3] Metaphors, particularly ones that have become so operationalized in the specialized cultures of research as well as wider cultures, can begin to function as traps. They have a way of locking in our practices of conceptualization. Ultimately, they become invisible to us. So, I think a critical problem in our field is not so much an inability to see and react to *new* metaphors. After all, these are all too apparent in their status as a threat to older paradigms. The problem lies in people not being able to see their own metaphors as such. What they see is "the truth."

Notes

1. "Organicism is a better general metaphor than machine for what we know about language as a medium of developing interaction among humans. Machines are constructed, whereas organisms grow. Machines have precision; organisms have plasticity. Machines have linear inter-connections; organisms have cyclical interconnections. And perhaps most important of all, machines are sterile, whereas organisms are fecund ... To the great extent then that we may ascribe to language these characteristics of growth, change, plasticity, fecundity, genetics, regen-eration, etc. – to this extent we may quite naturally conceive of language as an organism." Rutherford, W. (1987) *Second Language Grammar: Learning and Teaching.* London: Longman, p. 37.
2. Jeffares, N. (ed.) (1996) *Yeats's Poems* 3rd rev. ed. London: Macmillan.
3. Chomsky, N. (1996) *Powers and Prospects. Reflections on Human Nature and the Social Order.* Boston: South End Press, pp. 12–13.

Part Two

Language development as a mediated, social semiotic activity

Becoming a speaker of culture

Elinor Ochs

4

Introduction

Over the past several decades, anthropology has expanded the locus of ethnographic interest to include a broader band of social identities beyond focal male members of a community. Due in large part to a sea change in the philosophy of social science, the lives and perspectives of women and transgendered persons have been incorporated into analyses of power, labor, personhood, and other dynamics of society and culture (Brown 1976; Foucault 1990; Gal 1992; Haraway 1988, 1989, 1991; Keenan 1974; Kulick 1992; Ortner 1974, 1984; Strathern 1987). Yet, an important sector of the human population continues to be marginal to anthropological research. Specifically, young children are nearly invisible in ethnographic studies (Goodwin 1997).

The marginal status of children within anthropology is linked in part to their reduced visibility in settings in which political decision-making, economic exchanges, and religious rituals take place. Across many social groups, small children are considered to lack the knowledge and skills needed to fully participate in core community activities and they tend to be relegated to female-dominated domestic and educational settings. Moreover, young children, especially those under the age of five, are less than ideal informants for ethnographic field researchers. To understand the cultural organization and everyday business of childhood requires researchers to shadow children for long stretches of time as they engage people and objects in the world (Harkness and Super 1983; Heath 1983; Schieffelin and Ochs 1986). Finally, the marginality of children as objects of anthropological concern is likely rooted in a view of infants and young children as natural rather than cultural beings. This perception is so strong that anthropologists who conduct research on early childhood are often viewed as tackling issues of developmental psychology rather than anthropology or, at best, straddling the two fields. The distancing of child-oriented research from anthropology is even greater when the children under ethnographic study have mental disabilities.

The study of children presents a colossal challenge to ethnographers in that they are faced with articulating society and culture through the eyes of children as well as of those who attend to them. Children are often described as objects of care, and childhood is treated as an ideology and a life phase. But what does the social world look like from the perspective of the children themselves? How do children across the world's societies think and feel about relationships, actions, activities, places, artifacts, moral values, and so on? Ethnographers are distinguished by their desire to capture the perspective of the "other," and much has been written about the complexities of this enterprise (Clifford and Marcus 1986; Haraway 1988; Marcus and Fischer 1986). While ethnographic perspective-taking is daunting regardless of the object of study, attempting to capture the perspective of young children requires not only proximity and sustained observation but also literally getting down to children's level and viewing situations as they do, stepping into their shadows. I am usually stooped behind a child with a video camera capturing an unfolding scene faced by the child and a remote microphone picking up the child's vocalizations to the self and to others.

An ethnographic account of children with mental disabilities further taxes the perspective-taking capabilities of anthropologists. In addition to the challenges of capturing a child's point of view and entry into society, the ethnographer's goal is to assess how a particular psychopathology helps to configure how the child thinks, feels, and acts in the world. For three years, clinical psychologist Lisa Capps and I collaborated on an ethnographic study of intelligent children diagnosed with autism. Autism is a disorder characterized by social, cognitive, and communicative impairments (Frith 1989; Happe 1994; Sigman and Capps 1997). Even high-functioning children with autism display only a limited ability to take the perspective of others, recognize and express certain emotions, construe the relation of parts to whole configurations, and grasp certain pragmatic meanings of language (Baron-Cohen, 1996; Hobson 1986; Loveland *et al.* 1990; Sigman *et al.* 1986, 1992; Ungerer and Sigman 1987; Wulff 1985). Nowhere is the import of culture more evident than when observing children with autism attempting to participate in social activities. They strive to display and interpret the appropriate physical and psychological stances and actions for activities and identities, sometimes failing, sometimes succeeding with a little help from those around them.

To illustrate this social dynamic, consider the knowledge and skill that Erin, a young girl with autism, needs to play the game of softball at school and the ways in which Erin's teacher and unaffected classmates respond to Erin's limited abilities. The first time that Erin is up at bat, she hardly swings and strikes out. The next time Erin approaches home base for her turn at bat, Gary, one of the boys on her team, advises her on how to swing the bat:

Gary:	All *right!* (.) Erin you're *up.*
	[Come ↑o::n↓
	[((approaches Erin))
Erin:	((walks behind boy toward home base))
Gary:	((picks up bat and faces Erin))
Erin:	((turns around toward boy))
Gary:	**Erin (.) [Swing [like that okay?**
	[(((swings bat horizontally))
Erin:	((approaches, reaching for bat))
Gary:	**[Not like *this***
	[(((swings bat angled more vertically))
	[Straight like *that* okay?
	[(((swings bat horizontally))
	((hands Erin the bat))

When Erin does not swing at a ball, Gary continues to instruct her:

Gary:	**Erin! Don't swing at *anything* you don't *like!***
	((Pitcher throws ball; Erin does not swing))

Eventually, Erin hits the ball lightly to the immediate right of home base. She begins to run holding the bat, then hesitates, gazing toward the teacher, who initially tells her to go to first base, then changes her mind and declares the hit a foul. As Erin returns to home base, the teacher asks her classmates if the ball had hit Erin, in which case she is entitled to walk to first base. What transpires is a dispute between Erin's team mates and the opposing team. No one consults Erin herself:

Teacher:	**Did it hit he:r?**
Team mates:	Yes!
Teacher:	[That's what I thought.
Opp. team:	[No! (?)
Catcher:	n-
Gary:	((touches his own wrist, indicating where the ball hit Erin))
Catcher:	[No, it hit the [*bat* Miss Ruby
	[(((takes off face guard and hurries toward teacher))
	[(((Gary and team mates walk toward teacher))

Gary +
Team mates: **It hit her on [the *hand***
                               [((*pointing to hand*))
                  ((*Opposite team members shout objections*))
Catcher: No, (.) I saw it hit- it

As the dispute ensues, one of Erin's team mates approaches Erin, points to first base and directs her to go there. While Erin walks toward first base, the catcher convinces the teacher that the ball hit the bat and not her hand. Eventually, as Erin returns to home base, Gary asks if the ball hit her. Erin says nothing but slightly shakes her head negatively. The catcher uses this gesture to declare victory:

Gary: ((*approaches Erin*))
                  (Did it hit you?)
Erin: [((*picks up bat and walks toward home plate*))
Gary: **[(Erin? Did it *hit* you?) Did it hit you Erin?**
                  [((*following Erin*))
Erin: **((*Slightly shakes head horizontally while
                  walking*))**
Catcher: **See! She even said it. almo::st.**

Once again at bat, with the stakes high, Erin is given more instruction. One of her team mates stands behind her and positions her body for hitting the ball.

In addition, Erin's team mates move behind the catcher to monitor her judgment:

Team mate: [I'm standin' right here.
                  [((*stands behind fence right behind catcher*))
Catcher: I'm tellin' the ↑*tru:th.*

To the delight of her team mates and teacher, Erin hits a legitimate ball. Although the ball is thrown to first base before Erin arrives and she is declared out, Erin is applauded and she appears pleased:

Team mates: (GOOD!)
                  (GO ERIN!)
                  GO:::!
                  RUN ERIN!
                  ((*Ball is thrown to first base before Erin
                  reaches there*))
Teacher: YAY – ERIN YOU'RE *OUT*
                  [BUT THAT WAS YOUR FIRST [*HI::T!*
Erin: [((*walks back toward home base, smiling*))

Team mates:	[YA ::::::Y!
	[((clap))
Teacher:	[YA::Y! ALRI:::GHT!
Team mate:	[Good hit Erin!
	[((Erin walking toward outfield, smiling))

What can Erin's encounter with softball tell us about what a member needs to understand about society and culture? First, Erin needs to know the *categories* and *rules* of activities: For example, in the game of softball there is first, second, third, and home base and specified player positions, the batter tries to hit the ball, run the bases in order and return home, three strikes/four balls and you are out, three outs and your team takes to the field, and so on. These are rules that anyone who knows softball could articulate for a novice.

But Erin also needs to know much more. She needs to know *expectations* and *strategies* for positioning the body and bat, when to swing and not swing, how to swing, where to direct the ball, when to run and when to stay put and more. Knowledge of and skill in rules and strategies is critical both to playing the game of softball and to establishing Erin's social identity as a member of a team and player in this game. Here we see how classmates try to apprentice Erin into these roles, such that she animates their authorial prompts, and they ventriloquate her voice: "See she even said it - almost!"

Despite the profoundly organizing role of culture in our lives, researchers often have a difficult time discerning culture outside the more structured arenas of rituals and games. Those of us trying to understand children as social creatures, i.e. as *members*, have had to come to grips with the fact that cultural expectations about how people are to act, feel, and think in specific situations do not typically take the form of *explicit instructions* but rather must be *inferred* from performances of conventional, socially co-ordinated activities, and interpretative practices. The problem for us is also the problem for children like Erin. And imagine what a problem that must be.

To infer situational expectations, Erin must *minimally track and interpret goal-directed acts* (e.g. swinging a bat, running to base, declaring a pitch as ball, strike, foul and the like) and *take note of participants' psychological stances toward these acts* (e.g. positive or negative alignment).[1] She must *also link acts and stances to what is expected of particular participants* (e.g. batter, catcher, referee, team mates, opposing team). All this requires perspective-taking and empathy of a magnitude difficult even for a high-functioning autistic child like Erin to attain.

Erin must also *contextualize actions, stances, and participants in terms of what just occurred and what is anticipated to occur next.* That is, *she must understand the more general activity underway.* Here again autistic children have great difficulty in that they have problems grasping the relation of a part to a whole. They lack what Uta Frith (1989) calls "the drive for coherence."

Erin's task is made all the more complicated by the ethnographic fact that typically *more than one activity* is occurring. Within the activity of playing softball, for example, Erin's team mates are engaged in advice-giving while she is responding to the pitcher's throws. The team mates also simultaneously argue with the opposite team and try to persuade the teacher they are right, at the same time as someone directs Erin to run to first base. Off the softball field, in everyday social interaction, people routinely interweave several activities: They talk while carrying out some physical task, for example. And the talk itself is usually a complex overlay of discourse activities. Interlocutors may, for example, embed arguments and explanations within stories, or stories within arguments, explanations, prayers, or apologies. Being a competent interlocutor entails interweaving and disentangling such overlapping enterprises.

To push the envelope of cultural requirements even further, Erin cannot usually count on participating in a stable, sustained activity whose rules and strategies for participation are predetermined. While this may hold to some extent in formal events (Irvine 1979), most of social life is informal, and informality is defined by *relative spontaneity* and *fluidity*. Informal interaction is systematic, but its systematicity resides locally at the level of the interactional turn (Sacks 1992; Sacks *et al.* 1974). Thus, once a particular kind of turn is produced (e.g. greeting, a request for information), a particular kind of next turn is expected (e.g. a greeting response, an answer). When it is not forthcoming, it is noticeably absent. The ordering of such turn sequences in conversational exchanges, however, is typically not predeterminedly scripted. Further, boundaries between sequences of turns are often not explicitly marked, so that one activity may evolve into another with no warning (Duranti 1992). What started out as an announcement sequence slips into storytelling, or storytelling evolves into a plan for future action and so on (Ochs 1994). Erin and all novice members of communities need to *monitor turn by turn the emergent, contingent interactional construction of social realities.*

To be counted as culturally competent, Erin has to learn in addition that *while communities establish conventional parameters for carrying out social activities and realizing social identities, members have play within those parameters for doing so.* Even an activity as codified as a softball game, for example, does not constrict participation to invariant acts and role realizations but instead allows for different kinds of team mate, batter, catcher, referee, and so on. Autistic children tend to overgeneralize norms for activities and identities. A father teaches his 10-year-old autistic son to look people in the eye and shake hands when he meets them. The boy extends this norm to all situations, shaking hands, for example, with all the kids on his soccer team at the beginning of each practice and each game.

Finally, Erin needs to know *how and when to modify or even abandon conventional ways* of participating in activities and conventional social identities. While the tenacity of convention is great, individual members, families, classrooms, sports organizations, and other institutions within a community do change, particularly when confronted with novel conditions and problems.

A perspective

An interest in the cultural organization of children's social and communicative practices has shaped my career as an anthropologist. In 1973, while completing a dissertation on Malagasy conversation and oratory, I thought it would be fascinating to understand how children come to be communicatively competent and began videotaping the conversations of my two-year-old twin sons over a period of nine months. Although documentation of children's communicative skills was part of the mission of the ethnography of communication paradigm developed during the late 1960s, only a handful of anthropologists were conducting research of this sort (cf., for example, Blount 1977; Kernan 1969). I found myself drawn to psychologists and linguists centrally concerned with children's pragmatic competence and spent my professional life from 1973–1999 in departments of theoretical and applied linguistics.

During this period I sought to position the study of communication by and to children more centrally in the panoply of anthropological concerns. The first breakthrough came after presenting a paper on children's conversational competence at the 1974 meeting of the American Anthropological Association. In a serendipitous moment that sparked over two decades of collaboration, I sat down next to Bambi Schieffelin, an anthropology graduate student who had studied developmental psycholinguistics. Schieffelin and I joined forces and soon developed a subfield we called "Developmental Pragmatics" (Ochs and Schieffelin 1979). This enterprise drew together scholarship across the social sciences on how young children, over developmental time, produced and interpreted language in context. Developmental pragmatic research analyzes children's competence to introduce topics, refer to old and new information, make requests, tell stories, engage in arguments, and other situated language practices (Bates *et al.* 1979; Gordon and Ervin-Tripp 1984; Garvey 1984; Ochs and Schieffelin 1983; Scollon 1976).

Schieffelin went to Papua New Guinea in 1975 to document child language development among the Kaluli people. Three years later, accompanied by Alessandro Duranti and Martha Platt, I went to Western Samoa to record children's developing linguistic skills. In the course of these field efforts, anthropological and developmental interests melded. Schieffelin and I became aware of systematic ways in which the language of children and language directed to children is grounded not only in the immediate discourse context but also in the context of historically and culturally grounded social beliefs, values, and expectations. As we have reported in depth, Schieffelin and I found that Kaluli and Samoan caregivers alike typically did not use simplified baby talk and generally did not try to interpret the unintelligible utterances of infants (Ochs 1988; Ochs and Schieffelin 1984, 1995; Schieffelin 1990). Supported by like-minded scholars such as anthropologists Shirley Brice Heath (1983), Karen Watson-Gegeo and David Gegeo (1986a, b), and psychologist Peggy Miller (Miller 1982; Miller and Moore 1989), we decided to create another subfield called "Language Socialization," dedicated to discerning the sociocultural patterning of child–adult and child–child communication (Schieffelin and Ochs 1986).

Premises of language socialization

Language socialization is rooted in the notion that the process of acquiring a language is part of a much larger process of becoming a person in society. As originally formulated, the discipline articulates ways in which novices across the life span are socialized into using language and socialized through language into local theories and preferences for acting, feeling, and knowing, in socially recognized and organized practices associated with membership in a social group (Schieffelin and Ochs 1986). Language socialization research analyzes how and why young children are apprenticed through language into particular childhood identities and activities and how older children and adults learn the communicative skills necessary for occupational and other community identities. Language socialization studies also examine how members of multilingual communities are socialized into using different codes, and how language socialization practices impact language maintenance and language change (Baquedano-Lopez, 2001; Kulick 1992; Schieffelin 1994).

Language socialization has become a fruitful tool in understanding how children may be socialized into mental disorders such as phobias. Lisa Capps and I, for example, examined how children of sufferers of agoraphobia may be socialized into anxiety through family narrative interactions (Capps and Ochs 1995). We found that children are often drawn into collaboratively recounting and reacting to narratives that depict protagonists as helpless in a world spinning out of control. We also suggest that such narrative practices may ignite and sustain fears associated with the panic disorder for adult sufferers.

In language socialization research, social interactions are mined for culturally rooted ways in which veteran and novice participants coordinate modes of communication, actions, bodies, objects, and the built environment to enhance their knowledge and skills. Drawing on the cultural psychological notion that human development is facilitated by participation in socially and culturally organized social interactions, an important unit of analysis in language socialization research is the social *activity* in which more or less experienced persons participate (Leont'ev 1979). Activities such as playing a game, sharing a meal, or planning an event are analyzed for the psychological stances and actions that experts and novices routinely provide or elicit. Such moves shape the direction of activities and apprentice less knowledgeable and less skilled persons into activity competence. In the softball game involving Erin, for example, members of each team and the referee use the following linguistic structures to both configure Erin's actions and mentor her into the rudiments of the game.

Novices become acquainted with activities not only from their own and others' attempts to define what transpires in an activity, but also from how those participating in the activity respond to them. Are the expressed stances, actions, and ideas acknowledged or ignored? Do others display alignment, as when the referee initially supports the judgment that the pitcher's ball hit Erin?

Teacher:	Did it hit her?
Team mates:	Yes!
Teacher:	**[That's what I thought.**

Or do others display nonalignment, as when members of the opposing team disagree with Erin's team mates?

Opp. team:	**[No! (?)**
Catcher:	**n-**
Gary:	*((touches his own wrist, indicating where the ball hit Erin))*
Catcher:	**[No it hit the [*bat* Miss Ruby**

And is the uptake minimal, as when Erin displays attention to Gary's explanation but otherwise offers no facial or vocal feedback? Or do others provide elaborate responses, including not only tokens of attention but also elaborate assessments, descriptions, justifications, explanations, analogies, anecdotes, and the like? For example, the catcher of the opposing team successfully convinces the teacher-referee that the ball hit the bat, not Erin's hand, through an eyewitness demonstration of what transpired:

Catcher:	**[Miss Ruby, (.) Miss Ruby**
	[*((standing opposite teacher))*
	I saw it hit [her on the bat right here.
	[*((looks down and taps bottom of her*
	face guard))
Teacher:	*((looks down to where catcher is*
	indicating))
Opposing team:	It hit her on the *ba:t.*
Team mates:	(?)
Teacher:	OKA:Y. IT'S COUNTED AS A:: (.8)
	stri::ke.

From this perspective, socialization is an interactional achievement, and language socialization researchers are in the business of articulating the architecture of such interactions.

Social interaction is a fascinating platform for discerning the moment-by-moment creation of social life. At the same time, if our goal is to discern how novices become competent members of communities, it is important to situate interaction between more and less knowing participants in past and present cultural ideologies and social structures. Thus, softball players' stances and actions are organized by historically rooted norms and expectations about how to play and negotiate the game.

Understanding social context

Vital to competent participation in social groups is the ability to understand how people use language and other symbolic tools to construct social situations. In every community, members draw upon communicative forms to signal social information; indeed, one of the important functions of grammar and lexicon is to key interlocutors into what kind of social situation is taking place (Gumperz 1982; Hanks 1989; Silverstein 1993). Four dimensions of the social context are particularly relevant to the socialization of cultural competence: the ability to signal the *actions* one is performing, the psychological *stances* one is displaying, the social *identities* one puts forward, and the *activities* in which one is engaged. A social *action* is here defined as a socially recognized goal-directed behavior, e.g. responding to a question, asking for clarification, hitting a softball with a bat, catching a softball, running the bases (Leont'ev 1979). Psychological *stances* include both affective and epistemic orientation toward some focus of concern. *Affective stance* includes a person's mood, attitude, feeling, or disposition as well as degrees of emotional intensity (Biber and Finegan 1989; Besnier 1990; Ochs and Schieffelin 1989; Labov 1984; Levy 1984). In the softball game, for example, participants use a variety of lexical and grammatical affect markers to assess Erin's actions:

> "It *did* hit the *ba::t*.
> "↑O::::H↓!
> "YA::Y! ALRI:::GHT!"
> "**Good** hit Erin!"

Epistemic stance refers to a person's knowledge or belief, including sources of knowledge and degrees of commitment to truth and certainty of propositions (Chafe and Nichols 1986). The softball players and referee used epistemic stance markers, for example, to establish the truth of the claim that the pitcher's ball hit Erin's bat:

> "Miss Ruby, Miss Ruby I **saw** it hit her on the bat **right here**."
> "OKA:Y, IT'S COUNTED AS A:: (.8) stri::ke ... (Claudia) said it hit the ba:t."
> "**See!** She even **said** it (.) **almo::st**."
> "I'm **tellin'** the ↑**tru:th**."

The contextual dimension of *social identity* comprises a range of social personae, including, for example, social roles, statuses, and relationships, as well as community, institutional, ethnic, socio-economic, gender, and other group identities. In the softball game, Erin is apprenticed into the identities of softball player and team member. At the same time, the way her peers mentor Erin and speak on her behalf construct her as a classmate with certain impairments and special needs.

Finally, *social activity* refers to at least two co-ordinated, situated actions and/or stance displays by one or multiple persons. Typically, these actions and stance displays relate to common or similar topics and goals. As noted earlier, activity is a vital unit of analysis in cultural psychology and language socialization research, because it establishes a social milieu or medium for less and more competent persons to perceive, collaborate with, and potentially be transformed by one another in culturally meaningful ways. A game of softball, in this sense, offers Erin repeated opportunities to watch, listen, have contact with artifacts (e.g. bat, ball, bases), and enact the game.

As this discussion implies, children and other novices are exposed to dimensions of social context not in isolation but in concert, as they are drawn into the life of the community. The four contextual dimensions of action, stance, identity, and activity are interdependent in that social groups associate particular stances with particular actions, associate these linked stances and acts with particular social identities and activities, and associate particular activities with particular identities (Ochs 1996):

Actions ∪ Stances
Actions ∪ Stances ∪ Identities
Actions ∪ Stances ∪ Activities
Activities ∪ Identities

Moreover, identities and activities are more complex than actions and stances, in the sense that particular social identities and activities culturally entail particular actions and stances. That is, actions and stances are the cultural building blocks of social identities and activities.

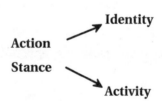

Thus, the activity of playing softball culturally entails such actions as pitching, striking, hitting, catching, and adjudicating. That is, such actions contribute to the constitution of the softball game. Carrying out these actions, in turn, helps to instantiate identities such as batter (hitter, strike-outer), catcher, referee, team mate etc., which in turn helps to instantiate being a child in this community.

The building of activities and identities is generative, in the sense that activities and identities themselves build more complex activities and identities. Thus, for example, the activity of one player being up at bat is part of the larger activity of one team being up at bat, which in turn is part of an activity unit called an inning, which is part of the larger activity of playing softball. Activity theorist Yrjo Engeström (1990, 1993) conceptualizes social structures such as medical clinics, courts, professions, workplaces, and schools as activity systems, i.e. a set of interconnected, situated activities. Thus, we might think of the activity of playing softball as one of many activities that structure the public school as a community institution. In this vein, Erin's competence and participation in the institutional life of the school depends on her understanding and participation in recreational activities such as softball. Similarly, social identities can help build other identities. Erin's identity as a more or less successful softball player helps to instantiate her as a more or less successful student and classmate in this school community.

As noted earlier, children with autism have considerable difficulty relating parts to a whole (Frith 1989). Even high-functioning children with autism stumble when directed to put together puzzle pieces of, for example, a horse or a ball. Similarly, they have problems linking actions and stances to create a larger, coherent narrative (Loveland *et al.* 1990; Solomon 2000; Tager-Flushberg 1995). One might expect, then, that these children would have difficulty discerning the links between actions and stances to identities and the relation of one kind of identity to broader identities. While a full study of how part–whole deficits associated with autism translate in the social realm, our ethnographic recordings indicate that high-functioning children with autism do seem to recognize which identity is expected of them in which circumstance, and that success in these identities is crucial to attainment of other desirable identities. In everyday classroom and playground activities, they are sensitive to the social implications of their own failures to act, think, and feel in expected ways. As the following interaction between 10-year-old Karl and his classroom aide demonstrates, children with autism can at times articulate a part–whole logic of identities that leads them to portray themselves as failures. In the middle of taking a math test, Karl expresses great frustration at not being able to solve the problem on the test, and turns to his aide for help:

Karl: [°Would you help me? **I don't know aa-nny-thing**
        [*((turns to his aide, whispers))*
Aide: [*((comes over to Karl's seat, squats))* What?

As the aide approaches him, Karl looks at the multiplication table on the wall and sees a possible answer. The aide quickly reproaches him:

Karl: It's thirty-six?
Aide: > **You're not supposed to be *lookin'* at that** (.)
       [Look <

At this point, Karl articulates his negative stance toward math and being a "math person":

> Karl: [I don't *like* math
>   [((*turning to/away from aide*))
>   I am not a *math* person.
>   .hh I am a *ro*bot person
>   not a [*math* person.

After Karl identifies himself as a "robot person," his aide first expresses surprise then attempts to redefine his identity appropriate to the activity at hand:

> Aide: [You ar::↑e
> Karl: Yes::!
> Aide: **Okay (.) right *no:w* (.) you are a *person* doing a**
>   **test (,) okay?**

But Karl resists this imposition of identity and follows it up with a declaration of his failure at "being a kid:"

> Karl: **He is *not* a test °person *anymore***
>   (.)
>   Eight
> Aide: **And you are [not supposed to be looking up on**
>   **that *cha:rt*.**
> Karl: [Two
>   **I am not *good* at being a *ki*- d.**
> Aide: You are good at *everything* you *wanna* be.

In this brief exchange, we see instances of how stances and acts help to constitute social activity and identity. The activity of taking a math test, for example, culturally entails that Karl displays certain types of stances and carry out certain acts but not others:

> Stances and actions that help realize activity of math test, and identity of test-taker, and math person, and child
>
> > *Karl is expected to:*
> > – be quiet, gaze down at his paper, attempt to solve problems, write answers and otherwise display involvement in the task;
> > *Karl can:*
> > – elicit some assistance from his aide;
> > *Karl cannot:*
> > – look at the math problem chart on the wall

Failure to adhere to these expectations leads Carl to deny or forfeit his identity as a "math person" and to retreat into a nonacademic identity as "robot person", which he has constructed for himself and which he frequently enacts while at school. Karl perceives that being a "math person" is a necessary condition for the more general identity of "being a kid" like everyone else around him. Notice that the aide tries to contradict his attribution of identity with the admonishing assessment, "You are good at *everything* you *wanna* be." While this evaluation is a form of cultural empowerment, it does not acknowledge Karl's limitations or handle his specific frustrations.

Language and social context

Where does language fit into this perspective on the construction of and socialization into culturally and situationally organized actions, stances, activities, and identities? Every social group has available to its members a repertoire of linguistic forms. Like a communicative palette, members draw upon this repertoire to portray particular stances, acts, activities, and identities. I have argued, however, that few linguistic forms explicitly and exclusively encode activities or identities. Rather, linguistic forms generally encode psychological stances and actions that are linked to activities and identities:

$$\text{Linguistic Form} \rightarrow \begin{bmatrix} \text{Stance} \\ \text{Action} \end{bmatrix} \rightarrow \begin{bmatrix} \text{Activity} \\ \text{Identity} \end{bmatrix}$$

For example, linguistic forms that express negative psychological stances are linked to the activity of disagreement, yet these forms index this activity only indirectly because they encode a stance that is culturally associated with disagreements. This does not mean that everyone who engages in disagreements always uses certain negative forms, but rather that if one wants to engage in disagreement, one can do so by using linguistic forms such as "No!" and "not" in English.

The relation between language and the construction of social context can be useful in understanding the emergence of language and cultural competence across the life span. Most children and other novices learn to use and recognize linguistic markers of stance and actions, and learn how to use these stance and action markers to instantiate certain social activities and identities. We can use this framework to discern levels of sociolinguistic competence (Ochs 1993).

First, we can determine whether or not and how a child or other novice *linguistically indexes an action or stance.* Did he use action or stance markers that are part of the group's sociolinguistic repertoire? For example, does Karl use action and stance markers that are recognizable to the speech community? In Karl's case, he does use such forms. In other cases, sociolinguistic incompetence may be due to a lack of knowledge concerning local conventions for act or stance production. Second, we can examine whether or not and how novices linguistically encode actions and stances that are appropriate to particular activities and identities. For example, are the linguistically encoded actions and stances that Karl expresses appropriate to the identities he is trying to establish and annihilate? Even though his aide disapproves of his social logic, Karl appears adept at linking his inability to solve math problems to his inability to be a "math person" and this problem to his lack of success in "being a kid." To varying degrees of explicitness, Karl displays local understandings and expectations concerning what it means to be a test taker, math person, and child. In other situations, however, Karl and other novices may fail to linguistically signal the activity or social identity in play, not because they lack understanding of how to linguistically mark particular actions and stances but because they lack understanding of how a particular social group associates those acts and stances with particular social identities.

The research framework presented here is useful in understanding cross-cultural similarities and differences in the relation of language to action, stance, activity, and social identity and their implications for second-language socialization. In this perspective, there is considerable overlap across speech communities in how language users signal actions and psychological stances but considerable differences in how communities use actions and stances to realize particular activities and identities (Ochs 1993). For example, actions such as requests, contradictions, affirmations, and summons are marked similarly across languages (Gordon and Ervin-Tripp 1984; Gordon and Lakoff 1971; Grimshaw 1990). Similarly, psychological stances of certainty and uncertainty, emotional intensity, and politeness have corresponding forms cross-linguistically (Brown and Levinson 1987; Labov 1984; Ochs and Schieffelin 1989; Besnier 1990). These commonalities assist novice second-language acquirers who venture across geographical and social borders. Alternatively, those who enter new speech communities face cultural differences in the *kinds* of actions and stances considered appropriate in carrying out a particular activity or assuming a particular identity, and in the *frequency, elaboration, and sequential positioning* of actions and stances expected in carrying out a particular activity or assuming a particular identity. These cross-cultural differences often thwart the language socialization of novices trying to access second cultures. Communication breaks down because the action or stance is not expected by one or another interlocutor, or went on too long or too briefly or at the wrong time and place in the particular activity underway, or for the particular social role, status, or relationship attempted. Because *some* but not all relations between language and social context are familiar and expected, novice and veteran language users may be disturbed at how the other is communicating.

Coda

In developmental studies, the notion of culture has become quite fashionable. Witness the formation of the subfield of cultural psychology and a general awareness that thinking and feeling are situated in a culturally constituted life space. At the same time, the marriage between culture and developmental research is uncertain. While culture is considered important to fathom, it is obscure and difficult to analyze. You can't see it; you can't count it in any obvious way. Culture, like God, seems unknowable. Central to understanding the relation of language and culture in human development is long-term, rigorous ethnographic observation, recording, description, and analysis of displayed preferences and expectations for encoding and displaying psychological stances and social actions, and their historical and ontogenetic enduring and changing relation to social identities and activities. Without this ethnographic knowledge, it is difficult to grasp the realms of social meaning that novice and veteran members of communities are building when they interact, and the sociocultural fissure points that land them in tangled webs of miscommunication.

Notes

1. As will be discussed in later sections of this chapter, the term "psychological stance" here refers to a person's feelings or sense of certainty toward an object of concern. "Positive/negative alignment" describes a person's stance as affiliating or disaffiliating with the stance taken by another person (Ochs 1993; Ochs and Schieffelin 1989).

References

Baquedano-Lopez, P. (2001) Creating social identities through *doctrina* narratives. In A. Duranti (ed.), *Linguistic Anthropology: A Reader*. Oxford: Blackwell, pp. 343–58.

Baron-Cohen, S. (1996) *Mindblindness: An Essay on Autism and Theory of Mind*. Cambridge, MA: MIT Press.

Bates, E., Camaioni, L. and Volterra, V. (1979) The acquisition of performatives prior to speech. In E. Ochs and B.B. Schieffelin (eds), *Developmental Pragmatics*. New York: Academic Press, pp. 111–31.

Besnier, N. (1990) Language and affect. *Annual Review of Anthropology* 19, 419–51.

Biber, D. and Finegan, E. (1989) Styles of stance in English: lexical and grammatical marking of evidentiality and affect. *Text* 9(1), 93–124.

Blount, B. (1977) Parental speech to children: cultural patterns. In M. Saville-Troike (ed.), *Linguistics and Anthropology*. Washington, D.C.: Georgetown University Press, pp. 117–38.

Brown, P. (1976) Women and politeness: a new perspective on language and society. *Annual Reviews in Anthropology* 3, 240–49.

Brown, P. and Levinson, S.C. (1987) *Politeness: Some Universals in Language Usage*. Cambridge: Cambridge University Press.

Capps, L. and Ochs, E. (1995) *Constructing Panic: The Discourse of Agoraphobia*. Cambridge, MA: Harvard University Press.

Chafe, W. and Nichols, J. (1986) *Evidentiality: The Linguistic Coding of Epistemology*. Norwood, NJ: Ablex.

Clifford, J. and Marcus, G.E. (1986) *Writing Culture: The Poetics and Politics of Ethnography*. Berkeley: University of California Press.

Duranti, A. (1992) Language and bodies in social space: Samoan ceremonial greetings. *American Anthropologist* 94, 657–91.

Engeström, Y. (1990) *Learning, Working and Imagining*. Helsinki: Orienta-Konsultit Oy.

Engeström, Y. (1993) Developmental studies of work as a testbench of activity theory. In S. Chaiklin and J. Lave (eds), *Understanding Practice: Perspectives on Activity and Context*. Cambridge: Cambridge University Press, pp. 64–103.

Foucault, M. (1990) *The History of Sexuality: An Introduction*, Vol. 1. New York: Random House.

Frith, U. (1989) *Autism: Explaining the Enigma*. Oxford: Blackwell.

Gal, S. (1992) Language, gender, and power: an anthropological perspective. In K. Hall, M. Bucholtz and B. Moonwomon (eds), *Locating Power: Proceedings of the Second Berkeley Women and Language Conference*, April 4 and 5, 1992, Berkeley, California, Vol. 1, pp. 153–61. Berkeley Women and Language Group, University of California, Berkeley.

Garvey, C. (1984) *Children's Talk*. Cambridge, MA: Harvard University Press.

Goodwin, M.H. (1997) Children's linguistic and social worlds. *Anthropology Newsletter* 38(4), 1–4.

Gordon, D. and Ervin-Tripp, S. (1984) The structure of children's requests. In R.L. Schiefelbusch and J. Pickar (eds), *The Acquisition of Communicative Competence*. Baltimore: University Park Press, pp. 298–321.

Gordon, D. and Lakoff, G. (1971) Conversational postulates. *Papers from the Seventh Regional Meeting of the Chicago Linguistic Society.* Chicago: Chicago Linguistic Society, pp. 63–84.

Grimshaw, A. (1990) *Conflict Talk.* Cambridge: Cambridge University Press.

Gumperz, J.J. (1982) *Discourse Strategies.* Cambridge: Cambridge University Press.

Hanks, W.F. (1989) Text and textuality. *Annual Review of Anthropology* 18, 95–127.

Happe, F. (1994) *Autism: An Introduction to Psychological Theory.* Cambridge, MA: Harvard University Press.

Haraway, D. (1988) Situated knowledges: the science question in feminism and the privilege of partial perspective. *Feminist Studies* 14(3), 575–99.

Haraway, D. (1989) *Primate Visions: Gender, Race, and Nature in the World of Modern Science.* New York: Routledge.

Haraway, D.J. (1991) *Simians, Cyborgs, and Women: The Reinvention of Nature.* New York: Routledge.

Harkness, S. and Super, C.M. (1983) The cultural construction of child development: a framework for the socialization of affect. *Ethos* 11, 221–31.

Heath, S.B. (1983) *Ways with Words: Language, Life and Work in Communities and Classrooms.* Cambridge: Cambridge University Press.

Hobson, R.P. (1986) The autistic child's appraisal of expressions of emotion. *Journal of Child Psychology and Psychiatry and Allied Disciplines* 27, 321–42.

Irvine, J.T. (1979) Formality and informality in communicative events. *American Anthropologist* 81, 773–90.

Keenan, E.O. (1974) Norm-makers, norm-breakers: uses of speech by men and women in a Malagasy community. In R. Bauman and J. Sherzer (eds), *Explorations in the Ethnography of Speaking.* Cambridge: Cambridge University Press, pp. 125–43.

Kernan, K. (1969) The Acquisition of Language by Samoan Children. Unpublished Ph.D. dissertation, University of California, Berkeley.

Kulick, D. (1992) *Language Shift and Cultural Reproduction: Socialization, Self, and Syncretism in a Papua New Guinean Village.* Cambridge: Cambridge University Press.

Labov, W. (1984) Intensity. In D. Schiffrin (ed.), *Meaning, Form, and Use in Context: Linguistic Applications, GURT '84.* Washington, D.C.: Georgetown University Press, pp. 43–70.

Leont'ev, A.N. (1979) The problem of activity in psychology. In J.V. Wertsch (ed.), *The Concept of Activity in Soviet Psychology.* Armonk, NY: M.E. Sharpe, pp. 37–71.

Levy, R. (1984) Emotion, knowing and culture. In R.A. Shweder and R.A. LeVine (eds), *Culture Theory: Essays on Mind, Self, and Emotion.* Cambridge: Cambridge University Press, pp. 214–37.

Loveland, K., McEvoy, R. and Tunali, B. (1990) Narrative storytelling in autism and Down's syndrome. *British Journal of Developmental Psychology* 8, 9–23.

Marcus, G. and Fischer, M. (1986) *Anthropology as Cultural Critique: An Experimental Moment in the Human Sciences.* Chicago: University of Chicago Press.

Miller, P. (1982) *Amy, Wendy, and Beth: Learning Language in South Baltimore.* Austin: University of Texas Press.

Miller, P. and Moore, B.B. (1989) Narrative conjunctions of caregiver and child: a comparative perspective on socialization through stories. *Ethos* 17(4), 428–49.

Ochs, E. (1988) *Culture and Language Development: Language Acquisition and Language Socialization in a Samoan Village.* Cambridge: Cambridge University Press.

Ochs, E. (1993) Constructing social identity: a language socialization perspective. *Research on Language and Social Interaction* 26(3), 287–306.

Ochs, E. (1994) Stories that step into the future. In D. Biber and E. Finegan (eds), *Sociolinguistic Perspectives on Register.* Oxford: Oxford University Press, pp. 106–35.

Ochs, E. (1996) Linguistic resources for socializing humanity. In J.J. Gumperz and S.C. Levinson (eds), *Rethinking Linguistic Relativity.* Cambridge: Cambridge University Press, pp. 407–37.

Ochs, E. and Schieffelin, B.B. (1979) *Developmenal Pragmatics.* New York: Academic Press.

Ochs, E. and Schieffelin, B.B. (1983) *Acquiring Conversational Competence.* Boston: Routledge & Kegan Paul.

Ochs, E. and Schieffelin, B.B. (1984) Language acquisition and socialization: three developmental stories. In R.A. Shweder and R.A. LeVine (eds), *Culture Theory: Essays on Mind, Self, and Emotion.* Cambridge: Cambridge University Press, pp. 276–320.

Ochs, E. and Schieffelin, B.B. (1989) Language has a heart. *Text* 9(1), 7–25.

Ochs, E. and Schieffelin, B.B. (1995) The impact of language socialization on grammatical development. In P. Fletcher and B. MacWhinney (eds), *The Handbook of Child Language.* Oxford: Blackwell, pp. 73–94.

Ortner, S.B. (1974) Is female to male as nature is to culture? In M.Z. Rosaldo and L.L. Lamphere (eds), *Woman, Culture and Society.* Stanford: Stanford University Press.

Ortner, S.B. (1984) Theory in anthropology since the sixties. *Comparative Studies in Society and History* 26(1), 126–66.

Sacks, H. (1992) *Lectures on Conversation: Volumes 1 and 2*, Vol. 1. Cambridge: Blackwell.

Sacks, H., Schegloff, E.A. and Jefferson, G. (1974) A simplest systematics for the organization of turn-taking for conversation. *Language* 50, 696–735.

Schieffelin, B.B. (1990) *The Give and Take of Everyday Life: Language Socialization of Kaluli Children*. Cambridge: Cambridge University Press.

Schieffelin, B.B. (1994) Code-switching and language socialization: some probable relationships. In J. Duchan, L.E. Hewitt and R.M. Sonnenmeier (eds), *Pragmatics: From Theory to Practice*. New York: Prentice Hall, pp. 20–42.

Schieffelin, B.B. and Ochs, E. (1986) *Language Socialization across Cultures*. Cambridge: Cambridge University Press.

Scollon, R. (1976) *Conversations with a One Year Old: A Case Study of the Developmental Foundation of Syntax*. Honolulu: University Press of Hawaii.

Sigman, M. and Capps, L. (1997) *Children with Autism: A Developmental Perspective*. Cambridge, MA: Harvard University Press.

Sigman, M., Mundy, P., Ungerer, J. and Sherman, T. (1986) Social interactions of autistic, mentally retarded, and normal children and their caregivers. *Journal of Child Psychology and Psychiatry* 27, 647–56.

Sigman, M., Kassari, C., Kwon J. and Yirmiya, N. (1992) Responses to the negative emotions of others by autistic, mentally retarded, and normal children. *Child Development* 63, 796–807.

Silverstein, M. (1993) Metapragmatic discourse and metapragmatic function. In J. Lucy (ed.), *Reflexive Language*. New York: Cambridge University Press, pp. 33–58.

Solomon, O. (2000) Narratives of a different order: autistic children's use of connectives. Paper presented at the Sixth Annual Conference on Language, Interaction, and Culture, UCLA.

Strathern, M. (1987) An awkward relationship: the case of feminism and anthropology. *Signs* 12, 276–92.

Tager-Flushberg, H. (1995) "Once upon a ribbit:" stories narrated by austistic children. *British Journal of Developmental Psychology* 13, 45–59.

Ungerer, J.A. and Sigman, M. (1987) Categorization skills and receptive language development in autistic children. *Journal of Autism and Developmental Disorders*, 17, 3–16.

Watson-Gegeo, K. and Gegeo, D. (1986a) Calling out and repeating routines in the language socialization of Basotho children. In B. Schieffelin and E. Ochs (eds), *Language Socialization across Cultures*. Cambridge: Cambridge University Press, pp. 17–50.

Watson-Gegeo, K.A. and Gegeo, D.W. (1986b) The social world of Kwara'ae children: acquistion of language and values. In J. Cook-Gumperz, W.A. Corsaro and J. Streeck (eds), *Children's Worlds and Children's Language*. Berlin: Mouton de Gruyter, pp. 109–27.

Wulff, S.B. (1985) The symbolic and object play of children with autism: a review. *Journal of Autism and Developmental Disorders* 15, 139–48.

Cross-cultural learning and other catastrophes

5

Ron Scollon

"What's that? That's a boat."

"Mommy chodai."

There are two utterances here, both spoken by a mother to her one-year-old infant, though said at different times. The first raises some questions about the interaction between systems of representation and social action; the second raises some questions about what it means to say that an utterance is spoken in a language. Taken together I would like to use these two utterances to reopen a discussion begun two decades ago in a working paper by Suzanne Scollon (1977) under the title "Langue, idiolect, and speech community: three views of the language at Fort Chipewyan, Alberta."

To do this, I will look first at these utterances which are, I hope, simple enough that we can isolate the problems to be addressed. Then I will review the central argument of Suzanne Scollon's paper, which was that in order to understand language in use we need a rather more complex model than we have been accustomed to using in linguistic research – a model of multiple models or, in fact, an ecological model. Then I will return to the problems of representation on the one hand and of the identification of utterances as *being in* a language on the other, and sketch out a model which I have been calling *mediated discourse analysis*, which addresses some of these questions.

"What's that? That's a boat"

A child aged one shows little ability to use language, even when prompted by her mother who would like to put on a good display for the visiting researcher. In this case (Example 1) the mother is engaged in the group of practices which are common within this particular social group of pointing to things and asking the child to name them (Scollon 1976, 1979; Scollon and Scollon 1981; Heath 1983). A common formula for this is, "What's that?" which is followed by the same speaker saying, "It's an X," and the objects cover a wide range of things from material objects in the immediate environment to represented objects in books, in paintings or drawings, or on television.

Example 1

1. AGE: 1:0.2		
Brenda	*Mother*	*Context*
[neːneː] [kaː]	What's that over there? What's that, hm? What's that, hm? [eːː] What's that, hm? You're not sick? Nene? Hm? That's a hakata doll. Yeah. Doll. What's that? That's a boat.	M pointing to hakata doll. B looks at doll, M points to painting.

Brenda, the child in this case, is just one year old. She shows little ability to nominate objects within these pedagogical practices of pointing and naming. We can see in her utterance [kaː] what might be an imitation of the stressed syllable of M's "hakata doll" but, as I have argued in my extended study of this child's language (Scollon 1976, 1979), at this age she had not yet arrived at the so-called one-word stage of language development.

Elsewhere I have developed an analysis of the processes by which such a child comes to be construed as a communicating social actor within the first year of life (Scollon 2000, 2001). There I have taken a single, narrowly defined social practice, that of handing an object from one person to another, and argued that this practice comes into the life of the infant as a pre-existing social practice. That is, I have argued that ontogenetically this practice predates the social actor's participation in that practice. More to the point here, these social practices of pointing and requesting that names of objects be given as well as the systems of representation which include the nomination of objects – hakata doll, boat – predate the infant's ability to participate in them. Brenda is asked to name objects before there is any real expectation that she can give their names.

Here, however, my interest is not in the broad questions of language socialization which have been treated in much detail by others. I am specifically concerned in the two problems of representation that we see in this example, the nomination of objects "hakata doll" (coupled with gaze direction, pointing practices) and the nomination of represented objects. That is to say, in this case we see the linguistic/discursive/pedagogical conflation of what are two very different ontological objects, the hakata doll and a painting of a boat. The hakata doll is a physical object – a Japanese art object – that is displayed on a shelf in the room but the "boat" is the painting of a boat, a reproduction, which is hanging on the wall. One is an object and the other is the representation of an object. The answer given to the question, however, is not "That's a painting," the answer is "That's a boat."

The question that I believe needs to be addressed in this case is: What is the role of the system of representation in this conflation of represented object with object? I would like this very primary example to stand in for the much more complex question of how systems of representation from visual design practices of artists to the grammatical systems so central to formal linguistics, applied linguistics, and sociolinguistics figure into our day-to-day, moment-by-moment social actions.

Example 2

2. AGE: 1:0.9			
Brenda	*Charlotte*	*Mother*	*Context*
{silent}	Momma, look. Give me another one.	Yeah, this is yellow, yellow crayon. Thank you. Thank you. Oh. Give it to Charlotte. Thank you.	B holds out yellow crayon toward mother

Example 2 can be used to illustrate the sort of complexity we encounter in trying to develop a systematic link between these systems of representation (the nomination of objects "hakata doll" or nomination of represented objects, or double representation "boat") and social practices of pointing and pedagogization; in many cases such representations are indirect and presupposed. As I have argued in my fuller treatment of this material (Scollon 2000, 2001), Brenda cannot be imagined to be a social actor exercising any sort of agentive force here.

At the time of this action she was still months from attesting the separation of self and objects, or from any sort of cognitive construction of objects as permanent and independent of herself. In other words, at this moment we cannot construct Brenda as someone who could hand a crayon to her mother or to her sister because we cannot support the notion that she even perceives the crayon as separable from her hand. All this comes a few months later. Nevertheless, in this example we see that the mother constructs Brenda as:

1. A hander; that is, as an agent who can hand a crayon to her sister.
2. A language learner; that is, as a child who can learn both the noun "crayon" and the color "yellow."
3. A socially competent actor; she says "Thank you" to her and thus attributes intention and social grace to the child.

In this one moment of social interaction we see an inseparable melding of linguistic and social pedagogy, of representation, and of cognitive, agentive independence, all of which is constructed socially by the mother and the older sister out of the most minimal of movements on the part of the infant with the crayon.

To rephrase this within the habitus model of Bourdieu (1977, 1990), we can see that there is no basis in Brenda's behavior to attribute to her the rather complex set of behavioral, social, and linguistic actions which are being constructed upon the site of this act of holding up the crayon. Nevertheless, as I have argued in my longer treatment of this material, within a year we can construe Brenda to be a highly agentive social actor who can name these objects, who can hand them to others as well as receive them, and who does so for highly social purposes such as controlling the conversational topic (Scollon 1976). That is to say, whatever objectivist analysis we might make overall of a "system" of handing on the one hand and a "system" of representation on the other, in the ontogenetic development of the child we see that the system of representation is taken one piece at a time, beginning by being construed by the caregivers – the social world – as something which can be taken for granted.

If we focus more closely on the boat before moving on, we could subject this painting to a representational analysis along the lines of any number of semiotic systems of analysis, whether derived from art-historical frameworks of analysis or from more social semiotic ones such as Kress and van Leeuwen's (1998) recent visual semiotic system, but in this case it is only really the realism that is being appropriated by the mother. That is to say, for this little piece of pedagogical display, virtually any realistic representation of a "boat" would suffice, whether it was a painting, a drawing, or a photograph across a very wide range of styles, periods, and genres. The history of artistic representation is swept aside in this brief pedagogical move. From this point of view – the point of view of this one social action – the rest is simply irrelevant. At a minimum this suggests that whatever complexities of systems of representation an analyst might discover in this painting, from the point of view of the social actor – the mother in this case – there is another and very different sort of analysis going on. It is this disjunction between what we might call *universalistic* or *objectivist* analysis and *analysis in use* that is the center of the problem of representation I would like to come to understand.

"Mommy chodai"

There is a second problem, however, which is ultimately related to the first, though perhaps not at first glance. This is the problem of social organization. We have come through various historical and analytical processes to identify systems of representation with social groups. We have come to think of systems of representation, say the Japanese language, as coterminous in some way with social systems or organizations, say the Japanese culture/nation/people. I have chosen "Japanese" in this case because of Example 3. I might as well have said that we have come to identify a perspectival system of realist representation in art with the European Renaissance and thus to identify realist art with premodern European people. The problem is in establishing the basis for making such identifications.

Example 3

3. AGE: 1:0.9		
Brenda	*Mother*	*Context*
	I found candy. I found candy, Brenda.	M brings box of candy, gives to B. B shakes box of candy.
	[rɛturɛtu:] (3x)	
[op:pʰ] [n n]	Up. Up. Nice, hm? Mommy chodai, Mommy chodai. Oh. Thank you, thank you. Now. Oh, you want to open it but. Open. So nice.	B cannot open the candy box.

Turning again to the social exchanges between Brenda and her mother, this time one week later, just a week and two days after Brenda's first birthday, we find the mother again encouraging Brenda to hand her an object by saying, "Mommy chodai." The question here is: What language is "mommy chodai"? Of course we are inclined to say that this is Japanese, but why? The mother was born a Japanese citizen and lived her early years in Japan, though by this time she had become a US citizen. She continues to use Japanese in speaking to her friends and relatives, but as her husband, Brenda's father, is Hawaiian Chinese and does not speak more than a few words of Japanese, she rarely uses any Japanese at home. In my data, utterances "in Japanese" are extremely rare.

More to the point, for Brenda we cannot construe this utterance to be *in* any language. At this time, as I have said, we cannot attest any but the most minimal of language ability. We cannot attest even active social agency in most cases. Nevertheless, the utterance itself (or at least "chodai") has a clear historical provenance in the representational system we might call "the Japanese language." That even M does not imagine this "chodai" to be available for Brenda is proved in Example 4.

In Example 4, from the same week, we see that Brenda does actively pursue food. The surprise comes when she "says" "[tɕoːda]". I put "says" in quotes because I believe there is good evidence that this is what we might call an erratic, by analogy with the geological use of the term for a rock that appears very far from any possible source in the bedrock. Elsewhere (Scollon 1976) I have argued that such erratics often occur months before there is any attestation of a phonological base for such utterances. Clearly the mother is equally surprised by Brenda's utterance. She rather paradoxically addresses Brenda as a conversational interlocutor ("Hear what you said?") while simultaneously denying by implication that Brenda is competent to have noticed her own utterance.

I believe I can argue that "chodai" is not spoken by M *in* the Japanese language, though it is certainly possible to argue that it has this provenance. When Brenda speaks the word, it is much less arguable that this is a Japanese utterance; even M denies this. But in Example 5, we see that "chodai" has migrated even further afield.

Example 4

4. AGE: 1:0.9				
B	M	R	S	Context
[nanana] [ene] [xx] [na:na:nan] [nannanna]	Do you want juice? Do you want juice?	You should write down that she's trying, first tried to get my taco and then tried to get your juice.	How can I write? ☺	B crawls toward S's juice glass. B is pulling on S's juice glass in S's right hand.
[ɛnnannan]		I've got it now. Where can I put it so you won't get it? I don't have it. I hid it.		Left hand has taco on plate.
[tɕo:da]	☺ O.K., give it to you. ☺ xxx Chodai! ☺ She said "Chodai."	See, Suzie's got it again.		
	That means to give me please.	What's that?		
	Um hm, Yes. ☺ Did you hear that? Chodai. ☺	Oh, is that right?		
		Well I can't resist that. She just asked me like that. What can I say?		
	Yeah. Hai. You want juice? Hm? Hear what you said? You said, "Chodai." Hm? That's too big. Chodai. Mommy throw that.			

Example 5

5. AGE: 0:8.23			
Rachel	R	S	Context
xxx [riðəbʊ] ("read the book") xxx xxx xxxxxx	 xxx the book?	chodai? chodai? huh? chodai? chodai? Thank you.	Not clear what object is being requested. ["read the book" is "tune before the words."]

Some two years after Brenda's "chodai," Suzanne Scollon was recorded saying "chodai" to her own daughter, Rachel. While it is true that she had studied some Japanese at university, this utterance has its clear provenance, not in the Japanese language but in the Brenda recording sessions of my dissertation research two years earlier. The question, then, is under what circumstances are we willing or interested in speaking of such things as "the Japanese language" but not equally interested in speaking of such things as "Ron-Brenda-Brenda's mother's language"? It should be clear enough that for Brenda's mother this little piece of culture came into her habitus through somewhat earlier mother–child interactions between herself and her own mother in Japan. Thus we need to ask why certain social groupings and categorizations – nations, ethnic groups, cultural groups and the like – are privileged as "having" languages and others are not?

To address these issues, then, I will turn to the ideas of language, idiolect, and speech community as sketched out by Suzanne Scollon (1977).

Langue, idiolect, and speech community

In a working paper entitled "Language, idiolect, and speech community: Three views of the language at Fort Chipewyan, Alberta," Suzanne Scollon argued that a minimum of three different units of analysis would be required to achieve a useful analysis of language in use. These are the *langue*, the *idiolect*, and the *speech community*. This paper, which formed a two-paper set with a paper of my own (R. Scollon 1977), was stimulated by the Presidential Address given at that year's annual meeting of the American Anthropological Association by Richard Adams, "I can feel the heat, but where's the light?" in which Adams reviewed the possible interest in and impact upon anthropology of the work of the Belgian physicist, Ilya Prigogine, on dissipative structures.

Adams argued that the characteristics described by Prigogine for the dissipative structure were, in fact, those characteristics long since understood by anthropologists to be the nature of such organic structures as the social organization or culture. As he argued, there was a polarity in analysis between closed systems (systems near equilibrium) and open or dissipative systems (systems far from equilibrium). The pendulum clock was an example Adams used of the closed system. The pendulum pulled to one side swings in ever decreasing arcs until it comes to a standstill. On the other hand, a pendulum clock with a spring puts energy into the system and keeps it in wide and systemic fluctuation. Ultimately, of course, the spring winds down and so a human puts energy into the spring. The human, in turn, requires feeding in order to have the energy to wind the clock. Adams used this and other examples to argue that a closed-systems analysis of social and cultural systems was doomed to failure because ultimately we would lose sight of the sources of external "energy" which were the "cause" of the maintenance of the internal fluctuations of the system under study.

S. Scollon, basing her thinking on Adams' Presidential Address (Adams 1977) as well as on Prigogine (Prigogine 1976; Glansdorff and Prigogine 1971; Holling 1976; Jantsch and Waddington 1976; Grace 1981), argued on the basis of language acquisition data from Fort Chipewyan, Alberta that the "language that has traditionally been the object of our linguistic descriptions is only one part of the picture" (74). She argued that, on the whole, linguists had sought to treat languages, *langues*, as closed, rule-based systems which operate quite independently of their sociocultural and biological environments. Based on her Fort Chipewyan data she argued that there were, in fact, four such ontological entities at Fort Chipewyan: Chipewyan (Athabaskan), Cree (Algonkian), English, and French. Nevertheless, as we argued elsewhere (Scollon and Scollon 1979) and as she put forward in that paper, none of these appears in anything like the standard, full, or normative variety of the *langue*. In fact, from the point of view of any single one of these four languages, any one of Chipewyan, Cree, English or French by itself would appear to be in a moribund state at Fort Chipewyan.

Contrasted with this view of languages at Fort Chipewyan, if one looks at the language use of any particular individuals living there, they seem competent linguistically in their ability to move with ease not only across registers of any one of these languages but also across the languages themselves. For this complex competence S. Scollon argued, following Grace (1981), that we need the concept of the idiolect. By this she meant the full linguistic ability of the person, without particular reference to historical or named linguistic varieties. In speaking of this notion of the idiolect, Grace, and Scollon, contrasted it with the *absolute monoglot idiolect* of Bloch. That is, the focus of idiolect in this usage is not on the individual's particularistic knowledge of, say, English, but the whole language of the experience of the person, including as well the ability to translate from one language to another. In terms of Prigogine's dissipative structures, the idiolect would be a system far from equilibrium, one in which extensive exchanges with the environment are characteristic, and which is highly adaptable in terms of that environment.

Finally, Scollon argued that neither the *langue* (e.g. Chipewyan or French) as a bounded, closed rule-based objectivized entity nor the *idiolect* (e.g. Ben Marcel's language ability) as an open dissipative structure in active exchange with its environment is sufficient to develop an understanding of language use and language acquisition at Fort Chipewyan. She argued that we must also account for the structures of social systems such as the speech community itself. At Fort Chipewyan, this would have to include the histories of those four languages in that region and of the people who identify themselves through the use of those languages. It would have to include community-wide practices such as dual-lingualism (Lincoln 1975) in which two (or more) persons would carry on a conversation in which each speaks in a different language (langue) but is able to listen to the other(s) in whatever language they might speak. Such community-wide structures of social interaction and of genres cannot be properly said to be located either in the idiolect of the individual, though of course, one aspect of this idiolect would be to come to know how to perform in such speech situations, or in the langue – there is nothing in the grammatical structure of English which would tell me how to interpret an utterance in Cree, or how to translate between them.

Scollon's argument, then, is that it has been a counterproductive move to seek to reduce our understanding of language phenomena to any one of these three broad systems or system types, *langue, idiolect,* or *speech community.* As she argued, a more productive model is to consider these three systems to be in active engagement with each other as a complex dissipative structure of languages. Fluctuations within the speech community interact with fluctuations in the idiolect that exert pressures on the relatively closed systems, the langues present within the speech community.

Chaos and complexity twenty years later

In the twenty years since these working papers were written, there have been several cyclones of chaos and complexity. In 1977 it was a striking new idea at the American Anthropological Association that models used in physics, chemistry, and biology would resonate with more traditional anthropological analysis. Now a national chain bookstore has a book section labeled "Complexity." Unfortunately, one looks in vain for anthropology or linguistics in this section. Instead one sees that in anthropology, with the exception perhaps of Rodseth (1998), it is apparently still a very new idea. For example, a Brandeis anthropologist and a Harvard physicist (Shiveley and Ertas 1996) have raised the question of "Possibilities and limitations of complexity theory in anthropology." It is interesting that in this paper from the 1996 annual meeting, which cites much popular literature on chaos and complexity theory, there is no mention and apparently no memory of the Presidential Address at that same association's meeting 19 years earlier.

It is not my wish to make much of whether or not there are resonances with complexity theory in our analyses of language in use. What I believe is important is that in various disciplines there have been rather reductionist moves. The two most common are 1) the reduction of all symbolic or semiotic activity to the analysis of the systems of representation, and 2) the reduction of language to nothing but a social habitus. The first of these is most strongly seen in linguistics and the Saussurean spawn of semiotics. One could argue that it is the essence of both science on the one hand and of art on the other to theoretically isolate phenomena for the analytical and esthetic contemplation of the internal, rule-based structure of its composition. Linguists have done this with languages, and artists have done this with framed paintings, bounded musical compositions, and tight poetic forms. However, reducing language to nothing but a system of representation fails to account ecologically for its use in the world.

The second form of reduction is most strongly represented by Bourdieu. At about the same time as Adams was giving his address in Houston, Bourdieu was launching his *Outline of a Theory of Practice* (1977) which consisted in great part of a critique of such rule-based, closed system models of social action. There he argued for his concept of the *habitus* which was the largely unconscious structure of the human life experience out of which social action is taken. This practice theory of action focuses on the conflict in analysis between seeking to understand human social activity as rule-governed on the one hand or as practice-based on the other. Without developing Bourdieu's argument here, as it is likely to be well understood by most readers, I would like to suggest that this notion of habitus is very much the notion which S. Scollon and Grace were trying to capture with their notion of the idiolect. That is, to bring about a closer alignment of the Scollon/Grace terminology with Bourdieu's terms, one could define the idiolect as the language habitus. Elsewhere (Scollon 2001) I have argued that this idea has other historical antecedents in the work of Bateson (1972) whose classes S. Scollon attended at the University of Hawaii, and in the writing of Nishida Kitaroo (1958), especially his concept of the historical body (*reishiki teki shintai*). The danger in this line of analysis, however, is an equivalent, though contrasting, reduction of social phenomena to nothing but the emergent structures of ongoing social interactions.

My argument in this chapter is that neither the reduction of social phenomena, including language, to rule-based conceptual structures, nor the reduction to ongoing, lived experience is likely to be able to make sense of how social actors construct their worlds in real-time social interactions. I would argue, as Suzanne Scollon argued, that at a minimum we need to account for the dialectical interaction of objectivized structures and the structures of habitus in a model of interacting complexity which would include both very different types of structures:

1. The rule-based analytical structures of our representational systems, and the social structures of our communities, organizations, and social groups.
2. The habitus-based structures of practice.

I believe that a fully developed ecological model of language socialization for adults or children will need to account not only for these different types of structures in isolation but also for the complex interactions among them in a dissipative structure model.

Mediated discourse

If we wish to avoid an idealist account of human social reality, it seems we have little choice but to locate representational systems, social groups, and habitus structures of practice in what are really just two places: the habitus of social actors and the material world. Mediated discourse analysis takes the position that structures are available only as the embodied habitus of social actors or as material objects (and complexes of objects) in the world. The relationship between these two ontological primes is established in the social actions or, as Wertsch (1991, 1998) calls them, mediated actions, of social actors.

As a practice-based theory of social action, mediated discourse works with five basic conceptual tools:

- mediated action
- social practice
- site of engagement
- mediational means (objects, persons, structures, systems of representation as embodied in objects)
- nexus of practice.

Elsewhere (Scollon 1998, 2001) I have begun to elaborate a theory of mediated discourse. I can illustrate the way these concepts are used within that perspective by returning to the examples with which I began. Brenda's mother tries to get her to name several objects; in this stretch it is the "hakata doll" and the painting of a boat ("a boat"). This action of trying to elicit words forms the focus of a mediated discourse analytical approach to this social interaction.

Mediated action

In a way this action is particularly instructive of the nature of mediated action, simply because Brenda is largely incompetent to take any agentive role. The mediated action is virtually always mutually constructed among multiple participants, never (perhaps rarely, if we want to be a bit less energetic in our claims) a matter of discovering the *a priori* intentions. We can be quite sure that Brenda has no intentions in any meaningful sense here, and yet we can see how actively the mother is working to construct a mutually participatory social action.

Social practice

In any event, within a mediated discourse understanding of mediated action, an action is defined within a social practice. That is to say, a movement, a noise, a sound, a behavior is a mediated action to the extent it is recognized as such (Gee 1999) by participants as being located within a social practice. It is because I understand this bit of pointing and talking on the part of the mother as the characteristic pedagogical practice of nomination that I see it as a mediated action. My reasons for doing this are, of course, based on the mother's own speech and actions. Thus in this case it is my dual status as researcher and participant that allows me this recognition of practice, and it is Brenda's infancy that (at this point in her life) seems to disallow it.

Site of engagement

This mediated action is multiply located at the intersection of several, not just one, social practices. At a minimum we can see pointing as a social practice which is used here in trying to produce objects around the house as suitable objects for nomination. But such a practice is also seen in the book game (Scollon 1976; Heath 1983), when a caregiver points to pictures and asks questions about the pictured objects. More generally the practice is used to direct behavior, "Go get the crayon," or to indicate social relations, "That's your cousin." A second practice here might be called "caregiving" and this is seen in the phrase, "You're not sick?" Yet a third practice is the nomination, "That's hakata doll" or "That's a boat."

As I have argued in my longer analysis of this data (Scollon 2001) as well as in my earlier development of mediated discourse (Scollon 1998), any particular mediated action forms the intersection or linkage among multiple social practices. One looks in vain for fixed, regular, and invariant linkages among nondiscursive practices and discursive ones, for example. The site of engagement makes reference not just to the mediated action itself but to the practices that are instantiated at the moment of social interaction. This concept focuses on the real-time, unfinalized, unidirectional, and unique co-occurrence mode of social interaction (Bakhtin 1981; Gumperz 1977).

Mediational means

The mediational means by which actions are carried out are both the physical, external material objects by which we take action (including our bodies, in pointing gestures and other social actors), and the internal, psychological structures of the habitus which enable our use of the physical world. Here we have seen several mediational means called upon by the mother. She has used the hakata doll and the painting, but she has also used pointing, as just mentioned, and language. A bit further afield, but not at all insignificant, are the room itself (her living room, in which the objects are all very familiar to Brenda), and my tape recorder which is in an important way the instigator of this particular sequence of pedagogization.

What is important from the point of view of mediated discourse analysis is that these objects in the world – let's focus on just the hakata doll and the painting of the boat – are not mediational means for Brenda at this stage, but just for the mother and, of course, myself. Wertsch (1991, 1998) has developed Vygotsky's notion of the cultural (psychological) tool, which is a historical/psychological process by which external objects and semiotic means are appropriated over time by the user. To the extent that psychological tools remain external and unappropriated, we would want to refer to them simply as material objects, the doll and the painting, whatever internal structural or semiotic characteristics they might have. As they become appropriated through a series of mediated actions such as the one we have observed here, they come to take on meaning for Brenda as mediational means through which she herself can take action.

From this point of view we would want to say that the doll and the painting (as well as the mother's speech, of course) are simply objects at this stage for Brenda but mediational means for the mother. By the end of the year in which I studied this child, these had become mediational means for Brenda as well. That is, she had come to appropriate some aspects of their existence which she could use for at least this nomination function: she called the doll a "hakata doll" and she called the painting "a boat."

Nexus of practice

Finally we come to the point which will be of use in addressing the question of whether "Mommy chodai" is an utterance in a language. Based in the concept of the mediational means, "chodai" was a mediational means for the mother from the beginning of the data which I collected. Like the doll and the boat, however, I believe we could argue that it was not a mediational means for Brenda. Over a series of mediated actions in which the practice of handing was constructed by the mother out of Brenda's moves and acts and in which "Mommy chodai" was sometimes linked within those sites of engagement, this became for that dyad a mediational means. We see in Example 4 that for R (that is, for me) it was still nothing but a word, though it was at least identifiable as that.

M: She said, "Chodai."
R: What's that?
M: That means to give me please.

We can see further in this little exchange that in the first place the mother assumed I would know (be able to appropriate) this mediational means. I could not, and so she brought it one step closer to usability for me. I have already pointed out that within two years, this had become "standard" within the repertory of the Scollon household.

I am using the concept of the nexus of practice to indicate connected groupings of practices which never by themselves produce a social group but which, over time, produce what Bourdieu has called "homologous habitus" (1977, 1990); that is, habitus which is shared by members of a group or class. In this case I would want to say that Brenda, her sister, her mother, Suzanne, and myself formed a nexus of practice over the year of the recordings. Early in the year, as this recent example has shown, I do not know what "chodai" means; it is not a mediational means available for me to appropriate, even though it is being used within my presence relatively frequently at first. Early in the year, Brenda is entirely unaware not only of the tape recorder and its function but of handing, nomination with pointing, and the whole host of practices that are constructed by her mother (and by us) around her actions. By one year and 10 months, however, we had the following conversation:

B:	Tape 'corder.
R:	Yeah.
B:	Use it.
	Use it.
R:	Use it for what?
B:	Talk.
	'corder talk.
	Brenda talk.

It is clear from such examples that not just the tape recorder but much more broadly the nexus of practice which we might call "recording young children for research" has been quite distinctly constituted. I would argue that such nexus of practice are the stuff of our identifications of words as being words in a language. For the mother, "chodai" is a very different object than it is for me or for Brenda or for Suzanne. For the mother it is a mediational means which can be appropriated within multiple nexus of practice – her home in caregiving as well as in social interactions with strangers from the same home country. For me it is a mediational means which can be appropriated within the rather narrow nexus of practice of doing my research project. A mediated discourse analysis of such structures as this word would argue that they have ontological status as mediational means only within such nexus of practice. That is another way of saying that there is no meaning of the word "chodai" outside of social actions within practices.

Cross-cultural learning and other catastrophes

Because they tend to imply closely bounded social groups, the phrases "cross-cultural" and "intercultural" seem to me particularly problematical in trying to come to an understanding of human learning (Scollon 1999, forthcoming), at least within a mediated discourse perspective. Within this perspective, learning is understood to be a process of appropriation in the habitus over time of the knowledge of and ability to use the external, objective world. I believe the very partial and slow accumulation of such habitus as I have only sketched out here argues for a concept of mediational means, including language and other objectivized systems of representation, as always being ambiguously structured and partially constructed systems of representation. That is, not only is it problematical to seek to reduce language and other semiotic systems to simple systems of representation, but the purported systematicity of those reductions is also problematical. It is never a question of whether one is "speaking a language" (or a member of a culture) so much as it is a question of, What are the multiple practices within which this particular mediational means can be appropriated by a particular social actor and, from that, what are the nexus of practice within which social actors come to recognize themselves as sharing homologous habitus?

An objectivist, rule-based structure such as a language (Japanese, English, Chipewyan) or an esthetic system (late eighteenth-century realist European art) can certainly be analyzed by examining the multiple products of human social actions – paintings, dictionaries, school grammars, art history books, and the like. The structure of the habitus of a particular social actor can also be analyzed through a particularistic and historical study of that person's actions. It seems to me that the time has come, however, to problematize the often easy equation of the first type of structure with the internalized structure of the habitus. Much work remains to be done to show how structures which are inferred on the basis of a much broader semiotic base than any human can possibly internalize can be related to structures within the individual habitus which are inferred on the basis of the particularistic and concrete experience of the individual.

As Suzanne Scollon argued, I believe we need a model along the lines I have sketched out here which can account for three things: objectivized, rule-based structures of systems of representation, practice-based structures of the habitus, and the interactions between them in social action. I believe mediated discourse analysis is one such possible model.

References

Adams, R. (1977) I can feel the heat, but where's the light? Presidential Address, 76th Annual Meeting of the American Anthropological Association, November 30.

Bakhtin, M.M. (1981) (originally published in 1934–5). *The Dialogic Imagination*. Austin: University of Texas Press.

Bateson, G. (1972) *Steps to an Ecology of Mind*. New York: Ballantine.

Bourdieu, P. (1977) *Outline of a Theory of Practice*. Trans. by R. Nice. Cambridge: Cambridge University Press.

Bourdieu, P. (1990) *The Logic of Practice*. Stanford: Stanford University Press.

Gee, J.P. (1999) *An Introduction to Discourse Analysis: Theory and Method*. London: Routledge.

Glansdorff, P. and Prigogine, I. (1971) *Thermodynamic Theory of Structure, Stability and Fluctuations*. New York: Wiley-Interscience.

Grace, G.W. (1981) *An Essay on Language*. Columbia: Hornbeam Press.

Gumperz, J. (1977) Sociocultural knowledge in conversational inference. In M. Saville-Troike (ed.), 28th Annual Round Table Monograph Series on Language and Linguistics. Washington, D.C.: Georgetown University Press, pp. 191–212.

Heath, S.B. (1983) *Ways with Words*. New York: Cambridge University Press.

Holling, C.S. (1976) Resilience arid stability of ecosystems. In E. Jantsch and C.H. Waddington (eds), *Evolution and Consciousness: Human Systems in Transition*. Reading, MA: Addison-Wesley.

Jantsch, E. and C.H. Waddington, C.H. (1976) *Evolution and Consciousness: Human Systems in Transition*. Reading, MA: Addison-Wesley.

Kress, G. and van Leeuwen, T. (1998) *Reading Images: The Grammar of Visual Design*. London: Routledge.

Lincoln, P.C. (1975) Acknowledging dual-lingualism. University of Hawaii: *Working Papers in Linguistics*, 7(4), 39–46.

Nishida, K. (1958) *Intelligibility and the Philosophy of Nothingness*. Tokyo: Maruzen.

Prigogine, I. (1976) Order through fluctuation: self-organization and social system. In E. Jantsch and C.H. Waddington (eds), *Evolution and Consciousness: Human Systems in Transition*. Reading, MA: Addison-Wesley, pp. 93–133.

Rodseth, L. (1998) Distributive models of culture: a Sapirian alternative to essentialism. *American Anthropologist* 100(1), 55–69.

Scollon, R. (1976) *Conversations with a One-year-old: A Case Study of the Developmental Foundation of Syntax*. Honolulu: University Press of Hawaii.

Scollon, R. (1977) Dissipative structures, Chipewyan consonants, and the modern consciousness. University of Hawaii: *Working Papers in Linguistics* 9(3), 43–64.

Scollon, R. (1979) A real early stage: an unzippered condensation of a dissertation on child language. In E. Ochs and B.B. Schieffelin (eds), *Developmental pragmatics*. New York: Academic Press, pp. 215–27.

Scollon, R. (1998) *Mediated Discourse as Social Interaction*. London: Longman.

Scollon, R. (1999) Intercultural communication: Problem, solution, new problem. Talk presented at the University of California, Berkeley Language Center, March 12.

Scollon, R. (2000) On the ontogenesis of a social practice. Paper presented to the Workshop on Theory and Interdisciplinarity in Critical Discourse Analysis, Institute on Discourse, Identity, and Politics, University of Vienna, July 6/7, 2000 as a pre-session to the 7th International Pragmatics Conference in Budapest (July 9–14, 2000).

Scollon, R. (2001) *Mediated Discourse: The Nexus of Practice*. London: Routledge.

Scollon, R. (2002). Intercultural communication and ethnography: Why? and Why not? In C. Barron, N. Bruce and D. Nunan (eds), *Knowledge and Discourse: Towards an Ecology of Language*. London: Longman, pp. 300–13.

Scollon, R. and Scollon, S. (1979) *Linguistic Convergence: An Ethnography of Speaking at Fort Chipewyan, Alberta*. New York: Academic Press.

Scollon, R. and Scollon, S. (1981) *Narrative, Literacy and Face in Interethnic Communication*. Norwood, NJ: Ablex.

Scollon, S. (1977) Langue, idiolect, and speech community: three views of the language at Fort Chipewyan, Alberta. Department of Linguistics, University of Hawaii: *Working Papers in Linguistics* 9(3), 65–76.

Shiveley, K. and Ertas, D. (1996) Possibilities and limitations of complexity theory in anthropology. Paper presented at the 95th annual meeting of the American Anthropological Association, San Francisco, November 24, 1996.

Wertsch, J.V. (1991) *Voices of the Mind: A Sociocultural Approach to Mediated Action*. Cambridge, MA: Harvard University Press.

Wertsch, J.V. (1998) *Mind as Action*. New York: Oxford University Press.

6 An ecological-semiotic perspective on language and linguistics

Leo van Lier

The transgression of disciplinary boundaries is a prerequisite for scientific advance.

Pierre Bourdieu

Introduction

The goal of this chapter is to describe an ecological perspective on language that is relevant to the activities of language education. When teachers teach and learners learn language – a second or foreign language, or specific normative (including academic) aspects[1] of their own language – we can assume that some idea of what language is underlies the activities that take place for the purpose of language education. But what is this idea of language?

While there is great variety in basic assumptions and actual practices, certain themes are ubiquitous in the language teaching profession, and in Table 6.1 I attempt to capture some of these. In each case I start with the practical view as commonly expressed in teachers' books and course syllabuses (the middle column), and link it to what may be underlying theories – which are often unexpressed and perhaps not explicitly known in their full extension – and to some typical instantiations one might expect to encounter in conversations among teachers and learners, and in applied linguistics guides (the arrows indicate "points to" or "relates to;" no linear causality is implied).

I do not suggest that any or all of these views and practices are fundamentally "wrong" in some way, and that this wrongness can be fixed by a new theory of language that I will be presenting here. All of the things mentioned in the table have some plausibility and merit (although some may be based on popular but false assumptions, and some may be in or out of fashion), and all the classroom practices listed may be useful at some times and in some places. However, I do think that they do not tell the whole story of what language learning is and what it entails. Even more strongly, I suggest that all of the items in the table (in all three columns) can lead to ineffective practices and counterproductive initiatives if they are decontextualized; that is, if they are not seen as part of a rich and deep understanding of what language is and what language does. This rich and deep understanding, this contextualizing of language, cannot be taken for granted; it is not always automatically "there" in students, teachers, and course providers. It needs to be developed. This development is the topic of this chapter, although I do not pretend to offer more than a sketchy map of the territory here.

Offering the suggestion here that teachers – including language teachers – and learners do not know enough about language may sound arrogant and presumptuous. So let me qualify my statement and say in apparent contradiction to this that everybody knows a lot about language, and that this knowledge can be of enormous benefit in teaching and learning. How can we resolve this contradiction?

In any account of good teaching, subject matter knowledge plays an important role. For the language teacher, therefore, knowledge of the subject matter of language is a requirement. Now, if we decide that current teachers do not have sufficient knowledge, the result may be that more preparatory courses or in-service workshops are offered on linguistics and applied linguistics. "Exactly!" a sympathetic teacher educator may comment. "I have seen many teachers who cannot spell and who are bad writers, and whose knowledge of grammar is inadequate. It's high time that they get proper training in linguistics."

At this point I must dissent, and I move to my second statement, the one that says that teachers know a lot about language. While appreciating the need for "training in linguistics," I will argue that the knowledge teachers need is not that of theoretical linguistics, prescriptive grammar, and formal accuracy, but a knowledge that starts from everything they already know about language, that connects this knowledge to all that their students already know about language, and then builds bridges to deeper understandings of the uses and processes of language in personal, social, academic, and professional contexts. So, what teachers and learners need is, to use the distinction made by Lee Shulman (1995), *subject matter knowledge* that is connected to *pedagogical subject matter knowledge*.

In earlier writings (van Lier 1991, 1992, 1994, 1996) I have made the case for a re-examination of the language education that is provided for language teachers, both in-service and pre-service. My recommendations are not unique in this respect (Brumfit 1997; Carter

Table 6.1 Teachers' and learners' knowledge about language.

UNDERLYING THEORY	←COMMON ASSUMPTIONS→	PRACTICES
The conduit metaphor; sender-receiver model; information processing; "telemention" (Harris 1996)	COMPUTATIONAL Assumption Language use is information exchange, consisting of inputs and outputs	Information gap tasks; tasks where crucial information is hidden from one or more participants
Language as acquired habit; language as internal, mental competence (innate or learned); representation	STORAGE Assumption Language learning means acquiring competence, i.e. internalizing knowledge and skills pertaining to a "fixed code"	Memorizing lists of words; sentence practice; individual tests; building schemata and scripts
Structural, generative linguistics; speech act theory, functionalism	EITHER-OR Assumption Language consists of two separate things: form (structure) and meaning (function)	Focus on form(s); input enhancement; consciousness raising; content-based teaching; "natural" approach
Descriptive linguistics; survey courses, e.g., "Introduction to Linguistics"classes	COMPONENTIAL Assumption Language consists of pronunciation, vocabulary, grammar and meaning (including discourse, pragmatics), as building blocks	Skill building exercises; practice in all skill areas; moving from small items (sounds) to larger items (texts), or vice versa
Normative linguistics; sociolinguistics; dialectology	CORRECTNESS Assumption Language use can be correct or incorrect, standard or non-standard	Error correction; formal essay structure; accent reduction; standard tests
Early cognitive science; contrastive linguistics; behaviorism	WARRING LANGUAGES Assumption Languages compete with one another in our brain, for our attention, or for storage space	Avoidance of use of L1 in L2 classes; arguments against bilingual education; time on task

1990; Halliday 1993; Rutherford 1987), however, I would like to elaborate some of the principles behind them as a background against which to introduce an ecological–semiotic perspective.

For both teachers and learners, it may be useful to distinguish between everyday knowledge of language and school knowledge of language.[2] So, for example, it is well known that we can all use our native language proficiently in most circumstances of everyday life.

More than that, we may have well-developed skills in certain areas, such as telling jokes and stories, writing funny letters, chatting expertly with friends on the phone or in Internet chat rooms, doing crossword puzzles, and so on, although there are also many among us who have problems in one or several of these areas. Similarly, it is often said that children aged five or six have mastered their native language in all its essentials. Not so, say many educational linguists, since in that case why would children have to spend year after year in school studying the language they need for academic success?[3] I would say that both camps are right, but they mean something different by "language."

Everyday linguistic dexterity is quite separate from the kinds of linguistic knowledge that are required in academic contexts. Required by whom and for what purpose, you may ask? That is a good question, to which two answers must be given. Answer number one is that academic contexts (especially in native language and foreign language classes) require metalinguistic knowledge of a technical nature, regarding grammatical rules and terminology. Despite its persistent popularity in educational circles, the utility of such technical metalinguistic knowledge is unclear (Alderson *et al.* 1997; Brumfit 1997; Mitchell and Hooper 1992), indeed, it is possible that this sort of knowledge falls under the category that Alfred North Whitehead referred to long ago as "inert" school knowledge (1929). Answer number two is that academic success requires language understanding and control which is cognitively demanding and decontextualized, not just in language (native and foreign) classes, but also in all other subject matter classes.

According to Cummins (1986), the cognitively complex and contextually reduced language required in school work takes a long time to develop and is quite distinct from everyday context-embedded conversational language.[4] Thus, many teachers working with non-native speaking immigrant students report that language and academic development appear to stagnate – to hit a "road block" – after basic conversational ability has been achieved and when academic language use for different subject areas is required, i.e. when the student is mainstreamed. Vermeer (1985) and Verhoeven (1990) also report from studies in the Netherlands that at such points divergence increases; that is, immigrant children's performance gradually falls further and further behind that of successful native speaking students, regardless of whatever particular educational programs may be in place to counter-act this growing gap. However, and interestingly, Verhoeven (1990) reports a study suggesting that carefully designed native-language maintenance programs appear to be capable of counteracting this divergence and narrowing the gap.

In conclusion, teachers and learners have a vast amount of everyday knowledge of and about language, but this knowledge is different from that required in academic work, both from the perspective of explicitness of rules and terminology (metalinguistic knowledge), and from the perspective of the context-reduced special discourses required in various academic subjects. There are three observations I would like to make on the basis of this discussion:

- Knowledge about language of the technical, academic variety (metalinguistic knowledge) is not proven to be of direct and/or lasting benefit in complex academic performance, yet is widely advocated and promoted in educational programs.
- Every academic subject has its own registerial and discoursal variety that requires specialized forms of language use and understandings that do not flow automatically from being a proficient speaker.
- In the professional development of teachers, everyday language knowledge and practices might be exploited more systematically to underpin and connect the professional language knowledge and practices required for teaching.

These three points form the background against which I will discuss an ecological – semiotic perspective on educational linguistics.

Ecology and educational linguistics

Ecology is the study of the relationships between all the various organisms and their physical environment. It's a complex and messy field of study about a complex and messy reality. Its primary requirement is, by definition, that the context is central, it cannot be reduced, and it cannot be pushed aside or into the background. The context is the focal field of study.

Sociolinguistics, pragmatics, the sociology of language, and discourse analysis are therefore relatives of ecological linguistics. However, they are philosophically very different, because they start out from a selection or system of rules and therefore address only one tiny corner of the ecology. Ecological research cannot afford to do that, since the context is then no longer the context. Ethnography, ethnomethodology,[5] and discursive psychology are closer to an ecological science.

Looking back to the previous section, we can state that language learners have a lot of linguistic knowledge in one sense, but often very little in another sense. The gap between what they start out with as members of a speech community, and what they are supposed to end up with as academically successful and well-educated individuals, is huge. This is the gap between the "playing with German" that Rampton reports in inner London (1999), and that I have seen on numerous occasions when adolescents imitate Schwarzenegger or Hollywood cartoon representations of Germans (or Spanish speakers, etc.) in linguistically very precise ways, and the skills and knowledge required in the foreign language class or on tests. That is, the linguistic proficiency in everyday settings is incommensurably different from the linguistic proficiency in classroom settings, I would say even in those classrooms that purport to be communicatively oriented.

One answer to this conundrum is to say that the lack of knowledge about language must be addressed by specifying what it is that teachers and learners need to know, and then designing courses to fill those needs. This would seem reasonable, yet I argue that this is precisely the wrong approach. It reminds me of the cultural literacy approach of E.D. Hirsch (1988) some years ago (which was hugely successful at the marketing level, but I would argue misguided at the pedagogical level). It looks at the subject matter of language as an object (or group of objects) to be enumerated, classified, sorted, and delivered via instructional means. And here I come closer to an ecological approach to language education. I argue that educational linguists – including the language teacher and the language learner – must not be linguistic vivisectionists or paleontologists, but rather linguistic ethologists; so that, instead of dissecting the language and operating on the cadaver, examining the bits and pieces in the manner of Rembrandt's Anatomical Lesson, the educational linguist must observe the living entity, and learn to understand critically what it does to whom, by whom, and for whom in the multiplexity of semiotic ecosystems in which it (language) operates, or rather co-operates with other meaning-making processes.

In an ecological approach (as in biology, complexity theory (Cilliers 1998), and some recent approaches to physics; see Heelan and Schulkin 1998), educational linguistics becomes the study of relationships, not of objects. This changes the whole complexion of the field, from our conceptualization of what language is, what it does, how it relates to the world, and how it is to be taught and learned. In the next section I will outline some of the characteristics of this type of ecological linguistics.

Ecological linguistics

I propose that there are four basic constructs in ecological linguistics:

1. Language *emerges* from semiotic activity.
2. Language does not arise from input that is processed, but from *affordances* that are brought forth by active engagement, and which enable further action and interaction.
3. Language is not transmitted from person to person by way of monolog or dialog,[6] but arises from indicational processes occurring in *triadic interaction.*
4. Linguistic activity in particular contexts can be analyzed in terms of *quality.*

I will briefly elaborate on these four constructs of emergence, affordance, triadic interaction, and quality, using illustrations from real life.

Emergence

When M arrived in the US from Peru, aged three, he was essentially monolingual in Spanish (even though his parents speak both Spanish and English, he was predominantly exposed to Spanish in the home and in day care). For about two or three months he went through a silent period in which he spoke no English, and was clearly, in some sense, in a state of language shock (particularly in the Montessori preschool program in which he was the only non-native speaker of English). Then, one day he was being wheeled through the local supermarket, sitting in front of the shopping cart in which so far the only item was a box of Rice Krispies. At that point he spotted another cart coming down the aisle, and this cart had also just a box of Rice Krispies in it. Noting this coincidence, M produced his first utterance in English: "Look! This on this!"

We can note that the first word establishes joint attention (see Triadic interaction opposite) and the remainder indicates the state of affairs that is the focus of attention. Words are used, but these words function only in conjunction with gestures (a pointing finger), gaze, and the parts of the physical surroundings staked out. The whole scene can be referred to as semiotic action, and in this semiotic action language emerges and becomes a constitutive part. So, speaking is always a part of a context of meaning-producing actions, interlocutors, objects, and relations among all these. In other words, language emerges as an embodied and situated activity.

Affordance

Consider how language learners (and native speakers for that matter) describe actions and events to others, such as how they got into an accident, how they go about making sushi, how the steps work that they were taught in a salsa lesson, etc. Observing such speech events clearly illustrates that language is not just a sequence of sentences put together in a coherent and cohesive discourse. Any speech event is a semiotic complex of rememberings, enactments, and interactions. Language is brought forth and carried along by a complex process involving physical, cognitive, and social actions. Language is one strand woven into this web of meaning making.

A context in which language is part of the action provides an ambient array of opportunities for meaning making. An actively engaged participant is offered a myriad of opportunities for meaningful action and interaction, and these opportunities are called affordances (Gibson 1979). Affordances are meaningful ways of relating to the environment through perception-in-action. They are neither linguistic objects that are received and taken into the processing mechanisms of the mind, nor are they linguistic objects that are retrieved from memory and packaged syntactically for output. So, what is language then if it is not inputs and outputs of linguistic units such as sounds, words, and sentences? We could give a more or less radical definition in the Bakhtinian style, that language is a process of sign-making to relate the self to the world. Or we could be slightly less radical and grant that, yes, language is also the structural reality of linguistic units in rule-governed combination, but that its ecological study focuses on the ways individuals relate to the world and to each other by means of linguistic and other sign systems.

Triadic interaction

Two students are sitting at a computer and are engaged in finding some information on a Website. These are beginning ESL (English as a second language) students and their linguistic resources are relatively limited. They are working side by side, one of them using the keyboard, the other helping out with the mouse. Similar to M's "Look! This on this!" their interaction is heavily embedded in pointing, establishing joint attention, and commenting on what they see. Then they suggest to each other what to do next in terms of getting the information they need, how to write it down, what to cut and paste, what to bookmark, and so on. As in the above examples, language is just one of the sign systems in operation. What strikes us here especially is how heavily their interaction is structured by the objects of their joint attention. The students are not speaking face to face bridging some sort of information gap, but they are working side by side, with a joint focus of activity, the object (the computer screen) as a third interlocutor of sorts. In other words, they are engaged in triadic interaction.

The linguistic processes going on in this triadic interaction are indicational, that is, they are focused on naming and commenting, i.e. the indexical or deictic functions of language. I will elaborate further on this in the section on semiotics.

Quality

Finally, we address the elusive quality of linguistic experience. Let's look for it in a fourth-grade elementary classroom, where children are using computers to put together a Website of class poetry. Since there are not many computers, the class is divided into rotating shifts. The students are so keen that they have to be almost forcibly removed from the room at the end of their shift, while the next shift is pushing at the door and peering through the windows, impatient to get in. In the room students work in pairs, learning from each other and teaching each other. One little girl teaches me (the so-called expert!) how to get layers of a picture to go forward and backward. Students learn how to be patient, how to help others, how to be helped, how to deal with the unexpected (which is guaranteed to happen in a quirky computer classroom), and so on.

In terms of the products of learning, say the quantity and quality of the poetry produced, it is not clear that working in this way has been superior to a more traditional desk-based writing project. So, by educational standards there may not be all that much gain. But in terms of the quality of educational experience, there may have been a great improvement. Thus, we can draw a distinction between educational standards and the quality of education. This distinction parallels that made by the founder of the deep ecology movement, Arne Naess, between standard of living and quality of life (1989). It is unfortunate that educational policy makers and politicians rarely seem to be capable of (or interested in) grasping the distinction (and dynamic relationship) between standards and quality, much less acting upon it.

Educational standards, as measured and quantified by outcomes on tests, are clearly important, or let's say at least that society tends to place a great deal of importance on them. But there is more to the quality of educational experience than scores and objectives. We can think back to our experiences of school, those that we found memorable, to understand this point.

Ludwig Wittgenstein (1980) said that there are remarks that *sow* and remarks that *reap*. Paraphrasing that, we can say that there are learning opportunities of a "sowing" kind and of a "reaping" kind. Traditional educational design, research, practice, and evaluation have exclusively addressed the latter. Ecological research will also investigate the former, difficult though that may be.

In sum, ecological–educational linguistics has a job list that consists of the systematic investigation of emergence, affordance, triadic interaction, and quality. There is more, but this is clearly a substantial set of tasks, requiring conceptual clarification, the location of new forms of evidence through description and analysis, the elaboration of contextual research procedures, and plausible documentation. The remainder of this chapter will address some aspects of these tasks.

Semiotics

Semiotics can be defined as the study of sign-making and sign-using practices. This includes traffic signs, clothing, and gestures, as well as language. Indeed, everything can become a sign, as Bourdieu noted in his work with the Kabyles: "Morning is the time when everything becomes a sign announcing good or ill to come" (1977:152).

Not only does the study of semiotics include many other signifying processes besides language but, as I noted above, language generally occurs intertwined with various other sign systems, anchored in the practical and social world. In traditional linguistic theory these other systems, and the physical world, have been regarded as relatively minor or trivial add-ons or as backgrounds, as words such as "paralinguistics" suggest. But this may be a mistake, a product of a way of theorizing that regards one linguistic phenomenon (e.g. the "word," the "sentence," the "rule," or whatever) as the key or essence of language, and the rest as peripheral or padding of some sort. In actual fact, it may make as much sense to separate language from other semiotic processes as it does to separate the swaying of the tree branch from the wind that moves it.

Semiotics has been around for a long time (see Nöth 1995), but in recent decades two traditions have become prominent, both of them originating around the start of the twentieth century: a European tradition starting with F. de Saussure, and an American tradition starting with C.S. Peirce. The similarities and differences between these two strands have been much debated over the years, but I will not go into this here (see Nöth 1995; Thibault 1997). Here I will take the Peircean perspective, since this has gradually been emerging as the most influential theory of signs, and it leads directly to an ecological approach to communication.

Peirce (1992, 1998) bases his semiotics on three universal categories: *Firstness, Secondness,* and *Thirdness.* Firstness is just what is, in itself, with no reference to anything else. This is often called Quality (not in the more practical sense that I used it above); Secondness is reaction, relation, change, experience; Thirdness is mediation, habit, interpretation, representation, communication, signs.

The sign is a triadic process that has no beginning and no end. It continually evolves in various directions, growing into other signs. It is triadic because it consists of the dynamic interaction between the *Representamen* (sign or sign vehicle; signifier in Saussure (1907/1983), the *Referent* or object, that which it stands for, and the *Interpretant,* the meaning or outcome of the sign (which is another sign, of course). Each of these three correlates can be characterized in terms of Firstness, Secondness, or Thirdness, and thus the total number of possible signs according to this scheme is huge. This need not concern us here, however, since we need to move from the abstractness of this semiotic theory to the practical affairs of language and education.

To illustrate the kaleidoscopic nature of sign making, here is the word "pozzie." I am in a busy Australian store, I'm carrying a bulky shopping bag, and I'm looking for a place to put the bag down so that I can have both hands free to examine the merchandise. The assistant sees me looking around and says, pointing to a bench in a nearby corner: "There's a good pozzie." And that's where I put my bag.

There are a large number of semiotic processes going on here, but let's just focus on the pozzie. To be a good pozzie, an object (or location) in the environment must fulfill several criteria that are unique to each situation and purpose. So, in this case it must be out of the way but in view, big enough to hold the bag, safe from shoplifters, clean and dry, and so on. But I have not even mentioned that this is the first time I have ever heard the word "pozzie," so there is pozzie-interpreting going on, followed by pozzie-based conversation between sales assistant and shopper. Then of course similarities between pozzie and other Australian words come to the fore: barbie, pokie, garbo, smoko, darl, dunnie, and dinkie. And when I get to my hotel room I ask myself what might be a good pozzie for my Powerbook.

Where does all this lead us? When we are active in a setting, affordances are created by our activity and the surrounding world. The world is beginning to signal relevances, to offer affordances because of who we are and what we are doing, and we perceive these affordances. In nature these affordances are perceived directly, immediately, since they express the "fit" between organism and ecosystem. I suggest that the same is true for humans, even though the *immediate* becomes intertwined with the *mediate* (mediated) ever more rapidly as we grow up. The word "pozzie" becomes a linguistic affordance because it allows me to connect my needs with the physical resources (affordances) in the environment. It also affords storytelling, and exploring the wonders of Australian word-making.

Activity, perception, and affordance are the ingredients, the raw materials out of which signs grow and from which language emerges. In early childhood a child's random hand movement becomes a grasp when the hand encounters the mother's finger (Vygotsky 1978), a vocalization becomes a call when the mother answers it, an eye movement becomes intersubjective engagement (Trevarthen 1990). Thus the child's actions become "acts of meaning" (Halliday 1993). At first there are iconic Firstnesses, becoming indexical expressions (Secondnesses) when they are shared, and ending up as symbolic Thirdnesses when they turn into games, grow into speech, or form rituals.

Signs are not objects out there, nor thoughts in here, but relationships between the person and the world, physical and social. Signs are mediated affordances, thus they start out as dialogical relationships between the person and "something out there." At first the kaleidoscopic confusion of the world must be uninterpretable and unmanageable to an infant. But just as in a thick fog that is slowly lifting, shapes gradually appear, become recognizable, interpretable, usable. Once signs have created the infrastructure to grow language, we use language to reassure ourselves that we know where we are. There is thus a conceptual congruence between Gibson's ecological theory of perception, Peirce's theory of signs, and Bakhtin's theory of language – to which I will later add Vygotsky's theory of mental development.

I am finally ready to bring the discussion back to second language learning. In Figure 6.1 (adapted from Merrell 1997b), Peirce's basic "decalog" of 10 types of signs is presented.

In Figure 6.1 we see three interrelated realms (planes) of signs (cf. Merrell 1997a, b):

- **iconicity**, which represents feeling, direct perceptual experience, qualia, the inner self, holism;
- **indexicality**, which represents linearity, synchronicity, division, otherness, the social world;
- **symbolicity**, which represents mediation of the mind, reason, logic, representation, integration.

The figure shows the dynamic flow from one sign type to another. Language and language learning in general are concentrated in secondness to begin with: linguistic action in the world, especially social interaction with others. Several iterations of semiosis (meaning-making,

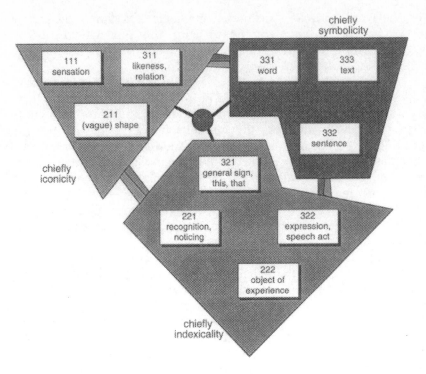

Figure 6.1 *Peirce's decalog of signs (adapted from Merrell 1997, p. 210).*

i.e. sign-making) are required before an affordance in the world can become a word. The central process of language at this beginning moment is *anchoring*, the tying of language to the world, the grasping of the world through language, and tying the self to the world, resulting in mind. The general term for this semiotic process is deixis, or pointing (Clark 1996; Hanks 1995; Levinson 1983). Gibson (1979) called this the *indicational* process of language, as opposed to higher-level *predicational* processes (see Reed 1996). Deixis has several functions, the most important of which include indexing, referring, and naming. The indexical functions of language are instrumental in sorting out the world, and here the incipient language user explores Firstnesses for affordances that can become signs, and these signs can become engendered[7] into higher signs, including symbolic signs, chiefly through interaction with other users of language.

My suggestion is that the indexical plane is the key to language, and from there these early language signs "pick up" signs from the iconic substrate (in the way that a hurricane picks up power from warm ocean waters) and move into symbolic territory, with both immediate and socially mediated affordances that provide signs of increasing as well as decreasing complexity. And every sign invokes and evokes other signs. Language, though it begins in Secondness,[8] soon begins to engender signs that incorporate iconic, indexical, and symbolic qualities in various combinations and emphases.

Through language we jump straight into the sign world, on the indexical plane. This plane becomes a workbench or desktop from which we make sense of experience and become part of a socio-cultural-historical world (Cole 1996). Language is thus a way of gaining access, both to the physical world of space, time, and objects (physical fields, Lewin's *life space* (1943) and Bakhtin's *chronotopes* (1981), and to the social world of people, events, and societies (symbolic fields, cf. Bourdieu and Wacquant 1992).

Signs continually develop into other signs, they "leak" or "pour forth" into each other, as Merrell puts it (1997b:210–11). Language development involves both the use of ever more complex constellations of signs (from indicational to predicational, in Gibson's terms, from lexical pointers and heuristic speech acts to texts and arguments), and the simplification of complex (symbolic) signs into indices and icons (rituals, routines, metaphors, idioms). So, signs develop "upwards" (engenderment) and "downwards" (de-engenderment) along specific routes of semiosis (Merrell 1998).

If language learning, both first and subsequent, proceeds in some way as suggested here, there are certain instigative and debilitative circumstances that might occur. For example, routes to engenderment (and subsequent de-engenderment and re-engenderment) may be blocked, ruptured, or denied, in a number of ways. One such way is insufficient proficiency or, in more general terms, insufficient access to significant signs and sign systems in the surrounding world. Another way might be lack of engagement, in extreme cases anomie. In such circumstances of insufficient access to and/or engagement with indexical language work (and in all cases this also includes non-linguistic action), signs may be predominantly channeled toward iconic and indexical aspects of the world: anxiety, pain, food, survival, danger, work-for-survival. A culture's or society's Thirdnesses (symbolic systems) are cut off, flattened, or funneled into iconic and indexical realms. Or in some cases alternative symbolic systems are set up, in the form of countercultures, imported ethnic cultures, or "oppositional cultures" (Ogbu 1991).

Language and other communicative processes thus essentially depend for their success on the open flow between iconic and symbolic systems, activated through the "desktop" of indexicality. Indices (indexicals, deictic expressions, including pronouns, demonstratives and names) play a key role in this, and often can be used analytically as indicators of the success or failure of a person's linguistic sign work (see e.g. Wortham 1994). Indexing can also be used to control (either deny or facilitate) access by constructing group membership, drawing boundaries (e.g. through constructing discourses of otherness, or "othering," Riggins 1997), or more positively by prolepsis (Rommetveit 1974).[9] Connecting these suggestions to Bronfenbrenner's ecology of human development, indexing can be instigative or inhibitory or, in Bronfenbrenner's words, the "activity milieu" can "stimulate or stifle psychological growth" (1979: 55). As mentioned, close examination of the use of pronouns (e.g. inclusive versus exclusive uses) and practices of naming in discourse can provide significant clues in this respect. Types of interaction that can be particularly revealing are stories, jokes, and conversations, all of which are prime vehicles for indexing, and thus the integration of iconic and symbolic systems. Access to such speech events, and the ability to participate in their creation and enactment, are crucial for the developing person. See in this respect the insightful work of Bonnie Peirce, which discusses "the right to speak" (1995; Bourdieu 1977), Bourdieu's economic metaphors of linguistic and cultural "capital" (Bourdieu 1991; Bourdieu and Wacquant 1992), and the work of discursive psychologists (Harré and Gillett 1994; Edwards 1997; see also Mercer 1995).

To conclude this section, I suggest that sign systems provide the individual with keys to enter into the world, but sometimes the keys are broken, lost, or withheld, for a multitude of reasons (including racism and other forms of discrimination, lack of resources, ineffective educational practices, lack of opportunities for participation, excessive psychological distance, and so on). The most important key to becoming a member of a community is the indexing or deictic one, the one that allows for pointing, referring, and participating. It allows for the creation and use of relevant affordances and signs, but more importantly it is the workbench or desktop on which the learner may negotiate the free flow among signs and the construction of options for life. Without the deictic key, the learning person remains an outsider, but with that key an invitational culture of learning is possible, and the learner may become a "signatory" to that culture.

Learning as emergence

How does language emerge in learning? From the above it is already clear that I propose three phases that are sequential in L1. I will argue that they are concurrent in L2, and that therein lie many of the much-debated differences between L1 and L2 learning.

The three phases proposed for L1 development are as follows:

1. The development of mutuality (reciprocity)
2. The development of indicational language
3. The development of predicational language.

In each of these phases one of the three chief categories of signs is prominent: Iconicity (Firstness), Indexicality (Secondness) and Symbolicity (Thirdness), respectively. The development of mutuality, while culminating in Secondness, finds its origin in Firstness, the direct sensation of voice, touch, vision, and smell (see Eco 2000), which becomes Secondness when it is reciprocated. As I mentioned above, when the child's vocalization is answered by the mother's response, the random hand movement becomes a grasp (and so on), Firstness reveals the way to Secondness, action becomes *inter*action. This Firstness is hard to capture, since it is indescribable until it hitches a ride on Secondness yet, paradoxically, the more this original sensation of emotion is mediated, the less it is directly and deeply felt. As we mediate our Firstnesses through language and cultural procedures, we may feel a loss of depth in our emotions or close connections to the objects of those emotions. As a simple analogy, writing "hugs and kisses" in an email is obviously different from the actual acts to which the words refer. Some people try to get back to these original feelings (called Dharma in ancient Indian philosophy) through meditation or varieties of religious experience. Oliver Sacks, in his account of healing his torn leg (not by medicine, surgery, or exercise, but by inner forces stimulated by music) after being badly mauled by an angry bull in Norway, calls it *grace*: "... full-bodied vital feeling and action, originating from an aboriginal, commanding, willing, 'I'" (1984:121–12).

Mutuality is a precondition for the development of indicational language. Pure feeling, that which Sacks calls "grace," and Eco calls "voice" (2000: 100) surely exists even before mutuality fully develops, but as soon as it encounters the other it becomes wrapped in Secondness. During the prelinguistic phase of an infant's development, Firstness is still close to the surface, and communication is phatic, prosodic, corporeal (Ruthrof 2000). The senses are used to establish patterns of reciprocity. In Peirce's scheme, pure Firstness is 111, i.e. Firstness of sign, Firstness of object, and Firstness of interpretant. As mentioned earlier, this is pure existence or feeling. As soon as it is perceived and reacted to, it becomes connected with Secondness.

Secondness becomes the driving force, but this does not mean that Firstness disappears or that Thirdness is not yet present. As I mentioned above, Secondness, including indicational ways of language use, is necessary to incorporate Firstness into language. And as soon as two or more people use triadic, side-by-side ways of talking about the world, Thirdnesses in the form of symbolic signs inevitably develop. Predicational language allows the child or learner to talk about events located outside of the here and now, about feelings, and about abstract, hypothetical, or imagined arguments and states of affairs.

For the first phase (mutuality), language is not necessary, even though it is used in a phatic sense. For the second phase, language is essential, but mainly in the sense of fixed phrases, speech acts, and indexical expressions closely linked to action and gesture. It is only in the third phase that grammar, in the sense of complex propositions expressing tense, aspect, modality, and voice, becomes necessary.

A baby goes through these phases in order, developing mutuality in the first six months of life, adding indicational processes around nine months, when locomotion is achieved and objects can become a joint focus of attention, and predicational processes around the age of two, when the reasons for things are beginning to be examined, and syntax becomes relevant. As Bates and Goodman put it: "The successive bursts that characterize vocabulary growth and the emergence of morphosyntax can be viewed as different phases of an immense nonlinear wave that starts in the single-word stage and crashes on the shores of grammar a year or so later" (1999: 41).

Halliday calls this moment of the emergence of grammar the "magic gateway" (1993: 98). I have already mentioned how societal forces can limit an immigrant's access to symbolic sign engenderment, and confine a person's signifying opportunities to a reduced menu of iconic and indexical relationships. Now I want to suggest some implications for the design of classroom activities that follow from an ecological–semiotic perspective.

Given the content of linguistic theories, it is no surprise that applied linguistics has focused on the predicational (or grammatical–structural) aspects of language. Language teaching methods have been based on grammatical or functional specifications, thus limiting the curriculum to predicational concerns, and largely ignoring the other two phases, mutuality and indicativity. The consequences of this neglect are not clear, but they may be substantial and they may be detrimental. I am not suggesting that second language teaching must mirror first language development. Indeed, I suggested above that the three phases may simultaneously be present in all but the youngest second language learners. That does not mean, however, that any of the three can be neglected or ignored.

The canonical participation structure of communicative language teaching is that of face-to-face communication, the classical speaker–hearer configuration, where inputs and outputs flow in alternating fashion. A central participation structure from an ecological perspective is that of working side by side, as mentioned earlier (see also Rogoff 1995). The side-by-side organization of talk encourages joint action, exploratory talk, and the use of indexical language which is more lexically than syntactically based. It also encourages the development of mutuality.

When learners work side by side in triadic interaction (or dynamic interaction, as Reed preferred to call it: 1996:137), they share affordances with the environment. Language and gestures combine to indicate objects, places, and events. It is in dynamic, triadic interactions of this sort that language emerges. The sharing of the perceived world, activity, and experience is increasingly done linguistically. From a semiotic perspective, language is here imbedded in and supported by other signifying material (gesturing, posturing, drawing, facial expression, the local or remote objects of joint attention, etc.), and from these indexical activities predicational language gradually emerges.

In a second-language context, the three phases – mutuality, indicativity and predicativity – become strands that are simultaneously developed in tasks permitting triadic interaction. Other tasks may separate language from the body or the object, often deliberately (as when, in two-way information gap tasks, the information each has is hidden from the other, or when students are told to sit back to back while describing a Lego structure),[10] and it is possible that such separation promotes dysfluencies rather than stimulating development.

Conclusions: an ecological curriculum of teaching, learning, and teacher research

At the start of this chapter I suggested that an improved language education for both teachers and learners requires a reconceptualization of what language is and a close examination of the contexts in which language and learning occurs. I then argued for an ecological–semiotic perspective on language that will facilitate the development of pedagogical subject matter knowledge for both teaching and learning. This perspective leads to a language curriculum that is experiential, contextualized, activity-based, and developmental. By way of summary, let me address these aspects of the curriculum in turn.

Experiential

I proposed that teachers and learners have a vast amount of everyday linguistic knowledge and skills, and probably a certain amount of technical knowledge as well. The everyday knowledge is generally not "legitimate" in the language classroom. I have taken high-school students home from school who were failing in their foreign language classes, and who hated these classes more than any other subject, yet in the back of the car they produced highly skilled – if nonsensical – renditions of the target language in song, rap, or pure banter. The "official" business of the language classroom does not connect with existing everyday expertise. Teachers are supposed to know their grammar, especially when it comes to such delicacies as tense backshifting in reported speech and discontinuous constituents, and learners have to demonstrate their knowledge of arcane points of syntax and remote lexical items on test after test. Yet their vernacular dexterity is never tapped or appreciated.

Contextualized (situated)

Modern linguistics has convinced us that we can only get to the essence of language when we consider it away from any context. But this is really the same as saying that we can get to the real onion if we peel away all the layers. Language is located in the world around us as well as in the brain. When we speak it is about something and for something – or someone – in the world, not just a by-product of firing brain cells. When we are mindful, we are in tune with our surroundings, not with our brain. Sure, the brain is important, and so is the heart. We think, feel, and speak, but we think with our brain in the same way that we feel with our heart, and speak with our tongue.

Language, as Bakhtin reminds us, is always dialogical, about something, reflecting other voices as well as our own. It is shaped by the context and at the same time shapes the context.

Current debate in educational research between cognitivists and situationists is especially instructive for language education (Lave and Wenger 1991). The decontextualized language of words and sentences has to be recontextualized in order to become meaningful. But why decontextualize at all? Through critical language awareness projects, teachers and learners can examine language in the context in which it is used, through field work, printed texts, movies, songs, Internet resources, etc. Some technical (metalinguistic) knowledge will be useful in such projects, but it can be acquired as it is needed, rather than transmitted as autonomous subject matter (it then becomes useful, rather than remaining inert).

Activity-based

Activities require action, interaction, perception, and reflection, and language is a part of all four. When we design our lessons using activity as the focal unit, language becomes a constituent alongside movement, gesture, experiment, manipulation, focusing, planning, judging, and so on. Language is naturally supported *by* and supportive *of* social activity, and in these two senses naturally scaffolded, that is, within human activity language gives and receives just as much support as is needed.

Developmental (emergent)

Language proficiency develops in certain natural ways, i.e. there are emergent properties that depend on prior conditions. I have suggested that mutuality or reciprocity is a prerequisite for language to develop, and that it allows for basic emotions to be shared through all the senses, including voice. Language proper develops with indexicality, when objects become the focus of joint attention (triadic interaction). Predicational language and grammar subsequently emerge to allow for language to become a tool of higher-order social and mental activities. In other words, intersubjectivity supports joint action, and joint action supports rational expression. It seems that planners of language education go straight to the ideal end stage, break that down into bits and pieces, and line these up in some sort of order. Whether these bits and pieces are words, grammar rules, pragmatic functions, or social skills, makes very little difference (as Widdowson saw in 1979), because the basic mistake here is that learning is an accumulation of bits and pieces until they are all in place. But that is not how we build a butterfly, to use an analogy. If we looked only at a butterfly and had to decide how to achieve such an animal, we would be thinking of long skinny legs, delicate colored wings, a long curled tongue, and so on. We would never come up with the idea of an egg, a caterpillar, and an ugly pupa with a pulpy substance inside.

Language also develops in surprising ways, and we hardly know yet how this happens. We can emphasize innate developmental powers and say that the environment is "trivial," (see Chomsky 1986; Pinker 1994), but this is unhelpful to the teacher and learner. Neither can we say that language develops from the imitation of correct pieces of language. Rather, it is a nonlinear process of phases and transformations. Not every phase and transformation looks unambiguously like a step closer to the goal of proficient language use. By analogy, not every phase in the transformation of a caterpillar into a butterfly looks to the naive observer like a step toward the goal – quite the contrary.

The wonders of language and language development are very closely tied to the ways in which we use language every day. Theories of linguistics have often ignored that, but there is no reason for language teaching and language learning to be based on decontextualized or prescriptive grammars.

Notes

1. Proponents of Universal Grammar frequently point out that children acquire their L1 by the age of five. Even if we grant this point in substantial ways, there is no doubt that children have to spend numerous subsequent years in mastering many aspects of their L1, in all areas of proficiency: phonological, lexical, syntactic, discursive, and pragmatic. These normative aspects of language are by no means trivial in terms of the overall definition of language, and it would be quixotic to regard them as unfair impositions by oppressive societies and institutions.
2. This mirrors Vygotsky's distinction between spontaneous and scientific concepts (1986).
3. These are the normative aspects of language mentioned in note 1.
4. Cummins' point is supported by the work of Halliday and associates on grammatical metaphor; see e.g. Halliday 1993.
5. Paradoxically, since its doctrine of "indifference to context" would seem to be diametrically opposed to ecology – but I argue that it is actually an eminently ecological way of doing social science.
6. I agree with Bakhtin and others (Wold 1992) that language is inherently dialogical and not monological. What I argue here is that it is not a transmission of "packets" of information from one person to another in monological or dialogical speech events, but a result of co-constructing meaning, working together.
7. Peirce used the term engenderment to refer to the growth of signs from other signs, into "new and higher translations" (Merrell 1997a); conversely, signs can de-engender into imbedded, entrenched, automatized, or habitual signs (Merrell 1997a). Peirce also used the terms generate and degenerate, but given the common negative connotation of the term "degenerate," these latter terms are not commonly used now since they might be misleading. Both engendering and de-engendering are processes of meaning-making or semiosis.
8. Actually, language originates in the Firstness – iconicity – of mother's voice and other voices, and it resonates deeply through the first experiences of being, gradually separating from other perceptual experiences, and taking acoustic shape in the wake of taking emotional shape, but it cannot be expressed or grasped until it has become Secondness.
9. In general, prolepsis means speaking of a future state of affairs as if it already existed. Bakhurst notes, in a remark he attributes to Vygotsky, that

"treating children as if they had abilities they do not yet possess is a necessary condition of the development of those abilities" (1991:67).
10.   Another rather alarming example was recounted by an Italian student of English who told me that in one class the teacher forced her to sit on her hands so that she was unable to use them while speaking English.

References

Alderson, J.C., Clapham, C. and Steel, D. (1997) Metalinguistic knowledge, language aptitude and language proficiency. University of Lancaster, *Language Teaching Research* 1(2) 93–121.

Bakhtin, M. (1981) *The Dialogical Imagination*. Austin: University of Texas Press.

Bakhurst, D. (1991) *Consciousness and Revolution in Soviet Philosophy: From the Bolsheviks to Evald Ilyenkov*. Cambridge: Cambridge University Press.

Bates, E. and Goodman, J.C. (1999) On the emergence of grammar from the lexicon. In MacWhinney, B. (ed.), *The Emergence of Language*. Mahwah: Lawrence Erlbaum, pp. 29–80.

Bourdieu, P. (1977) *Outline of a Theory of Practice*. Cambridge: Cambridge University Press.

Bourdieu, P. (1991) *Language and Symbolic Power*. Cambridge, MA: Harvard University Press.

Bourdieu, P. and Wacquant, L. (1992) *An Invitation to Reflexive Sociology*. Chicago: University of Chicago Press.

Bronfenbrenner, U. (1979) *The Ecology of Human Development*. Cambridge, MA: Harvard University Press.

Brumfit, C. (1997) The teacher as educational linguist. In L. van Lier and D. Corson (eds), *Knowledge about Language*. (Encyclopedia of Language and Education, Vol. 6.) Dordrecht: Kluwer Academic, pp. 163–72.

Carter, R. (ed.) (1990) *Knowledge about Language and the Curriculum*. London: Hodder & Stoughton.

Chomsky, N. (1986) *Knowledge of Language*. New York: Praeger.

Cilliers, P. (1998) *Complexity and Postmodernism: Understanding Complex Systems*. London: Routledge.

Clark, H. (1996) *Using Language*. Cambridge: Cambridge University Press.

Cole, M. (1996) *Cultural Psychology: A Once and Future Discipline*. Cambridge, MA: Harvard University Press.

Cummins, J. (1986) Language proficiency and academic achievement. In J. Cummins and M. Swain (eds), *Bilingualism in Education*. London: Longman, pp. 138–61.

Eco, U. (2000) *Kant and the Platypus: Essays on Language and Cognition*. New York: Harcourt Brace.

Edwards, D. (1997) *Discourse and Cognition*. London: Sage.

Gibson, J.J. (1979) *The Ecological Approach to Visual Perception*. Boston: Houghton Mifflin.

Halliday, M.A.K. (1993) Towards a language-based theory of learning. *Linguistics and Education* 5, 93–116.

Hanks, W.F. (1995) *Language and Communicative Practices*. Boulder: Westview Press.

Harré, R. and Gillett, G. (1994) *The Discursive Mind*. Thousand Oaks, CA: Sage.

Harris, R. (1996) *Signs, Language and Communication*. London: Routledge.

Heelan, P. and Schulkin, J. (1998) Hermeneutical philosophy and pragmatism: a philosophy of science. *Synthese* 115(3), 269–302.

Hirsch, E.D. (1988) *Cultural Literacy: What Every American Needs to Know*. New York: Vintage Books.

Lave, J. and Wenger, E. (1991) *Situated Learning: Legitimate Peripheral Participation*. Cambridge: Cambridge University Press.

Levinson, S. (1983) *Pragmatics*. Cambridge: Cambridge University Press.

Lewin, K. (1943) Defining the "field at a given time." *Psychological Review* 50(3), 292–310.

Mercer, N. (1995) *The Guided Construction of Knowledge: Talk Between Teachers and Learners in the Classroom*. Clevedon: Multilingual Matters.

Merrell, F. (1997a) *Peirce, Signs, and Meanings*. Toronto: University of Toronto Press.

Merrell, F. (1997b) Do we really need Peirce's whole decalogue of signs? *Semiotica* 114(3/4), 193–286.

Merrell, F. (1998) *Sensing Semiosis: Toward the Possibility of Complementary Cultural "logics."* Basingstoke: Macmillan.

Mitchell, R. and Hooper, J. (1992) Teachers' views of language knowledge. In C. James and P. Garrett (eds), *Language Awareness in the Classroom*. London: Longman, pp. 40–50.

Naess, A. (1989) *Ecology, Community and Lifestyle*. Cambridge: Cambridge University Press.

Nöth, W. (1995) *Handbook of Semiotics*. Bloomington: Indiana University Press.

Ogbu, J. U. (1991) Immigrant and involuntary minorities in comparative perspective. In M.A. Gibson and J.U. Ogbu (eds), *Minority Status and Schooling: A Comparative Study of Immigrant and Voluntary Minorities*. New York: Garland Publishing, pp. 3–33.

Peirce, B.N. (1995) Social identity, investment, and language learning. *TESOL Quarterly* 29, 9–31.

Peirce, C.S. (1992 and 1998) *Selected Philosophical Writings*, Vols 1 and 2. Bloomington: Indiana University Press. (Vol. 1: edited by N. Houser and C. Kloesel, 1992; Vol. 2, edited by The Peirce Edition Project, 1998.)

Pinker, S. (1994) *The Language Instinct*. New York: Morrow.

Rampton, B. (1999) Inner London *Deutsch* and the animation of an instructed foreign language. *Journal of Sociolinguistics* 3(4), 480–504.

Reed, E.S. (1996) *Encountering the World: Toward an Ecological Psychology*. New York: Oxford University Press.

Riggins, S.H. (1997). The rhetoric of othering. In his, *The Language and Politics of Exclusion: Others in Discourse*. Thousand Oaks, CA: Sage, pp. 1–30.

Rogoff, B. (1995) Observing sociocultural activity on three planes: participatory appropriation, guided participation, and apprenticeship. In J.V. Wertsch, P. Del Rio and A. Alvarez (eds), *Sociocultural Studies of Mind*. Cambridge: Cambridge University Press, pp. 139–64.

Rommetveit, R. (1974) *On Message Structure*. New York: John Wiley.

Rutherford, W. (1987) *Second Language Grammar: Learning and Teaching*. London: Longman.

Ruthrof, H. (2000) *The Body in Language*. London: Cassell.

Sacks, O. (1984) *A Leg to Stand on*. New York: Harper.

Saussure, F. de (1907/1983) *Course in General Linguistics*. La Salle, IL: Open Court.

Shulman, L. (1995) Fostering a community of teachers and learners. Unpublished progress report to the Mellon Foundation.

Thibault, P.J. (1997) *Rereading Saussure: The Dynamics of Signs in Social Life*. London: Routledge.

Trevarthen, C. (1990) Signs before speech. In T. Sebeok and J. Sebeok-Umiker (eds), *The Semiotic Web*. The Hage: Mouton, pp. 689–755.

van Lier, L. (1991) Language awareness: The common ground between linguist and language teacher. *Georgetown University Round Table*. Washington, D.C.: Georgetown University Press, pp. 528–46.

van Lier, L. (1992) Not the nine o'clock linguistics class: investigating contingency grammar. *Language Awareness* 1(2), 91–108.

van Lier, L. (1994) Educational linguistics: Field and project. *Georgetown University Round Table*. Washington, D.C.: Georgetown University Press, pp. 199–209.

van Lier, L. (1996) *Interaction in the Language Curriculum: Awareness, Autonomy and Authenticity*. London: Longman.

Verhoeven, Ludo (1990) Language variation and learning to read. In P. Reitsma and L. Verhoeven (eds), *Acquisition of Reading in Dutch*. Dordrecht: Foris, pp. 105–20.

Vermeer, A. (1985) Moroccan and Turkish children in the Netherlands: the influence of social factors on tempo and structure of L2 acquisition. In G. Extra and T. Vallen (eds), *Ethnic Minorities and Dutch as a Second Language*. Dordrecht: Foris, pp. 49–64.

Vygotsky, L.S. (1978) *Mind in Society*. Cambridge, MA: Harvard University Press.

Vygotsky, L.S. (1986) *Thought and Language*, Trans. by A. Kozulin. Cambridge, MA: Massachusetts Institute of Technology Press.

Whitehead, A.N. (1929) *The Aims of Education and Other Essays*. New York: Macmillan.

Widdowson, H.G. (1979) *Teaching Language as Communication*. Oxford: Oxford University Press.

Wittgenstein, L. (1980) *Culture and Value*. Chicago: University of Chicago Press.

Wold, A.H. (ed.) (1992) *The Dialogical Alternative: Towards a Theory of Language and Mind*. Oslo: Scandinavian University Press.

Wortham, S. (1994) *Acting out Participant Examples in the Classroom*. Amsterdam: John Benjamins.

Commentaries

Editors: Edward Bodine and Claire Kramsch

Language development as a mediated, social semiotic activity

In what ways would an ecological approach allow us to explore new dimensions of language-in-social interaction? What are the technical implications of studying language development in this way?

LEMKE   I found Elinor Ochs' analysis of emergent phenomena in and among groups of interacting kids fascinating. In the dimensions that you were using – identity, activity, and stance – all except activity seem to be referents to the level of individual organism and individual performance. I wondered if you had some thoughts regarding the level of *group*.

OCHS   First, I should point out that actions and stances are not essentially psychological; they are social and interactional. They are not just located *within* an individual. I think an extremely useful unit of analysis is the activity. In the context of the research I've presented here, the softball game as the overarching activity defines the boundaries of analysis. Of course, within this larger unit there are multiple activities going on simultaneously. We need to be able to peel those things apart along an interactional continuum, not just at one particular time and in one particular place. What's more, we need to be able to look at the range of competencies being exercised through this complex configuration of activities.

LEMKE   In your work, then, do you develop a sense of which patterns of interaffective stance are typical of an activity? In other words, what you are looking for is not necessarily the way a particular individual is expected to respond to another's affective stance but rather a particular *social type* of response.

OCHS   Yes, one does develop this sense over time. Working ethnographically means that you spend quite some time in a community. After a while, you get a good sense of how things are weighted. You come to an understanding of a community's system of weighting by talking with people, observing and recording the linguistic indexes that they use. These indexes mark things according to their relative salience. Once you have a clear idea of what they are, you can begin to investigate an array of social practices, including such things as sanctions, positive and negative assessments, etc. that surround particular behaviors and speech. When you follow 16 autistic children around over a period of two and a half years, as I have just done, you really get a sense from their perspective of what is important. Autistic kids are constantly breaking social rules. I find their rule-breaking a departure point for some fascinating research. Of course, impairment of social ability is a hallmark of autism. Most research focuses on autistic children's interpersonal capabilities, such as their ability to develop intimacy, to form friendships, and so forth. But to my knowledge, no one has studied them as members of classrooms, families – or softball teams for that matter. There has been little investigation into the ways they acquire institutional knowledge or are socialized into various micro-institutions. This is where, I believe, an ecological approach to developmental research could be of great value.

What constitutes complex, triadic interaction? How do various types of media and modes of mediation shape interaction in distinctive ways?

CANDLIN   When it comes to putting kids and computers together, a high degree of interactivity would seem inevitable. Spontaneous interaction seems almost inherent in any activity for kids involving computers. But I wonder if you can get a good measure of interactivity even if kids are operating with some relatively static object, say, a book?
VAN LIER   Yes, I think you can get a lot of interactivity between kids and books. The third interlocutor doesn't have to be a computer; it could be a book, or something else entirely. In fact, it could be something that is not even physically present, such as a joint remembering of some kind. Whatever it might be, I think we need to look at the learning context as consisting not of two interlocutors but three. This, of course, adds a new dimension to the context.
THORNE   An important area to explore here is the mediational qualities of the artifact. How do qualitative aspects of this third party influence the nature of the interaction? For example, I think it would be interesting to compare one-to-one computer interaction with triadic computer interaction where you've got a pair of kids working together with the machine. What might we see in terms of mediational differences and interactional dynamics? At the same time, it's worth considering that there are "cultures of use" that grow up around the use of various types of artifacts such as computers. I wonder what you might find if you looked at these interactions with what Michael Cole

phrased "the double-sided nature of the artifact" in mind?[1] In other words, how might the ways such artifacts lend themselves to interaction develop according to particular user communities?

GEBHARD If you think about the computer and book as cultural tools, then how each gets used depends very much on the context and ideologies surrounding these tools. Brian Street, in his discussion of ideological perspectives of literacy, describes how books get used in ways that are greatly context-dependent and defined.[2] We really have to understand how these interactional contexts are socially and culturally configured.

VAN LIER Perhaps we can recast this triadic model in terms of a distinction between the tool and the content. In certain contexts, the content becomes the tool and the tool becomes the content. If you look at studies on the negotiation of meaning involving face-to-face group work, you find some very interesting results. Take two-way communication tasks in which information is hidden from one person but available to the other. Quite often, the task involves both learners putting pieces of a picture together. Examining the discourse that emerges from such a task, you begin to realize just how much the artifact itself structures the discourse.

What is the nature of activity? How is our understanding of activity broadened from an ecological perspective?

OCHS Engeström's notion of *activity system* has had a great influence on my thinking.[3] I've found his approach to analysis particularly useful. My own research on interactional stance and participatory roles has been oriented around the notion of embedded systems of activity. In some sense, you *are* what you *do*; you are defined by the multiple activities you participate in.

THORNE In the research you presented here, your focus is on the activity system of the softball game. In what ways do you see this system nested within the greater activity system of the school? Take your focal child, for example. For her, participation in the softball game may be a part of a year-long acculturation process of becoming a competent member of the school community. How does the softball game frame fit into the larger school community frame over time?

OCHS This is an interesting point. However, let me just say that I think there is a danger in being too homogenous when you start applying ever larger institutional frames to micro-interactional behavior. You're asking broad questions about how and where the child fits into the system, and how the system ultimately serves the child. The challenge of an ethnographic approach to studying children with disabilities in a community setting is trying to understand the world of the child *along its own vector.* Now, when there are a number of different research perspectives all converging on the study of the same activity, each looking at different dimensions of development, there's a tendency for the child's own perspective to get overlooked. I think we have to be particularly sensitive to this.

LEMKE   From my point of view, the real challenge of looking at development from an ecological perspective is tying these momentary participations in activities – be they ten minutes or an afternoon – to longer-term processes. How do behavioral patterns evolve, accumulate, and stabilize over time? In other words, how do moments add up to lives? The vector of time is the most complex, least understood aspect of ecological development. How is it that some things that happen can be looked at retrospectively and threaded onto the chain of our identity?

OCHS   Ah, well, that is of course the great existential question of how we create coherence in our lives! How do we create the experiential mosaics our lives become? At its core, this is perhaps a question of phenomenology.

What is the nature of mediation? How can we distinguish between mediated experience and immediate experience?

VAN LIER   I believe we have to start with the ways in which we are oriented in our physical environment. Ulric Neissler describes five dimensions of ecological self that may help us in thinking about this issue.[4] An important aspect of this orientation is how we relate to ourselves, that is, how we come to see ourselves *through* these places. I think physical space is perceived in accordance with what it *affords* the individual. This has to do with the structure of the physical space and also our orientation within it. Physical context determines the parameters of our experience. We have learned a great deal from the work of Gibson on this point.[5]

LANTOLF   But when we talk about physical space in this way, aren't we also talking about cultural space? I think it is important to recognize that there is an overlap between them. Perhaps it would be clearer to say that physical space and cultural space are configured through one another. It seems to me that we need to further clarify this concept of affordance. Are we calling affordances *unmediated*?

VAN LIER   I wouldn't say they are unmediated. They are *immediate.* Let me try to illustrate this point. A classic example of research in affordance theory was the study of walking through doorways. On the surface, it seems a rather mundane activity. However, there is actually a great deal of behavioral complexity to it. If you walk through a doorway that is more than 1.3 times the width of your shoulders, you walk straight through at an angle 90 degrees to your direction of motion. If the doorway is 1.3 times or less, you rotate your shoulders accordingly. Now, it seems to me few would call this *mediated*. Rather, there is a direct relationship between the size of the doorway and the width of your shoulders. This experience is direct; it's immediate or un-mediated, if you like. I believe this perceptional dynamic is based on an invariant quality of the physical world out there as it relates to the organism.

LANTOLF I'm not sure. I would disagree with this. My body movement may be unmediated in and of itself, but the door is a cultural artifact. This makes the situated action mediated.

VAN LIER Well, I think mediation *emerges* as particular movements become habituated or acculturated over time. But, even then, there is always an undercurrent of direct, immediate experience.

SCOLLON Not everybody walks through doorways in the same way: some pass on the right side, some pass on the left side. It seems to me the dimension of the doorway is mediated by a particular cultural perception of it. I would not take it as a raw given object. But I do think, when talking about the perceptional development of children, this aspect of being habituated or acculturated into use over time is an important one. I recently returned to look at data I collected years ago and reanalyzed the handing of objects from one person to another. In particular, I looked at the handling behavior of one child over the course of a year. Now, I am not a great enthusiast of the Piagetian scales by any means, but at some point this child seems to have entered a stage of discovery where she began to understand the independence of the object from her body through her repeated dropping of it. Perhaps we might call this the emergence of intentionality. From dropping the object and understanding its physical independence, she slowly progressed to using it strategically to control social interaction. With young children, I think this really speaks to the emergent quality of mediation.

OCHS There also is much we can learn about the mediated nature of physical space through the grammatical categories and pragmatics of language. I was recently looking at autistic children's spontaneous discourse, when I found something odd about their use of locative prepositions. Locative prepositional phrases reveal a great deal about how people organize themselves and others in physical space. The construction of these phrases is also highly contextualized in linguistic culture. When autistic children don't get these constructions exactly right, as they occasionally do, the results are not necessarily ungrammatical, but they would strike one as peculiar. Let me give an example. One child was telling a story about how he was walking home with a friend when his father pulls up in the car, and they all ride home together. He says, "I went home inside the car with my friend." This preposition use really struck me and got me thinking about the perceptual frames inherent in grammatical categories. It was a great realization for me because I had discovered, through this child's narrative reconstruction of an event, an important particle of culture. It was more than a mere semantic distinction. "Inside the car," unlike "in the car," emphasizes the interiority of physical space. This grammatical example shows us how the cognitive impairments of autism influence – perhaps skew – the cultural organization of space. So, I think the two points being made about the mediation of space are in some sense both right. We are organized by the physicality of our spaces, but the physicality is being organized at the same time through language and other semiotic resources.

What does "rule" mean from an ecological point of view? Do we need to start rethinking the conventional notion of rule-based systems?

VAN LIER   We don't have to discard the notion of rules *per se*, be they grammatical, cultural, institutional, etc. They are, after all, very useful. However, it is clear that there is a whole other area of social activity that is characterized not as *a priori* rule-governed but as spontaneous rule-making and rule-applying. Philosopher Donald Davidson makes an important distinction between rules that are used in a premeditated and rational manner and rules that are adaptively applied during the course of action.[6] He calls the former "prior theory" and the latter "passing theory." I think a great deal of language use and social activity involves "passing theory." Adaptive rules are functionally different from the kind of *a priori*, generative rules used to describe the grammatical structure of language.

SCOLLON   I don't believe we operate according to rule-based structures when we take actions. On the other hand, we certainly seem to have a taste for making rule-based systems to describe a wide range of phenomena. We continually generate semiotic systems for art and language. Every culture sets down various normative systems in one way or another. After all, this is a fundamental process of socialization. I think it would be unwise to take a radical practice-based position and disregard the function of rule-based systems altogether. We would be neglecting an important dimension of ordinary social activity. What we need to do, I believe, is examine the *interaction* of rule-based structures and adaptive rule-making. In what ways does the social technology of rules begin to exert an influence on moment-to-moment practice?

OCHS   Rules are also closely tied to moral beliefs about right and wrong. I have written extensively on the socialization of autistic children into the rules of school and family life. Since autistic children are constantly violating various social and institutional rules, their behavior draws our attention to the nature of the rules themselves. Rules are, to a large extent, reflections or expressions of systems of values. In that they are a way of indexing our values and thereby making them communicable, rules are invariably laced with morality.

LANTOLF   There is another very important aspect to rules that touches on their irregular application in certain contexts. Hubert Dreyfus conducted studies on the differences in problem-solving between experts and novices.[7] It would appear from his findings that experts and novices learn in qualitatively different ways, and this is very much reflected in how each group follows rules. One study looked at how airplane pilots learn to read instrumentation panels. During training, both groups were given explicit procedures to follow for reading these instrumentation panels. Researchers discovered that novices generally follow these procedures as they are instructed. Experts, on the other hand, do not follow the same procedures. Rather, they cut corners, take shortcuts, and generally improvise. In this sense, experts behave in a rule-less kind of way. They may signal to others that they follow the rules, but at some point it is clear that experts need to move beyond conventional, fixed rules to reach a higher level of competence.

SCOLLON   The bigger issue here, I think, is the transitivity between the *a priori* forms and the adaptive functions of rules. How do socially emergent rule-based structures become internalized in the dynamic functioning of the organism? One of the great obstacles to under-standing the complexity of social phenomena is the assumption that the logical systems we come up with to describe them are in fact how people act. I think that's an enormously wrong notion. The central question should be: if rule-based structures are not necessarily the basis for action, how do they come to *mediate* action?

LEMKE   There clearly are relations of power involved with mediation. We cannot talk about rules without getting into social and cultural politics. What we are really talking about is the issue of organizing social systems at higher scales where the construction, institutionaliza-tion, and maintenance of rule-based structures set up conditions for who rules and who is ruled. Claire Kramsch mentioned Levi-Strauss in terms of how rules could also be called myths.[8] I think we really need to be aware of how rules become internalized and power relations mythologized in such a way that they appear absolutely natural and taken for granted.

Notes

1. Cole, M. (1996) *Cultural Psychology: A Once and Future Discipline.* Cambridge: Harvard University Press.
2. Street, B. (1984) *Literacy in Theory and Practice.* Cambridge: Cambridge University Press.
3. Engeström, Y. (1987) *Learning by Expanding: An Activity-Theoretical Approach to Developmental Research.* Helsinki: Orienta-Konsultit.
4. Neisser, U. (ed.) (1993) *The Perceived Self: Ecological and Interpersonal Sources of Self-Knowledge.* New York: Cambridge University Press.
5. Gibson, J.J. (1979) *The Ecological Approach to Visual Perception.* Boston: Houghton Mifflin.
6. Davidson, D. (1986) A nice derangement of epitaphs. In E. LePore (ed.), *Truth and Interpretation: Perspectives on the Philosophy of Donald Davidson.* Oxford: Basil Blackwell, pp. 433–46.
7. Dreyfus, H.L. and Dreyfus, S.E. (1986) *Mind Over Machine: The Power of Human Intuition and Expertise in the Era of the Computer.* New York: The Free Press.
8. Levi-Strauss, C. (1963) *Structural Anthropology.* New York: Basic Books.

Part Three

Discourse alignments and trajectories in institutional settings

"I'd rather switch than fight": An activity-theoretic study of power, success, and failure in a foreign language classroom

7

James P. Lantolf and Patricia B. Genung

Introduction

This chapter reports on a case study of one student's failed attempt to learn Chinese as a foreign language during an intensive summer course at a major North American university. Our primary focus will be on the issue of power as wielded by the course instructors and program director which, from the student's perspective, appeared to conspire against her best efforts to learn the language. We will examine the ways in which the student undertook not only to resist but to openly, actively, yet unsuccessfully, challenge what from her viewpoint was abusive power and an impediment to her attempt to learn the language. We will consider how her ultimate submission to this power enabled her to obtain a satisfactory grade without learning the language and in so doing fulfill a requirement for her PhD degree, and at some level, therefore, to emerge from the experience as a successful student, albeit not as a successful language learner. We will argue that a major source of the struggle had its roots in the student's, and potentially, at least, the instructors' histories as learner and teacher.[1] To carry out our analysis, we rely on activity theory, as developed in the work of L.S. Vygotsky (1978, 1987) and A.N. Leontiev (1978, 1981) and recently expanded upon in the writings of Y. Engeström (1987, 1999). We believe that this theoretical framework allows the analyst to develop a rich and robust understanding of concrete human activity because it brings into focus the interaction of a complex array of factors that reveal the unstable and dynamic nature of this activity.

Activity theory

Ehrman and Dörnyei (1998: 261) note that situated learning, and other socioconstructivist theories, including *activity theory*, find their inspiration in the work of Vygotsky and A.N. Leontiev.[2] According to Ehrman and Dörnyei, "proponents of these theories, such as Lave and Rogoff, suggest that effective learning and motivation are always socially imbedded" (*ibid.*). As will become clear, ineffective learning is also socially imbedded. It is not embedding that makes learning effective; it is the quality of the social framework and the activity carried out within that framework that determine learning outcomes.

Traditional approaches to the social and behavioral sciences are essentially dualistic to the extent that they have "cherished a division of labor" between the individual and the surrounding socioeconomic forces (Engeström 1999:19). Although some approaches acknowledge the relevance of the social environment in individual development, they fail to build a framework in which there is a necessary, dialectic, link between individuals and social structures. For instance, Ehrman and Dörnyei (1998) attempt to overcome the separation of individuals and social groups by drawing on two distinct theoretical perspectives: psychoanalysis and social psychology. Activity theory, however, "has been elaborated" as a unified theory of individual and societal behavior (Engeström 1999:19).

At the core of the theory resides the concept of *mediation*. All human activities are mediated by culturally created artifacts (i.e. physical or symbolic tools) and social relationships. It is this notion, according to Engeström (1999:29), that "breaks down the Cartesian walls that isolate the individual mind from the culture and society."[3] Mediation imbues individuals with the agency to regulate their own mental and physical activity, from the *outside*. In this way, the theory avoids the need for internal "biological urges" (such as in Freudian psychoanalysis) or some type of "inherent free will" or external omnipresent social forces as sources of control of human activity (*ibid.*).

With regard to the second-language classroom setting, several participants and processes come into play. Classroom communities are generally organized according to a division of labor. For example, it is tacitly assumed that certain individuals are assigned the role of teacher and others take on the role of student. However, while this might be the basic division in most classroom communities, how the specific tasks, powers, and responsibilities of each role are distributed and negotiated (see Cole and Engeström 1993:7), and perhaps even if they are negotiated, varies across time and space. What is negotiable and how negotiation is conducted is very much influenced by the beliefs of those participating in the community of practice, including not only those physically present in the classroom (i.e. teachers and students), but also those less visible participants in the community, including administrators, curriculum developers, textbook authors, parents, etc.

In any activity system, and emerging from the division of labor, are the rules that the community and, by implication, individual members, follow when interacting with each other and the mediating artifacts made available to the community. These rules may either be tacit, with their origins in the cultural-historical circumstances in which the community is imbedded, or they may be explicit, as in the case of the course syllabus. Normally, only certain individuals (e.g. teachers) have the power, and responsibility, to set down explicit rules of interaction. The syllabus prescribes the sequence of topics to be studied, sanctioned behaviors, and appropriate learning outcomes (see Auerbach 1995:14). In addition to overt rules of behavior set down in the syllabus, there are also at work unwritten rules of the general educational community. These rules define and constrain the role of "teacher" and "student" and provide a general framework for how these individuals may or may not interact with each other.

Complementing the social relationships at work in the community, we also find culturally constructed artifacts that serve to mediate learning activity. Included among these are textbooks, computers, videos, handouts, and the approved languages of interaction (L2, L1, both).

Finally, a critical feature of any activity system is history. According to Vygotsky, the sources of uniquely human behavior are to be found in history, not biology (Scribner 1985:123). As Vygotsky (1978:65) puts it, "it is only in movement that a body shows what it is." By movement, here, Vygotsky is referring to genetic (i.e. historical) processes that evolve over time. To eschew history is to potentially misconstrue human behavior. Although sociocultural theory is interested in four historical domains, our attention will focus on only two of these: *ontogenesis*, or the life history of individuals in society, and *microgenesis*, or the history of particular psychological functions over relatively brief time spans, such as occurs in classroom language learning.[4]

From an activity-theoretic perspective, all distinctly human forms of psychological behavior arise from some need and are directed toward some object, which, in turn, is projected to an anticipated outcome. The projection from object to outcome, even if vague, is the motive for an activity and it is this link between object and outcome that imbues our behaviors, mental or physical, with meaning

(Engeström 1999:31). Importantly, motives are not rigid phenomena predetermined prior to engaging in some activity, but are malleable and frequently established in the process of activity itself (Lompscher 1999; Häkkäräinen 1994).

Activity theory, power and resistance

In our opinion, research informed by activity theory has not paid sufficient attention to matters of power and how power is manipulated and resisted in sites such as language classrooms. We do not believe this to be a problem with the theory as much as a matter of researchers' interests. Clearly, because activity theory is concerned with the nature of communities and their rules of interaction, it is able to handle matters of power. In fact, according to Yaroshevsky (1989:222), for Vygotsky, "the volitional character of the psychical regulation of behavior distinguishing man from other creatures, man's power over himself, is rooted in the relations of power that take shape in society."

With regard to classroom settings, activity theory provides a fruitful way of making sense of what transpires. Classrooms are not "isolated spaces" in which the only things going on are teaching and learning, but are instead "social spaces" in which "social relations [including those circulating around power] are played out" (Pennycook 2000:90–94). In the analysis that follows, we will attempt to integrate a discussion of power into the activity theoretic framework.

As a working definition of power, we offer the following: power is the capacity (and privilege) to project and impose one's perspective on others without taking account of others' perspective. With regard to classroom settings, we often, and incorrectly, assume that the "actual teaching that goes on behind closed doors" entails "a neutral transfer of skills, knowledge, or competencies" (Auerbach 1995:9). Even though "the dynamics of power and domination may be invisible, they permeate the fabric of classroom life" (*ibid.*). At issue are such matters as, "Whose experience is valid? What counts as legitimate knowledge? And how is this knowledge transmitted/constructed?" (1995:11).

Analysis

In the analysis that follows, we will discuss how activity theory helps us to understand the experience of an individual who undertakes to learn an L2. On the one hand, because of conflicting views on what constitutes an appropriate community of practice for learning between the individual and those with power (i.e. the teachers and the program director) to strongly influence, if not *a priori* determine, how that community is to be constructed, the individual is thwarted in her goal to learn the language. On the other hand, in eventually opting to acquiesce to that power, she succeeds in her goal of complying with the programmatic mandate that she pass a course in a non-European language.

The student

The focus of our discussion is on an adult graduate student, PG, enrolled in a doctoral program in linguistics.[5] The particular program required that students complete six credits in a non-European language, which could be fulfilled through language courses or courses on the linguistic structure of the particular language. PG opted to complete the requirement through an eight-credit summer Chinese language course. Prior to her study of Chinese, she had extensive experience with other languages and had been a student of French, Latin, Russian, and German. She had spent time living and/or traveling in France, Germany, Switzerland, Austria, and Russia and spoke the languages of these countries with different degrees of proficiency. Her strongest second language was German, which she had studied both through the audiolingual method and in a communicative classroom. She had also spent approximately eight years living in Germany, where she used the language on a regular basis. PG was specializing in applied linguistics and was intently interested in the processes through which people learn languages beyond their first. She was also a colonel in the United States Army. We mention this final point, because we believe that PG's history as a high-ranking officer in US military culture was a central factor in her willingness to challenge, albeit unsuccessfully, the community structure and rules of interaction imposed by the instructional staff. We also believe that her background in second-language acquisition allowed her to formulate the challenge in terms of this discourse community.

The other players

The course enrolled a total of 16 students from a variety of linguistic backgrounds and with different reasons for taking the course. Some were interested in fulfilling the university's language requirement; some wanted to use the language in their research; some were interested in using Chinese in business; while others were heritage students with at least one Chinese-speaking parent. One student was a native speaker of an Indonesian dialect and another spoke Malay as his L1. Several students had previous experience with the language either through formal study or travel in Chinese-speaking areas of the world. One student had a Chinese spouse. The remainder were native speakers of English and, like PG, were first-time students of the language.

The course had four instructors: three female native speakers of Chinese responsible for directing drill sessions as well as listening, speaking, reading, and writing activities, and one male non-native (L1 English) speaker of the language, whose role was to explain grammar, vocabulary, and the writing system through English. This individual was also the director of the program. Each day students had one contact hour with each native speaker and two contact hours with the non-native speaker. Students were not permitted to use any English during their time with the non-native instructor, and they were not allowed to ask any questions during practice sessions with the native-speaking teachers. Since most of the students were not proficient enough to ask pertinent questions in Chinese, this rule effectively prohibited the students from asking any questions at all.

Two of the three native-speaking instructors were from the People's Republic of China. One had earned an undergraduate degree from Beijing University and a PhD in Chinese literature from a North American university. The other had pursued university studies in China, but had not completed a degree. The third native speaker had earned an undergraduate degree in education in Taiwan and held an MA in applied linguistics from a North American university. The NNS instructor had studied Chinese at university level and was nearing completion of a PhD in Chinese studies at a North American university. He had also spent a good deal of time in China.

All of the instructors had received training in the primary methodology that was used in the program. Two of the three native speakers had considerable experience teaching in the program, while the third was a relative newcomer. One of the two experienced native-speaking instructors had participated in several courses and workshops on communicative language teaching, and regularly attends meetings of the American Association for Applied Linguistics. To our knowledge, neither of the other two native speakers participated in such activities. The non-native speaker (NNS) had previous experience teaching Chinese as a graduate student. The programmatic philosophy as expressed by the instructors and director and manifested in the syllabus was that formal accuracy in all aspects of the language, including writing, is of paramount importance. Students were expected to produce correct forms from the outset, and as we will see, even if this came at the cost of producing interesting meanings.

The setting

The sixteen students were divided into two groups of eight. Each group was assigned to a different classroom for each class meeting. To add variety to the pairings, on a weekly basis students were reorganized into different groups of eight. The chairs in each classroom were arranged in a semicircle with the instructor positioned in the front at all times, which is the quintessential position of power, marking him as the purveyor of knowledge and manager of all talk (Auerbach 1995:13). Students were not permitted access to any physical artifacts, such as textbooks, during drill sessions. Note taking was only permitted during English language sessions with the non-native instructor.

The syllabus, goals, and artifacts

The goals of the course were "to develop culturally appropriate conversation and accurate reading." The students received a weekly schedule indicating homework assignments as well as the material to be covered during drill sessions. Classes met five days a week for seven hours (9 AM to 4 PM) each day over a period of nine weeks during the summer. Students were also required to attend an unsupervised lab session at the end of each day, which they could forego by checking out tapes for home study. During the initial four weeks of class, Chinese language films with English subtitles were presented on Friday afternoons following normal class meetings. Over the final five weeks, this time period was reserved for a Chinese calligraphy class.

The textbook and tape program, *Colloquial Chinese*, comprised sentence patterns, grammar explanations and exercises, vocabulary lists, one- to two-page situations written in *pinyin* (Latin alphabet) accompanied by English glosses, sketches, and dialogs on such topics as shopping and giving directions. The text was supplemented by a Chinese character text illustrating each character, its stroke order, its meaning and use, and sentences written in full-form characters. The tape program introduced syntactic patterns, vocabulary, and pronunciation, including tones.

Evaluation

Students were given daily quizzes requiring them to insert appropriate tonal diacritics into sentences written in *pinyin* and then to write out sentences in full-form character format. During this time the NNS instructor would give a quiz on tone recognition and on *pinyin* representation of various phonemes of the language.

Every two weeks students were given a unit test consisting of written English to Chinese *pinyin* translations, translation from full-form character Chinese to English, transcription of *pinyin* to full-form characters, and dictation of Chinese words to be written in *pinyin* with tones marked appropriately. Students were also individually evaluated for oral production by a team of two instructors. The course grade was based on three unit tests and a final exam.

The daily routine

In the drill sessions students practiced specific syntactic patterns that they were required to familiarize themselves with the night before each class period. The instructors called upon the students sequentially to respond to a question with the relevant pattern. Factual validity was irrelevant and only responses adhering to the requisite pattern were accepted by the instructors, whose task it was to correct pronunciation, grammatical, or lexical errors. Students were required to repeat the appropriate response incorporating all of the corrections. They were also required to memorize and recite dialogs either in conjunction with the instructor or with another student in a round-robin procedure.

Pronunciation exercises consisted of showing strings of words in *pinyin* on an overhead projector and asking individual students to read the words aloud. Errors were corrected immediately and students were required to reproduce the relevant lines until they became error-free. PG reports that while students struggled to utter each line correctly, her attention frequently strayed. Since instructors rarely varied the order in which they called on students, she could predict which lines were reserved for her; consequently, she paid no attention to her classmates' performance, unless they were struggling with a word she herself was unsure of. When a student completed a line, all were often required to read the same line in unison.

Ten new full-form characters were introduced each day by the NNS instructor. He would draw each character on the blackboard, occasionally presenting its etymology, and giving the root under which it could be found in the dictionary. Students practiced drawing each character on specially designed grids, which were submitted to the instructor for correction and feedback later in the day. Each afternoon the students transcribed Chinese sentences from *pinyin* to full-form characters.

Students were required to write five or six sentences in full-form characters in a daily journal. Here they were allowed some flexibility in making their entries. On occasion the instructors responded to the content of journal entries, expressing agreement, disagreement, or making a joke, etc. According to PG, "these responses were usually written in colloquial style, so that the students often had problems deciphering their meaning and had to ask the instructors for help. Students were neither required to incorporate corrections into their journals nor to use the corrections in future writing."

The data

The data that we will consider here are taken from two sources: a diary journal and retrospective commentary written down by PG at the immediate conclusion of the course. In the diary, PG recorded the events of the course along with her reactions, feelings, and commentary as well as some of the reactions and commentary of the other students and the course instructors as related to, or overheard by, PG.

PG'S ORIENTATION TO LANGUAGE LEARNING AND THE COURSE

At the time of the course, PG had not been enrolled in a beginning language course for nearly three decades. The dominant methodology in her history as a language learner had been based either on audiolingual or grammar translation procedures. Language had played a significant role in her life history and she was preparing for a career as an applied linguist. She remarks that even though she had had a long-standing interest in Chinese, she probably would not have taken a Chinese course at this time had it not been for the doctoral language requirement.

INITIAL EXPERIENCES AND PG'S (RE)ACTIONS

As it turns out, PG misconstrued the schedule as to when the class would begin. She had anticipated that it would begin on Monday, June 8 and had planned her personal schedule accordingly. In fact, the class began on Wednesday, June 3, a fact she only discovered on Tuesday, June 2. She had not yet purchased the required course materials. She reports, like Schumann (1980), a feeling of not being fully "nested" because she hadn't completed necessary and planned household chores. This created a good deal of anxiety and irritation, which she states did not subside for several weeks.

PG expresses "amazement" when she realized early on that virtually all classroom activity would be teacher-fronted and highly controlled by the instructors; moreover, it would entail heavy reliance on pattern practice exercises to the exclusion of more freewheeling, learner-centered communicative activities. The basis of PG's surprise is interesting. The dominant pedagogy within the Modern Languages department housing the Chinese language program was, in PG's opinion, communicative. Her previous experiences in advanced German courses in the same department had been with communicatively-based pedagogies. What is more, she had taken the methods course required of all new graduate teaching assistants and instructors in the department. This course was strongly biased toward communicative-based approaches that decentered the teacher. PG had also observed several communicatively-based classes taught by departmental faculty and graduate students. Thus, we observe a significant dissonance in PG's mind between the community of practice within the Chinese course and the community of the language department in which the program was imbedded. This, in our view, represents an intriguing twist on Pennycook's (2000:9) argument that classrooms generally reflect the social relations at work in the outside world. In the case at hand, the outside world is not the so-called everyday world beyond the walls of the educational institution, but the culture of the academic department in which the Chinese language program was situated. The Chinese program seems to have insulated itself from the dominant belief system about language teaching and learning that served to organize the department at large. Why and how this came to be is in itself an interesting matter that has much to do with history, but it is a topic beyond the scope of this study.

According to PG, she began her study of Chinese as a highly motivated and effective language learner (based on her history). She reports that she was "almost instantly transformed" into an ineffective learner by the instructors' attitudes and methodology. From an activity-theoretic viewpoint, there was a dissonance between what PG anticipated would be the rules of interaction and the rules that were actually imposed by the instructors. She reported feeling the need to impress her instructors with her language learning ability, but the rules of interaction and the division of labor at work in the community made it difficult for her to demonstrate her prowess. Noels *et al.* (1999:25) characterize this experience as *introjected* extrinsic motivation in which the person internalizes external pressure to perform in order to impress others.[6] Eventually she took it upon herself to speak with the director of the program about the situation. She expressed her disappointment at discovering "that the course was almost entirely audio-lingual 'drill and kill' methodology." She asked why the intensive Chinese course departed so radically from the approach espoused by the department. Her diary records that the director responded "that as he understood it, it had been shown that Chinese is so different from the languages already familiar to most learners, largely from Indo-European backgrounds, [that] communicative classroom methodologies were not effective." She then asked "why [he thought] my brain would function one way when learning an Indo-European language and quite another way when learning an Asian language." She records no response from the director.

PG also questioned the director about the grading policy, since the course enrolled students with sufficient proficiency in Chinese to allow them to do well on the oral exams. She did not believe it was fair to grade real beginners, such as herself, on the same basis as these students. The director responded that they used a so-called "fudge factor," which took account of students' oral performance in class, homework, and their progress in relation to their starting point. According to PG the "fudge factor" was not mentioned or explained in class. She was quite discomfited by this state of affairs. Although she earned B+ for the course, she did not believe this was accurate, since in her view, her performance was no better than average and was therefore worthy of perhaps a C+.

The impact of setting

PG reports that, like Bailey (1980), the physical setting in which the course took place affected how she responded to instruction. Although both classrooms utilized for the course were supposed to be air-conditioned, one air conditioner malfunctioned for the entire nine-week period. According to PG, the heat and humidity during a two-week period in July affected student performance in drill sessions held in the room without air-conditioning. PG became so irritated at the faculty's inability to rectify the situation that she took it upon herself to obtain permission from the person in charge of room assignments to use another air-conditioned room. PG considered this "failure by the faculty to ensure the physical comfort of the students, along with the 'unfair' grading procedures, as an indication of a lack of concern for the students' well-being."

Coping problems

PG had difficulty coping with the practice of students having to rise and greet their instructors in Chinese with "Hello" or "Good morning Old Master" and to take leave with "Old Master, thank you." According to PG, she felt that the expected behavior was "juvenile and demeaning and reminiscent of what might have happened in an elementary school." She again asked the director why it was necessary to follow the procedure. His response was that it was intended to familiarize students with a Chinese classroom atmosphere, should they ever study in China, to which she pointed out that "students in China were not allowed to drink coffee and eat breakfast in the classroom, and they did not routinely come late to class" as her classmates did.

PG and, as she reports, at least some of her classmates were thoroughly frustrated by the drill instructors' refusal to answer their questions, as the following diary entry forcefully illustrates:

> On July 28, the NS instructor was trying for the "umpteenth" time to instruct us in the use of the particle *le*. This particle had been a cause of confusion for over a week, and all of us were at our wits' end trying to get it straight. Part of our confusion arose from the insistence that we use only a specific pattern to answer on any given day. What we said the day before, which was perfectly acceptable and grammatically correct then, was, magically, not acceptable and not correct the next day, because the instructor was drilling a different optional form. One of the first-time learners had just given an answer, which was correct in the previous hour, but was no longer right because the pattern had changed. He did not pick up on this fact, so he was thoroughly confused and asked the NS, in Chinese, to explain his mistake. Refusing to depart from her recitation format, she told him, in Chinese, that she would answer his question after class, and she proceeded to the next individual. I was sitting three seats away from the man, and I had no trouble seeing his frustration. His face was red, his brow was furrowed, and under his breath he said (loud enough for me to hear three seats away), "Son of a bitch."

PG recounts another incident which she viewed as an affront to her integrity as a person. By the ninth day of the course, the class had studied vocabulary relating to the family, but they had not yet studied the word for "family," *jia*. PG was called on to discuss her *jia*, but since the word hadn't been presented, she was unable to respond. PG considered this a violation of the rules that she was willing to abide by, since the students were not to use vocabulary and sentence patterns that had not already been presented. She pointed out to the instructor that she didn't understand the meaning of *jia*, to which the instructor expressed surprise at her not having prepared for class. PG comments that she felt embarrassed by this reaction, since she had indeed prepared for the lesson. She opted not to make an issue of the matter until after class, when she attempted to assure the instructor that she had prepared and was quite certain that *jia* was not in the assigned lesson. PG reports that the instructor "turned on her," insisting that she never included words in her lessons if they were not first presented in the homework assignments.

According to PG's diary, the interaction between herself and the instructor became "quite stormy" as she defended her position. Her diary reflects her astonishment that an instructor would openly attack a student in front of other students. She remarks that she was furious and was unable to accomplish any productive work for the entire lab session that followed the incident. As it happened, PG was right about *jia.*

PG reports having observed another of the NS instructors intimidate a student who was unable to completely produce a line of dialog. According to PG, as soon as the student began his recitation, the teacher "snapped" at him in Chinese *"Bu hao!"* ("Not good!") but failed to give any hint as to the nature of the problem. The student then began again, and again the teacher responded with *"Bu hao!"* This exchange was repeated six times before the instructor specified that the source of her displeasure was the student's omission of an exclamatory word, which according to PG, was "unimportant to the meaning of the dialog." During the break in the session, the students commented that they felt "verbally abused" and "beat up."

From PG's perspective, the dominant tone of the community that emerged in this classroom was one of hostility. For a student to be forced to overtly mark in action and in words a distinct division of labor between students and teachers in which the teachers wielded almost absolute power was clearly distasteful. This of course is PG's take on the situation; other students might well have seen things in a different light. However, as we will discuss, at least some of the other students reported to PG that they also had difficulties with the rules of interaction set in place for the community by the instructors.

PG's reaction to the power differential is interesting given that at the time she was a high-ranking (colonel) member of the US military culture. At face value, we might suspect that she would therefore value and appreciate a hierarchical distribution of power. As it turns out, however, the situation is more complex and interesting. The military code of ethics requires that those imbued with the power that derives from rank treat all people, and especially subordinates, with respect and fairness. As PG saw the situation in the Chinese classroom community, her colleagues were being "intimidated and humiliated" as they tried to comply with the rules of classroom interaction. Paramount here was the fact that they were not given the freedom not to respond. This, along with "the refusal to find an air-conditioned space" and what she perceived as the questioning of her integrity with regard to the *jia* incident, compelled her to "speak out." If she had not done so, "I would have been failing in my obligation to look out for my unit [my class] and the other soldiers [students]."

Shifting goals and motives: success through submission

One particular aspect of PG's experience in the Chinese class, more than any other, appeared to contribute to her reorientation from learning the language to merely putting in time to fulfill the degree requirement. This had to do with her futile struggle to learn to produce full-form written characters. The situation came to a head when 12 points were deducted from her grade on a test for failure to produce accurate Chinese characters. If not for the characters, she would have missed only one point on the exam.

PG reports that her inability to produce accurate full-form characters changed from frustration to resentment. She asked the program director why she needed to produce written characters if the stated goal of the course was to develop culturally appropriate conversation and accurate reading ability in the language. She reminded him that since the communist takeover, simplified characters had replaced full-form characters in the vast majority of written texts produced in China. According to PG, the director responded that it was easier to first learn the full-form characters from which the simplified characters were derived. She did not react positively to the director's justification. As it turned out, the simplified characters were never introduced and PG observes that she is unable to read Chinese newspapers, menus, train schedules, signs posted in front of stores, etc. She remarked that she probably should have "refused to try to learn the characters" since she spent "valuable time on the useless effort which could have been spent learning vocabulary or practicing other aspects of the language." She states that her only reason for not abandoning the struggle was her embarrassment "at not being able to read the characters in the in-class oral reading exercises." When the class read a few pages from the required novel, *Lady in the Painting*, PG resorted to writing the meaning of every character she did not recognize in the margins and, instead of relying on her inferencing ability, she translated the text verbatim, a practice encouraged by the instructors.

Despite her frustration and resultant negative attitude, PG opted not to withdraw from the course. She reports that her focus shifted from long-term learning to presenting a performance that satisfied her instructors and that yielded a good grade on the unit tests. As she put it, "I had to pass the course, and the only way to do this was to learn what was put before me." She mentions that she continued to work hard, but the outcome she expected was no longer to develop an ability to converse and read in Chinese, but to "fulfill her obligation to the Army" to complete the PhD in the three-year time frame she had been given.

Considering this shift from an activity-theoretic perspective, we would argue that, at the outset of the course, PG's desire to succeed at learning languages had found its object in the Chinese course. Given her history as a successful language learner, she had anticipated yet another productive undertaking. This projection from object to anticipated outcome was one of her two original motives for enrolling in the course. Following her unsuccessful efforts to modify the rules of interaction, she realized that this motive and its affiliated goal/outcome had to be abandoned. Her second motive for enrolling in the course, however, was still available; consequently, she opted not to drop the course. PG's second motive arose from her desire to earn the PhD in linguistics, which required that she pass a course in a non-European language. In this case, her desire to obtain the degree found its object not in the language but in the prescribed and proscribed pedagogical practices of the classroom community in which she had membership. The anticipated outcome of her actions in this regard was now projected toward obtaining a passing grade. To achieve this, PG believed that it was no longer beneficial for her to behave in accordance with her history as a successful language learner, so instead she took on the behavior of a dutiful and compliant student. She focused on achieving short-term results rather than long-term learning.

According to Lompscher (1999), there are three general types of interrelated motives: social learning motives in which people set out to communicate and co-operate with others; self-related motives in which individuals are concerned with their own development and wellbeing; and cognitive motives, which are subdivided into lower- and higher-level motives. The former entail empirical thinking aimed at learning isolated facts, details, and surface relations and have the goal of obtaining a result. The latter arise from intrinsic interest in learning the object itself and prompt the learner to want to know how to reach a given result rather than being satisfied by the result itself. While higher-level motives are more likely to lead to intensive and recurring cognitive activity, lower-level motives are more likely to result in short-term and more superficial mental activity (Lompscher 1999:14). PG's account of her reaction to a change in classroom practice near the conclusion of the course nicely documents, we believe, her shift in motive and the consequential shift to mental activity aimed at obtaining short-term results and nothing more.

In the eighth week of the course she records an incident that marked a "sea change" in the class and which she characterizes as an "absolute disaster." On July 21, one of the NS instructors who had been "the most dedicated drillmaster" of the three NS instructors, directed one of the students, whom PG describes as "already quite proficient in

Chinese," to sit in front of the class and "commanded" the other students to pose questions for him to answer. In PG's words, "There was utter silence." The instructor then proceeded to ask a question, in response to which the student "rattled on for some time" but what he said was incomprehensible to PG. The instructor then called on the students individually to ask questions. According to PG, most students "stammered and stuttered" and ultimately resorted to telling the instructor in English what they wanted to say and she translated it into Chinese. This activity lasted the full hour, with PG understanding "two or three sentences." At the break, PG reports that several students came "flying out of the classroom" saying such things as, "What the hell was that all about?"

Although drilling continued for the final two weeks of the course, students were permitted, to the extent they were able, to use the language in a relatively "freewheeling" way. According to PG, the students improved somewhat in their ability to ask questions and to express some of their own thoughts. But, as she remarks, "fluency was still a long way off." Be that as it may, PG had, by the second last week of class, grown to "resent" any attempt to inject communicative activities because "they took me away from the comfortable routine of drill and threw me into the less certain waters of actually having to communicate in the language, which required my attention and a high level of involvement." She notes that she had gotten "good at the rote memorization format, and since I had not been given an opportunity to use Chinese in a communicative format previously, I was not good at it."

Further, and we believe, rather convincing evidence that PG's dominant mode of cognitive functioning was superficial and aimed at the short-term goal of passing the course is provided by her commentary on private speech. She reports having mentally rehearsed dialogs that were to be memorized and recited aloud in class. She also rehearsed English to Chinese translation exercises carried out in class. Here she silently practiced each translated sentence that she knew she would be called upon to provide. PG also recalls on occasion silently answering questions asked of other students and then mentally correcting their answers.[7] This behavior occurred, according to PG, only when she was interested in what was going on in class, or when she realized that she was about to be called upon to recite. Importantly, she recalls no incidents of private speech outside class during the first eight weeks of the course. She recalls that when she was learning German, she would often silently try to figure out how to say certain things in this language while walking around campus and, in so doing, she reports having manipulated words, sounds, and sentence patterns that she would later try out when engaged in conversations with German speakers. When the Chinese instructors finally introduced the more open-ended question and answer activities documented above, PG reports that she found herself on occasion engaging in the same kinds of mental play in Chinese that she had done while learning German. With the apparent exception of what began to emerge near the end of the course, PG's private speech was generally deployed in the interest of self-defense – a strategy which did not allow her to internalize the language but which did permit her to achieve her short-term goal of passing the course to fulfill the degree requirement.[8]

Conclusion

In recognizing that human activity arises from concrete, historically formed motives and is always goal-directed and, most importantly, dynamic, the foregoing activity-theoretic analysis showed that motives and goals are formed and reformed under specific historical material circumstances (i.e. division of labor, rules of interaction, and the community of practice that emerges from these). As these circumstances shift, motives and goals, and, in the present case, affiliated cognitive behaviors and outcomes shift as well. At first glance, it would appear that the material circumstances of the Chinese language class had changed very little throughout PG's experience. The community of practice in which she was expected to learn the language was rigidly organized in terms of student and teacher interactional patterns and response types, and she was unable to successfully challenge the institutionalized power structure which dictated these behaviors. However, history, as we have argued, plays a central role in shaping human activity, and PG's history not only allowed her to construct an identity as a successful language learner, but recent concrete learning experiences led her to believe that learning could only happen under more open and flexible circumstances than were present in the Chinese language classroom. Our argument, then, is that there was indeed a shift in material circumstances – the circumstances under which PG had been a successful language learner in the recent past, and the concrete circumstances that confronted her in the community of practice that she entered to learn Chinese. As we documented, this ultimately resulted in a shift in her motives and related goals for being in the class, which in turn gave rise to a shift in the ways in which she behaved mentally, and even physically, in the classroom community. Thus, motives, goals, and their affiliated behaviors are very much emergent. For this reason, we wonder about the value of attempts to measure the amount of motivation a learner supposedly possesses as a way of predicting learning outcomes. Things appear to be much more complex and unstable than we may have suspected.

As is no doubt apparent to the reader, this study has not considered the instructors' side of the story in any kind of detail. Clearly, to fully understand the dynamics at work in any activity system, including language classrooms, the perspective of all of the participants must be integrated into the analysis. Interestingly, according to Wells (1999:328), Vygotsky, despite his focus on the importance of instruction in the zone of proximal development, "had relatively little to say about teachers and teaching."[9] Teachers and the activity of teaching, after all, have to be taken account of, especially when matters of power are at issue. To cite Auerbach, once again:

> ... all classrooms are "teacher-centered" to the extent that it is the teacher's conception of education that shapes how the learning community develops. Clearly teachers have their own goals, their own understandings of effective L2 pedagogy, and, most importantly, they have power. To deny this is both irresponsible and disingenuous: students know it and teachers act on it whether or not they acknowledge it. (2000:144–145)

In the Chinese classroom, for example, the instructors rigorously insisted upon Initiation-Response-Feedback as the only sanctioned form of classroom interaction, and proscribed all other types of classroom activity until the very end of the course when an opportunity to engage in open-ended questioning was introduced, although this was controlled by the instructors. This situation is reminiscent of Bakhtin's notion of "authoritative" discourse, which assumes that utterances and associated meanings are not only rigid, unchangeable, and binding, but also "demand our unconditional allegiance" (Bakhtin, cited in Wertsch 1991:78). Thus, from PG's perspective, the unyielding authoritative posture adopted by the instructors and program director short-circuited her attempts to participate in authentic language activity (see van Lier 1996 for a discussion of authentic language). Her attempts to challenge the authoritative discourse failed and she opted to give her "allegiance" to their authority. At the same time, however, she still managed to be successful – she passed the course and fulfilled the degree requirement.

It is necessary to pay closer attention to teachers' intentions with regard to the kind of classroom community they set out to build, how they perceive their success or failure at doing so, and how they view student behavior within that community. This means uncovering teachers' motives and goals as they relate to specific classrooms and interact with specific learners within these communities and to focus on how, why and even if these change over time. It is important to keep in mind that while teachers wield a great deal of power, students also wield a degree of power, and here we include resistance to the teacher's power. Along these lines, it is not only necessary to understand how teachers see themselves as purveyors of power, but also how they interpret challenges and resistance to this power on the part of students. For instance, in the present study, we do not know what motivated the one instructor to modify the interactional rules so as to introduce some communicative flexibility into the classroom community near the end of the course. Was this planned from the outset, or was it a reaction to PG's persistent challenges to the rules of interaction and the rigidly stratified nature of the community? What were the teachers' beliefs about language, how it is learned, and how it is used? Some evidence of the director's perspective on this emerged in his response to PG's query about why a more communicative set of practices were not integrated into the curriculum from the outset.

An important lesson of activity theory is that communities and activities within them are rarely stable and smoothly functioning entities. They are characterized by shifting motives, goals, and rules of behavior and they normally entail struggle and conflict, including contestations of power, how it is deployed and potentially challenged. As Cole and Engeström (1993:8) remind us, "activity systems are best viewed as complex formations in which equilibrium is an exception and tensions, disturbances, and local innovations are the rule and the engine of change." While it appears that PG changed her orientation and behavior over the duration of the course, we do not know, other than from her perspective, what transpired with regard to the instructors.

Notes

1. Because we did not have access to the instructors' or the program director's point of view on the events that played out in the classroom, we are only able to consider in essence half of the story. To be sure, this is a significant half and, as we will show, there is much to learn about classroom communities from this side of things. However, it is only a part of the full picture. We return to this issue later in the chapter.
2. Although we cannot pursue the matter here, we do not agree that activity theory, with its roots in sociocultural theory, is a socioconstructivist theory. History and internalization of mediational means play a central role in activity theory, but to our knowledge they do not in socio-constructivist theories (see Valsiner and van der Veer 2000).
3. Although the classic Cartesian dualism is generally framed in terms of mind/body, we believe that here Engeström is acknowledging that other

dualisms, which have vexed philosophers and psychologists for centuries, have their roots in this fundamental Cartesian stance. Perhaps this is pushing things a bit far, but we tend to agree with him. In fact, the dualism at issue here is one that has recently come to the fore in the debate between Firth and Wagner (1997) and those in SLA working from the learner as "autonomous processor" metaphor (Ellis 1997:244), who recognize the social but do not theorize its necessity for language acquisition.

4. For obvious reasons, *phylogenesis* and *sociocultural history*, the two remaining domains, are not relevant to the present study. The interested reader should consult Vygotsky (1978) and Wertsch (1985) for a detailed discussion of the four domains.

5. The custom in the L2 literature is to refer to someone in PG's position as the "learner." In our view this implies an individual engaged in the activity of learning. We believe that as the discussion unfolds, it will become clear that PG was not, properly speaking, learning Chinese; rather, she spent most of her time trying to become a learner of this language, but without much success. For this reason, we prefer the term "student."

6. Schumann and Schumann (1977:243) discuss a similar reaction from a learner in an Arabic class. The student, who also documented her own attempts at learning, writes: "I hated the method. My anger bred frustration, a frustration which I acutely felt as my goal was to be a star performer in class, and I found it impossible to be so under these circumstances."

7. Ohta (2000) documents similar private use of language among adult classroom learners of Japanese as a foreign language.

8. On the potential relevance of private speech for internalizing an L2, see Lantolf (in press).

9. Even though in 1926 Vygotsky published a textbook for educators that comprises his lectures delivered at a Soviet teachers college in the early 1920s (see Vygotsky 1997), to our knowledge, he did not carry out research projects that focused on the activity of teaching in concrete educational settings, which is the point of Wells' remark.

Bibliography

Auerbach, E.R. (1995) The politics of the ESL classroom: issues of power in pedagogical choices. In J.W. Tollefson (ed.), *Power and Inequality in Language Education*. Cambridge: Cambridge University Press, pp. 9–33.

Auerbach, E.R. (2000) Creating participatory learning communities: paradoxes and possibilities. In J.K. Hall and W.G. Eggington (eds), *Sociopolitics of English Language Teaching*. Clevedon: Multilingual Matters, pp. 143–64.

Bailey, K.M. (1980) An introspective analysis of an individual's language learning experience. In R.C. Scarcella and S.D. Krashen (eds), *Research in Second Language Acquisition: Selected Papers of the Los Angeles Second Language Research Forum*. Rowley: Newbury House, pp. 58–65.

Cole, M. and Engeström, Y. (1993) A cultural-historical approach to distributed cognition. In G. Salomon (ed.), *Distributed Cognitions: Psychological and Educational Considerations*. Cambridge: Cambridge University Press, pp. 1–46.

Ehrman, M.E. and Dörnyei, Z. (1998) *Interpersonal Dynamics in Second Language Education: The Visible and Invisible Classroom*. London: Sage Publications.

Ellis, R. (1997) *SLA Research and Language Teaching*. Oxford: Oxford University Press.

Engeström, Y. (1987) *Learning by Expanding: An Activity-Theoretical Approach to Developmental Research*. Helsinki: Orienta-Konsultit.

Engeström, Y. (1999) Activity theory and individual and social transformation. In Y. Engeström, R. Miettenen and R-L. Punamake (eds), *Perspectives on Activity Theory*. Cambridge: Cambridge University Press, pp. 19–38.

Firth, A. and Wagner, J. (1997) On discourse, communication, and (some) fundamental concepts in SLA research. *Modern Language Journal* 81, 285–300.

Häkkäräinen, P. (1994) Learning motivation and activity contexts. *Scandinavian Journal of Educational Research* 38, 195–207.

Lantolf, J.P. (in press) Intrapersonal communication and internalization in the second language classroom. In A. Kozulin, V.S. Ageev, S. Miller and B. Gindis (eds), *Vygotsky's Theory of Education in Cultural Context*. Cambridge: Cambridge University Press.

Leontiev, A.N. (1978) *Activity, Consciousness, and Personality*. Englewood Cliffs, NJ: Prentice Hall.

Leontiev, A.N. (1981) *Problems in the Development of the Mind*. Moscow: Progress Press.

Lompscher, J. (1999) Motivation and activity. *European Journal of the Psychology of Education* 14, 11–22.

Noels, K.A., Clement, R. and Pelletier, G. (1999) Perceptions of teachers' communicative style and students' intrinsic and extrinsic motivation. *Modern Language Journal* 83, 23–34.

Ohta, A. (2000) Rethinking recasts: a learner-centered examination of corrective feedback in the Japanese language classroom. In J.K. Hall and L. Verplaeste (eds), *The Construction of Second and Foreign Language Learning through Classroom Interaction*. Mahwah: Lawrence Erlbaum, pp. 47–72.

Pennycook, A. (2000) The social politics and the cultural politics of language classrooms. In J.K. Hall and W.G. Eggington (eds), *The Sociopolitics of English Language Teaching*. Clevedon: Multilingual Matters, pp. 89–104.

Schumann, F. (1980) Diary of a language learner: a further analysis. In R.C. Scarcella and S.D. Krashen (eds), *Research in Second Language Acquisition: Selected Papers from the Los Angeles Second Language Research Forum*. Rowley: Newbury House, pp. 51–7.

Schumann, F.E. and Schumann, J.H. (1977) Diary of a language learner: an introspective study of second language learning. In H.D. Brown, R.H. Crymes and C.A. Yorio (eds), *Teaching and Learning: Trends in Research and Practice*. Washington, D.C.: TESOL, pp. 241–9.

Scribner, S. (1985) Vygotsky's uses of history. In J.V. Wertsch (ed.), *Culture, Communication and Cognition: Vygotskian Perspectives*. Cambridge: Cambridge University Press, pp. 119–45.

Valsiner, J. and van der Veer, R. (2000) *The Social Mind: Construction of the Idea*. Cambridge: Cambridge University Press.

van Lier, L. (1996) *Interaction in the Language Curriculum. Awareness, Autonomy and Authenticity*. London: Longman.

Vygotsky, L.S. (1978) *Mind in Society. The Development of Higher Psychological Processes* Cambridge, MA: Harvard University Press.

Vygotsky, L.S. (1987) *Collected Works, Vol. 1*, including *Thought and Language*. New York: Plenum.

Vygotsky, L.S. (1997) *Educational Psychology*. Boca Raton: St. Lucie Press.

Wells, G. (1999) *Dialogic Inquiry: Toward a Sociocultural Practice and Theory of Education*. Cambridge: Cambridge University Press.

Wertsch, J.V. (1985) *Vygotsky and the Social Formation of Mind*. Cambridge, MA: Harvard University Press.

Wertsch, J.V. (1991) *Voices of the Mind: A Sociocultural Approach to Mediated Action*. Cambridge, MA: Harvard University Press.

Yaroshevsky, M. (1989) *Lev Vygotsky*. Moscow: Progress Publishers.

Discoursal (mis)alignments in professional gatekeeping encounters

8

Srikant Sarangi and Celia Roberts

Introduction

In this chapter we take up the theme of adult socialization in the professional domain of language use. Our choice of the gatekeeping setting is motivated by the fact that such encounters put a premium on language performance in deciding "who is in" and "who is out" of certain discourse communities. In this sense, it has definitive consequences for people, and especially for people from different linguistic and cultural backgrounds. A competent performance in such a setting assumes socialization into the wider discourses of the institution which the gatekeeper represents as well as the more specific socialization required to do gatekeeping interviews.

The movement of professional labor has been a feature of the global workplace, and no less so in the UK where the need to import such labor is felt mostly in the healthcare sector. At the time of writing this chapter, there is an ongoing debate about the risks of public safety as a result of recruiting overseas doctors and nurses, even though they are badly needed to improve service delivery. The debate brings to the fore the question of what is seen as "linguistic incompetence" of professionals trained elsewhere and several responsive positions emerge: that we should train and educate more healthcare professionals; that we should set tougher criteria for language and proficiency tests; and that there should be closer and more continuous auditing of doctors. One issue that is given less attention is the interactional aspects of intercultural professional communication and the mix of language and professional socialization required for such communication.[1]

Intercultural gatekeeping encounters have been a topic of study for a number of years (see Auer 1998; Gumperz 1982, 1992; Roberts 1985, 2000; Sarangi 1994a, 1994b), with a focus on (mis)understandings that might occur because of differential use of "contextualization cues"

(Gumperz 1982, 1992), leading to inappropriate conversational and activity-specific inferences (Levinson 1979). In this chapter, we extend this line of inquiry to the medical setting which involves oral membership examinations at the Royal College of General Practitioners (RCGP) in the UK. Membership of the Royal College represents an important and prestigious milestone for GPs, both from within the UK and overseas, as well as contributing to the definition of general practice as a discipline in its own right. The college has a long tradition of developing and evaluating the selection examinations for its membership, and has been particularly concerned with issues of fairness as they relate to doctors from overseas (Lockie 1990; Wakeford *et al.* 1992, 1995; Roberts *et al.* 2000).

We proceed as follows: first, we briefly describe the key trends within language socialization studies and how these connect to notions of "indexicality" and "alignment" before moving on to the gatekeeping function of language in professional gatekeeping encounters. This is followed by a distinction made between three modes of talk – institutional, professional, and personal experience – that are char-acteristic of the discourse of medical oral assessment and which candidates are expected to orientate to strategically. We then analyze one particular case in detail involving a candidate of non-native English language origin. She has completed her undergraduate training overseas and has been practicing as a trainee doctor for a year in the UK. She is fluent in English but fails the exam. Our claim is that rather than put all misunderstanding down to linguistic and cultural differences in some general or dichotomizing way, one can examine the misalignments at the discoursal level – which include the three modes of talk listed above – in order to account for such an outcome.

Language socialization across the lifespan

Language socialization has the double function of learning to under-stand language through social experiences and of learning to under-stand social experiences through language.[2] It is through the everyday language practices of social life that children become part of a community (see, for instance, Tomasello's (2000) claim that young children also display their knowledge of discovering new objects in the real world through the activity of learning vocabulary). The role of the school is to take children through the process of secondary socializa-tion. If older children and adults move to a new country they then go through a process of what has been called "tertiary socialization" (Byram 1997). During such a process they learn to use the language of the majority community in meaningful and appropriate ways (cf.

Bremer *et al.* (1993) on the communicative paradox concerning adult migrants: they have to learn the target language in order to communicate, and they also need to communicate with the host population in order to learn the target language). Whereas child language socialization normally takes place in a supportive environment, the process of tertiary socialization, particularly in the case of adults, occurs within a less favorable ecology – usually in institutional contexts. The gradual process of taking on new roles and identities, of managing activities, and of presenting oneself in terms of knowledge and attitudes has to be accomplished without the active attention, tolerance, and long stretches of informal and relaxed interaction which typifies child language socialization.

Professionals who come to reside in a new country not only have to be socialized into the habitus of their profession in the new environment, but they also have to learn the institutional discourses associated with it and with institutional life more generally. The gatekeeping encounter is an activity type (Levinson 1979) around which both professional and more general institutional discourses coalesce. The vast literature and self-help manuals on the selection interview are evidence of how complex and demanding this duality is for candidates. They are assessed on the basis of their performance as socialized professionals – both in terms of their professional competence and in terms of their ability to manage the institutional activity of the gatekeeping interview.

Professional socialization: interface of indexicality and alignment

In order to examine gatekeeping interaction as an example of the problems of professional socialization in a new cultural and linguistic context, we want to link two notions: indexicality and alignment. Ochs (1996:431) suggests that indexicality is at the heart of language socialization: "... a theory of indexicality is a theory of socialization and ... a theory of socialization is only as strong as the theory of indexicality that underlies it."

Indexicality refers to the function of language to point to some object or association in the immediate situation. This may refer, as Ochs suggests, to aspects of social identity that the activity speakers are engaged in, and their particular stance or perspective, as well as more obvious pointers to time and space in the interaction. For example, Ochs suggests that, in English, "now" not only refers to a time dimension but also may indicate affect, often used as an intensifier in utterances such as, "Now look what you've done!" The ability to interpret the indexicality of speech – to understand and respond appropriately to the linguistic and paralinguistic cues which call up social knowledge and associations – is, therefore, central to the conversational involvement of speakers and to their evaluation as competent performers in the social dramas of everyday and institutional life. In stratified multilingual settings, the "contextualization cues" used by gatekeepers to index what kind of activity participants are engaged in can often be misinterpreted by candidates and the resulting "crosstalk" becomes the evidence on which their competence is based, as we shall see below.

The notion of indexicality helps us understand how the process of language socialization is both a matter of interpreting and responding in the local production of talk and a matter of learning how to be and act in social situations more generally (cf. activity-specific language games). Learning "how to be" and "how to act" involves developing an understanding of events, feelings, roles, and statuses and so on as relative newcomers participate in new social practices (Ochs 1996: 408). In participating, the novice both learns and contributes to the language practices which themselves help to form wider social structures. So, the candidates in the RCGP oral exams, however competent they are, contribute to the structuring of GP practice and the institution of medicine more generally. Even the low graded candidates, in not being adequately social, unwittingly help to refine and reconfirm what a gatekeeping interview of this type looks like. The examiners, in discussing candidates' grades, bring to scrutiny the boundaries of institutional knowledge and assumptions, thus requiring them to reflect on what kind of selection process this is (Luhmann 1990). For example, comments like "she didn't really run with us" and "[she talked] a fair bit of rhubarb [nonsense]" bring to the surface assumptions about both social relations and kinds of knowledge which feed into the specific practices of oral examinations and into the structuring of medicine as an institution. In this way, as Ochs suggests, language socialization draws on both interaction theory (Goffman 1972) and poststructuralist theory (Giddens 1979) in accounting for competent membership of a particular community.

Indexicality and contextualization contribute to our understanding of linguistic processes in interaction. If we add to them a more general social theory of interaction, we can begin to see how gatekeepers can so easily make judgments about candidates based on the quality and adequacy of the interaction. Stokes and Hewitt (1976:841–2) suggest the notion of "aligning actions" in order to account for social interaction generally, as well as explain the potential misalignments in problematic situations. They use the term "alignment" to encompass two meanings:

(a) how individual conduct accords with that of co-participants in the creation of social acts; and (b) how problematic situations involve discrepancies between "what is actually taking place in a given situation and what is thought to be typical, normatively expected, probable, desirable or, in other respects, more in accord with what is culturally normal" (1976:843). These two meanings often converge, as alignments at the local, interactional level are primarily an index of the sociocultural norms of acceptability. Alignment, therefore, has a normative, moral dimension and where misalignments occur, there is a built-in justification for querying the suitability of a person's membership in a community. So, viewed from the professional socialization perspective, discoursal alignments and misalignments between participants are of considerable significance in decisions about inclusion and exclusion of members to/from a community of practice.[3]

The gatekeeping functions of talk-in-interaction

Socialization and the lack thereof present themselves as crucial candidates in the context of gatekeeping encounters, where normative ways of talking and interacting become the basis for inclusion and exclusion. As Erickson and Shultz point out (1982:193) in their study of academic gatekeeping interviews:

> [G]atekeeping encounters are not a neutral and "objective" meritocratic sorting process. On the contrary, our analysis suggests that the game is rigged, albeit not deliberately, in favor of those individuals whose communication style and social background are most similar to those of the interviewer with whom they talk. One result is that in gatekeeping encounters the "gates" of encourage-ment and special help are opened wider for some individuals than for others.

The "someone like us" or "someone we would get along with" phenomenon assumes a level of sharedness and solidarity which overrides apparently objective procedures (Jenkins 1986). Alignment (or not) is thus implicated in, and inseparable from, communicative styles.

In the kind of medical setting we are looking at here, the common-sense response to this issue would be that, since both gatekeepers and candidates are doctors, sharedness and solidarity can be assumed. Indeed, the kind of interview illustrated below could not take place unless there was a high degree of shared knowledge of medicine and its associated procedures. The data, however, illustrate a much more complex communicative environment in which both the institutional discourse of gatekeeping and the long "rite of passage" of medical socialization play a part.

As an activity type, the gatekeeping encounter positions the participants in an institutional frame. The interviewers have to act ignorant in asking questions of the candidates, and the candidates are expected to infer the "language game" from the context. A candidate who is not adequately socialized into the institutional discourse of gatekeeping interviews may see the interviewer's content-based questions as signaling a lack of expertise (cf. Roberts *et al.* (1992) where an unemployed spinner painstakingly explains the whole spinning process to the local employment adviser who has faked her ignorance in order to encourage him to talk about what transferable skills he has). In the RCGP oral exam, as we shall see, some candidates may interpret a content-based question not as a cognitively demanding abstract knowledge question but as an elicitation of their professional and/or personal experience.

Candidates not only have to display cognitive competence, but also social and relational skills. This links with the extended professional socialization where such skills are required. In their classic study *Boys in White*,[4] Becker *et al.* (1961:4) point out:

> In training for medicine, great emphasis is laid upon the learning of basic sciences and their application in the diagnosis and treatment of the sick. But science and skill do not make a physician; one must also be initiated into the status of a physician; to be accepted, one must have learned to play the part of a physician in the drama of medicine. As in other dramas, learning the lines is not enough. One must learn what others expect of him and how they will react to his words and actions.

This can be linked to the notion of "aligning actions" as discussed earlier. It also resembles Lave and Wenger's (1991) notion of learning as a continual shifting from legitimate peripheral participation to full participation within a community of practice. In this view, learning constitutes a continual form of participation (see Bennert 2000). The examiners of the Spanish candidate, discussed below, repeatedly use strategies that convey their dissatisfaction with the way in which she is participating. But in most cases she fails to pick up on their contextualization cues. They, in turn, fail to understand her problem of misalignment, and simply continue with the same strategies.

In symbolic interactionist terms, we are talking here of the mechanism of role-playing which would account for the expectations of others with whom we interact. In the gatekeeping encounter, the candidates have to align themselves to the role of professional doctor as a social being as well as a scientifically competent medical practitioner. More crucially, they also have to align themselves to the gatekeeper who stands at the gates of the College and whose questioning indexes a culturally specific mode of interaction and acceptability.

Microethnographic studies (cf. Gumperz 1982, 1996; Erickson 1999) have shown the tensions in the interactional accomplishment of solidarity in intercultural settings. The modes of talk of gatekeeping discourse both reflect and construct this tension. Candidates are expected to know the examiners' expectations, and any discursively produced uncomfortable moments can rapidly feed into negative judgments. These inferential differences which cause misalignments produce more than local problems for the candidates. They serve to challenge moral assumptions about what is normal, allowable, and right so that, as we have suggested, low grades and negative evaluations are apparently justified. There are further tensions and contradictions in the selection interview surrounding the gap between the candidates' professional contexts (in all their materiality and functionality) and the institutional agendas in place to assess professional competence. The candidates have to show that they are professionally competent doctors, but do so by effectively performing the situated identity of an interviewee in an institutional context. The modes of talk that construct this ambiguous and contradictory space are, not surprisingly, hybrid ones.[5]

Different modes of talk: personal experience, professional, institutional

Elsewhere (Roberts and Sarangi 1999), we have argued that in the RCGP oral interview there is a configuration of three modes of talk: personal experience, professional, and institutional. These three modes of talk have been characterized as follows:

1. Personal experience discourse is talk concerned with the individual's experiences and feelings. It usually takes the form of a narrative, for example, anecdotes and reminiscences, and deals with the "here-and-now" experience of the concrete particulars of a case in hand and "the accumulated experience of a similar case over time" (Atkinson 1995).
2. Professional discourse is the talk of doctors in practice, in doctor–patient interviews, in case rounds, in hospitals and in a range of doctor–doctor discussions and meetings. It is the discourse of shared ways of knowing and seeing which

characterize the community of medical practitioners (cf. Goodwin 1994).

3. Institutional discourse is not the actual talk that GPs use in their consultations (i.e. professional discourse) but the more abstracted and analytical ways in which they *account for* this talk. This institutional talk covers more personal and emotional aspects of the candidate's professional life which have to be accounted for in ways other than personal experience mode. In other words, the everyday competencies and practices of the GP have to be presented in organizationally recognizable terms (cf. Sarangi and Slembrouck 1996).

Given the primacy of the institutional dimension of the gatekeeping encounter, the institutional mode is most likely to dominate. Let us summarize the main points of this earlier paper as follows. What is involved is a transformation of the "what" and "how" of general practice (professional mode) to the "why" of medicine, health, and illness (institutional mode). The "what" and "how" of the professional mode includes, for example, the diagnosis of symptoms, discussion of treatment, and the modes of talk around organizing a general practice. The "why" of medicine, health, and illness invokes a more abstract, analytic, or academic mode. The personal experience mode (Mishler's (1984) "voice of the lifeworld") is also common in doctor talk (Atkinson 1995).[6] It is therefore not surprising that the personal experience mode should appear in oral examinations and that this third mode adds further complexity to the event. But like the professional mode, candidates are routinely expected to answer questions about personal values, feelings, self-awareness, and so on in the more distanced and analytic language of the institutional mode.

We would argue that alignment needs to be accomplished at the level of modes of talk, i.e. candidates need to respond to the expected mode in their response to interviewers' questions. The questions are therefore likely to index preferred modes, although there is no guarantee that there would be an explicit signaling of this. So, candidates need to pick up the "contextualization cues" and shift between modes as smoothly as possible. In the oral examinations, as we have suggested, the professional and the personal experience modes of talk are laminated over with the third and more powerful one – the institutional mode. Whereas it is fairly straightforward to distinguish the professional mode from the personal experience mode, a distinction between the institutional and the professional is rather problematic. But such a distinction, as we see it, is an important one here since candidates are expected to be socialized into both modes of talk.

Let us begin with an example of how institutional, professional, and personal experience modes are imbedded in an oral examination (E = Examiner; C = Candidate):[7]

Data Example 1

01	E3	let's go back to something clinical (.) define premenstrual tension for me
02	C	um (.) it's a (.) I would call it a constellation of (.) symptoms (.) that happen (.) usually in in the few days prior to menstruation [(.)] it =
03	E3	[mhm]
04	C	= (.) although some patients complain of having the symptoms (.) also during menstruation [(.)] um (.) it's usually (.) uh (.) changes in =
05	E3	[mhm]
06	C	= moods (.) sensation of (.) bloating um (.) retained fluids
07	·E3	okay (.) anything you've read anything about it or (.) recently
08	C	.hh (.) I should have seen (some guide just now) (.) uh ((laughs))
09	E3	okay it doesn't matter (1.0) what how do you manage it (.) in general practice
10	C	um .hh (.) u- there are (.) various strategies um you can try um (.) oil of primrose [(.)] um (.) evening primrose oil (.) um (.) you can also =
11	E3	[mhm]
12	C	= try the patient with a contraceptive pill [(.)] sometimes that helps (.) =
13	E3	[mhm]
14	C	= um (.) or with other hormonal (.) preparations (.) um [(.)] (pre^^^^^)
15	E3	[okay] yes (.) anything else you can try
16	C	um (.) *I'm not sure just now*
17	E3	(.) okay (.) it's quite a number of treatments you've mentioned there (.) what does that tell you (.) about (.) the problem
18	C	*okay* (.) all from (.) I think that from definition it's only symptoms is is a- (.) it's not clear cut (.) er entity (.) it seems to be many (.) factors

contributing (.) um to it (.) th- (.) the treatment is
not (.) clear [(.)] =

19   E3   [mhm]
20   C   = the diagnosis is not clear (.) either (.) some
           people think that there might be a (.)
           (psychosocial) component to it [(.)] not just a a =
21   E3   [mhm]
22   C   = a physical hormonal (.) cause for it

E3 frames the question in turn 1 in the institutional mode, which requires C to define an entity in an abstract, scientific way. The definition itself (turns 2–6) however is accomplished through a display of C's professional knowledge – her understanding based on textbook knowledge. She frames her answer with the words "I would call it" as if she was bringing her professional experience to bear on the definition. E3's question in turn 7 ("anything you have read about it") is indexical in the sense that once again it re-establishes the institutional frame. But C responds to this in a personalized way (turn 8), which includes embarrassed laughter. E3's remark – "okay it doesn't matter" – reinforces this slippage into the personal mode before getting the interaction back on to the institutional/professional plane. The question in turn 9 ("how would you manage") appears to require a professionally informed description of treatment options, which C is able to supply. Although this is a professional question, she prefaces her medical knowledge with an institutional frame at turn 10: "There are various strategies you can try." E3's institutionally framed question in turn 15 ("anything else you can try") seems to imply, however, that C has not provided enough options. In other words, there is a misalignment here. In many of the other video-recorded candidates, there is a similar assumption that the preferred response will be an institutional one in which the candidate will produce a rapid list of possibilities or strategies. Perhaps C is seen here as not having covered the ground sufficiently comprehensively or quickly. E3 immediately acknowledges that C has already given a number of alternatives, but between these two turns C had to confess her weakness (turn 16). At a sequential level, the question–answer pattern (sometimes followed by an instant feedback such as "okay it doesn't matter") clearly brings out the institutional nature of such gatekeeping encounters. The actual content of the answers does not have real professional significance (there are no life-and-death situations in the examination room) but has clear institutional significance: the candidate has not performed satisfactorily. But a closer look at the framing of the individual questions and answers shows that different modes of talk are overlaid onto one another, thus giving rise to a complex interactional climate which the candidate is expected to manage.

The distinction we suggest between the different modes is not only an analytic distinction, it is also a distinction alluded to by the "lay" candidates. One candidate who was taking the exam for a second time had recognized that she needed to shift from professional mode ("what I would do") to institutional mode ("I would consider other options"), as can be seen from the following comment in a post-hoc interview: "[last time] I was more specific in what I would do – if they asked me one question, I would say this is what I would do instead of considering the other options available."

The point here is that the "how" and "what" of the professional mode (e.g. "I would check her blood pressure") has to be laminated over with a rational and analytic statement – "I would consider other options" – in which the candidate removes herself from direct action and presents herself as rationalizing her activities rather than just carrying them out (as in our above example when C lists various options for treating premenstrual tension in turn 10). The professional discourse mode invokes the professional's responsibility and so commitment to a particular treatment regime – a statement about what she would actually do – whereas the institutional mode distances the speaker and their immediate concerns by producing a more academic, scientific, or bureaucratic response. Through continual participation, candidates can become partly socialized into the expected discourses of the exam. But, of course, gatekeeping encounters of this kind occur only rarely and so opportunities for language socialization have to be found in other medical and institutional experiences where different modes of talk are also subtly indexed. It is one thing for a candidate to be explicit about what is expected but it may be quite another thing to accomplish alignment in the here-and-now situation. For this candidate, a switch from specific responses to "considering the other options available" has to be interactionally negotiated.

Most of the data from the oral exams suggests that this shift from talking about actual GP practice to reifying and analyzing the practice of medicine and the professional values and awareness that underpin it (i.e. from professional or personal to institutional discourse) creates the most problems. It is the most frequent cause of interactional negotiation and difficulty on the one hand, and of lower marks and negative comments on the other. However, the reverse case can also create uncomfortable moments, such as when the candidate offers an analytic response and the examiner is looking for a description of what the candidate actually does (i.e. move from institutional to professional; see Roberts and

Sarangi 1999). This occurs because the institutional notion of "mark-ability" includes an element of both "why" and "what"/"how" (see below).

A case study

In this section we focus on a candidate of Spanish origin (discussed in Example 1 above), who had her initial medical training in Spain, but has since moved to the UK where she had a year's clinical practice training. This is her first attempt at the examination. This is an interesting case because the examiners, after the oral, felt that the candidate had difficulty in expressing herself in English. Our analysis suggests that the examiner's low marks were the result of a more complex deep-rooted problem. In order to make our point, we will use three sources of data to illuminate our discussion: (a) oral exam interaction between the candidate and two examiners, (b) post-hoc interview with the candidate, and (c) talk between the examiners in deciding the grade. This is how the two examiners confer after the oral:

Data example 2

01	E3	she did one of your questions quite well I put a G for it
02	E4	((looking into the scoring sheet and writing))
03	E3	you're not allowed to go back and do this naughty boy
04	E4	I'll change it to an (N) (.) she didn't do very well at the end though
05	E3	I gave her an (N) that was awful
06	E4	she could have got it evening primrose oil et cetera prescription
07	E3	nothing that was the worst one
08	E4	so now then
09	E3	that one
10	E4	I don't think I wrote many on that ((discussion of how writing has come out on the other side – must cross it out so do not influence anyone))
11	E3	I didn't really write much
12	E4	well I thought I'd better write 'cause I thought she might be
13	E3	yes you're right well done
14	E4	I I think she'll be a fail (.) this afternoon

| 15 | E3 | she was very hesitant (.) it's not her first language |
| 16 | E4 | no |

(G = Good; N = Not Very Good, i.e. below a bare pass)[8]

It seems the candidate has good moments, but overall her performance was poor: she might be a fail, as E4 announces. E3 characterizes the candidate as hesitant, and puts it down to English being her second language. In the oral examination, we can hear some pausing and hesitancy, but it is hard to see how these alone can explain the situation. It is worth noting E4's decision to record in detail the reasons for giving a poor grade to the candidate. As we will see in later analysis, the notion of "hesitation" can be extended to include how the candidate was less forthcoming with her responses, especially when it came to backing up personal opinions with professional knowledge based on literature. There is an interesting slippage from hesitation in giving adequate answers to someone being linguistically hesitant (see Rampton 1997 on ideologies associated with first- and second-language speakers, see also Gal 1989; Gumperz 1997; Joseph and Taylor 1990; Woolard 1993). It is this ideology that gives the examiners a set of apparently unproblematic assumptions and reasons to believe that "she'll be a fail."

In a post-hoc interview, the candidate categorically denies her lack of competence in English. Indeed she claims to have done well, but acknowledges the occurrence of awkward moments, which has mainly to do with her inability to come up with source readings in order to back up her claims and opinions.

Data example 3

01	I:	I mean would you be able to pick out something that happened today that you think went well
02	C:	[long pause and laugh] I would like to think that I have done generally well
03	I:	any particular question or answer that you think … to bring out your best
04	C:	of the questions they had already asked me
05	I:	yeah
06	C:	no I cannot think of anything
07	I:	or anything that went badly for instance you felt that you weren't in your best
08	C:	I felt that they were asking too much in particular what have you read in particular and I feel that is a bit unrealistic in this exam because we all have

read so many things that at least in my particular case I find it very very difficult to name specifically what I have read yes I have read something but it's very difficult to name particular things and I got the impression that they were asking for that more than anything

09 I: so you didn't expect such specific questions about your readings

10 C: yes I didn't think they would ask so specifically about what journal do you have you read about such
[...]

11 I: so did you feel that you just saying you have read a lot didn't quite satisfy them

12 C: well I hope it did [laughs] oh well I have read about it but
[...]

13 I: I mean was there some kind of a mismatch between what you expected and what happened – how you were prepared for the exam and what actually happened

14 C: [long pause] I wasn't sure what I was expecting of the oral

15 I: you weren't sure

16 C: no I wasn't sure

17 I: is it the first time you're taking the oral

18 C: yeah

19 I: how many years have you been in practice

20 C: in general practice

21 I: yeah

22 C: just one this is my training year
[...]

23 I: what's your background and where did you have your training everything here in Britain or

24 C: no I was trained in Spain and I came here – I've never worked in Spain – I have been working in Britain after qualifying I came over here

25 I: right so you had your training initial training in Spain then you came and did your training here

26 C: yes my postgraduate training has been

27 I: so how long have you been here now

28 C: ehm five years

29	I:	hm do you see language being a problem in the in the
30	C:	| language
31	I:	hm mhm
32	C:	no – not to me anyway
33	I:	right so there was no problem today about
34	C:	no no not at all
35	I:	what about any differences in the way that you do things in Spain as opposed to here
36	C:	well that's not a problem to me as I have never worked in Spain so the only system I know is although my medical training in the university was in Spain it's much different when you're a student from when you're actually working
37	I:	right
38	C:	so I have only worked here …
39	I:	you don't have much to compare with
40	C:	that's right

As can be seen, C appears to be surprised when the interviewer (I) raises the issue about language being a barrier (turn 29). Clearly, C denies this and claims to have been socialized into the system of clinical practice in the UK (turn 36). For us, this could mean competence in both institutional and professional discourses of clinical practice and being able to move smoothly between them. However, as we will see, a lack of familiarity with the oral examination (i.e. what kinds of questions get asked and what count as preferred responses; see turn 10 above) may be the possible reason for her likely failure.

Elsewhere in the interview (not shown here), she does, however, point out other possible sources of misalignment: her experience in the clinical side at the expense of the managerial aspects of general practice may have contributed to a difficulty in responding to the whole range of questions in a balanced way. Most notably, she points out the mismatch in expectations: the interviewers insisting on a display of her knowledge of professional literature at critical points, for which she was not prepared, and this ultimately results in many uncomfortable moments. In socialization terms, because she did not expect specific questions about her background reading, as we will argue later, she treats such questions by examiners in a literal sense (which includes display of memory lapse, mitigated confessions, etc).

As we have indicated earlier, in these interviews, the general professional questions index a blend of institutional and professional response which this candidate fails to align herself to. For instance, a general question such as, "What do patients think of the computer in the consultation?" receives a generic response (e.g. "they are quite happy about it") in the personal experience mode instead of an institutional/professional response based on research findings (see Data Example 6a). Because the question is framed in an informal way, the candidate aligns to this, giving an answer based on her general impression rather than on any scientific basis or professional judgment.

Let us now consider how these uncomfortable moments and misalignments are interactionally accomplished in the oral examination. In the following example the examiner (E4) asks about the ways in which a nurse practitioner's workload can be increased.

Data example 4

01	E4	just supposing that you (.) as her boss wanted her [nurse practitioner] to do more for you (.) I mean how would you go about (.) assessing what more she could do
02	C	er within the asthma clinic
03	E4	within a chronic clin- (.) chronic disease clinic not particularly asthma
04	C	um (.) I mean she she could I'm sure she'd be (.) quite capable of er er running all all the administration of the clinic [(.)] like all the =
05	E4	[mhm]
06	C	= registers and (^^^^) non attenders
07	E4	[mm] [mm] is it good use of a nurse practitioner's time to be doing administration
08	C	um (.) I think it's probably better if a receptionist could do it [(.)] =
09	E4	[mhm]
10	C	= but (.) on the other hand uh (.) perhaps if you involve too many people [(.)] in running one thing [(.)] then it gets a bit disorganised =
11	E4	[mm] [mm]
12	C	= [um]
13	E4	[have] you read anything about (.) nurse practitioner workload and
14	C	(.) er y::es I have um th- there was a (.) a:n article in the BMJ um at the beginning of this year (.) which uh was about a nurse practitioner who ran

> a (.) sort of emergency clinic for minor illnesses
> [(.)] um (.) =

15 E4 [right]

16 C = that showed that the she was able to do it [(.)
there] was a high =

17 E4 [okay]

18 C = patient satisfaction (.) that there was a low
percent of patients who returned (.) to see the
doctor

19 E4 okay let's move back to this (.) ...

E4's opening turn signals the institutional mode: expressions such as "just supposing" and the choice of conditional modals cue the hypothetical nature of the question. The collocation of "how," "go about," and "assessing" all strongly point to a preferred answer which is both analytic and action-based. But C fails to pick up on the analytic mode to do with assessment. Instead her response in turn 4 – "she'd be quite capable of running all the administration of the clinic" – is cast as a personal opinion, with affect rather than with analysis. In other words, she thinks of her own experience with her nurse practitioner who would not need to be assessed since C believes her to be sufficiently capable already. Later, in turn 7, E4 challenges C's viewpoint: "Is it good use of a nurse practitioner's time?" This is not only a disagreement but it indexes a request for a defense of position (i.e. institutional discourse) which C fails to pick up on again. Rather than defend her earlier position, C shifts ground by saying a receptionist might be a better alternative, while offering a qualified mitigation in turn 10: "if you involve too many people in running one thing then it gets a bit disorganized." We can detect here a kind of noncommittal response which attracts a question about her source of knowledge. E4's question in turn 13 is an indication that C has not given an adequate response so far, and thus this question asking for supportive evidence can be taken as an act of metacommunication (i.e. C has not picked up on the indexical force of the question about reading which is that she has not given a sufficiently analytic or informed answer). However, C manages to cite a relevant study in order to back up her claim. Here the BMJ citation which only summarizes one nurse practitioner's experience does count as an institutionally appropriate display of professional knowledge, and moves beyond the realm of personal opinion. Notice, however, that the reading cited aligns with her initial opinion that nurses are quite capable of running some types of clinics independent of GPs. It may be that for the examiner "running" (turn 10) means administration duties and for C it may mean being independent of the doctor – and perhaps this is where they are on parallel lines. This, in a sense, overrides the earlier "U turn" where C first suggested that nurses could take up more administrative duties, and then retracted her opinion by saying that perhaps a receptionist might be better at this. In addition to this parallel talk and E4's dissatisfaction leading to turn 13, the candidate has not given an institutionally relevant answer about how to assess the nurse practitioner's capacity to take on more duties.

In the next example C is asked questions about teenage pregnancies. Although E3 poses a specific question about how to solve the problem, C first goes into a lengthy account of some causes of teenage pregnancy.

Data example 5

01	E3	okay thank you (.) I see in your practice that you have a (.) a problem with (.) a large number of teenage pregnancies
02	C	yes
03	E3	could we just look at that as a problem for your practice and how you're going to solve it
04	C	right um (.) I think that because the (.) practice where I worked in is (.) an area that is (.) it's a bit deprived (.) um (.) it's also it's not just teenage pregnancy (.) I think that (.) problems that might be contributing to teenage pregnancies that the (.) um (.) many of the children (.) (d^^^) school and they're (.) and also there's lots of sort of (.) peer (.) pressure (.) um (.) w- what I mean is uh (.) in in those areas (.) it's it's all right (.) as as you don't plan to have sex I mean everywhere can go (^^^) [(.)] and then have [sex] but uh if you are on =
05	E3	[yes] [okay]
06	C	= the pill or if you are carrying condoms then you are planning (.) um then you (^^^^^) (.) um so (.) [I think]
07	E3	[right] wh- what can you do as a practice (.) you had this problem what are you going to do about it (.) you've identified some of the (.) causes [(.)] what are you going to do about it (.) how are you going to =
08	C	[mhm]
09	E3	= tackle it

10	C	I think that the first thing I – I would like to educate (.) the the all the population in my practice not just the teenagers but uh (.) also the parents (.) [um] and (^^^^) school (.) [in it um]
11	E3	[yes] [right] who who's going to do that
12	C	um (.) I mean I'm not sure how schools work here but uh (.) maybe a biology teacher or even (.) [if] they have a (.) a nurse in the school or =
13	E3	[mm]
14	C	= [(.)] or a doctor (.) um (.) I could also (.) put posters in the school =
15	E3	[mhm]
16	C	= (.) or [(.)] in the surgery and uh I I wrote there that uh um (.) I =
17	E3	[mhm]
18	C	= would like (.) to u- because with computer it would be easy to identify for the (.) teenagers (.) uh who are going to be (sixteen) [(.)] and that day I could send them a (wee) sort of happy birthday =
19	E3	[mhm]
20	C	= card and (.) uh information about (.) teenage pregnancy (.) [(a- am I)]
21	E3	[how] would that go down
22	C	well I know some probably some parents wouldn't be too happy about it because they might think well this practice is encouraging (.) uh (.) children to have sex (.) and uh (.) well I would (.) before (.) writing any leaflets I would like to get (.) advice from my (.) (^^^^^^ local (.) [^^^^)]
23	E3	[what] evidence do you have that giving children information makes them more likely to have sex
24	C	I don't think there is any evidence (.) to (.) support that
25	E3	do you know anything about (.) sex education and (.) and people's sexual activity following it (.) have you read anything about that
26	C	uh (.) I can't think of anything

The nature of E's questioning (e.g. "what are you going to do about it?", "who is going to do that?") indexes a specific problem-solution scenario, but C's responses have generated a new set of problems. For instance, in turn 22, C provides the next question for E3, for which in fact C does not seem to have a response with any supportive evidence. Also, in her response C shifts to the personal opinion mode. Not only does she give a descriptive rather than an analytic account, she does not frame the description as a context-setting exercise. Rather fleetingly she introduces too many dimensions, and adds to the complexity by admitting her lack of knowledge of the school system. From the examiner's point of view, C's response may be seen as nothing more than a series of personal opinions loosely strung together. Using the strategy of hyper questioning (turn 7), E3 then has to bring C back to focus. Toward the end, E3 asks for back-up evidence and C fails to pick up the indexical force of the question which is to shift her response to an analytic level. Without such evidence, her responses retain the status of personal opinion and speculation, thus falling short of what the examiner is expecting at the institutional/ professional level.

One common aspect of examiners' questions in these gate-keeping encounters is that at the surface level the questions may appear to be eliciting a response in the personal experience mode such as, "What do you think of ...?" or "What do you feel about ...?" However, in asking apparently general questions, examiners are indexing an answer which assumes a shift in mode where they expect candidates to offer responses in an institutional/professional mode. Similarly, examiners may choose to frame a question in an institutional/professional mode, but expect a response in the personal opinion mode. In other words, most of the questions are formulated ambivalently, leaving the candidate to work out the exact mode of explanation (Roberts and Sarangi 1999). However, some questions do more explicitly index a shift in mode. For example, the shift from, "How would that go down?" type of question to "What evidence?" type of question (turns 21 and 23) is marked by lexical and syntactic changes to a more rational, scientific mode of discourse. But the shift is rapid – perhaps too rapid for the candidate to use it as an opportunity to move into the relevant mode. Or perhaps, as we have suggested above, she has not come to the examination expecting to draw on more general analytic knowledge. In the next example we can see how a question such as, "What do people think of the computer in the consultation?" is handled.

Data example 6a

```
01   E4   okay we'll move on to a different area (.) you
          mentioned in the last question (.) that you had a
          computer in your practice
```

02	C	that's right
03	E4	what do patients think of the (.) computer in the consultation
04	C	in (.) the particular patients that uh (.) are so
05	E4	well what you've read about
06	C	um (.) uh I I think in in general (.) patients (.) are quite happy they have accepted that (.) computers are here they are (.) part of our [(.)] =
07	E4	[mhm]
08	C	= daily lives they are everywhere um (.) and uh (.) I think most of the patients are (.) aware as well [(.)] that [they] can have
09	E4	[mm] have you read anything about (.) computers in the consultation
10	C	um (.) I have no I have read *things* (.) but I couldn't (.) tell you
11	E4	okay (.) so you've said that all the patients are (.) quite happy (.) what WHAT might be their worries

The question about reading is again formulated in a generic fashion because the examiner has not received a sufficiently analytic answer. But he again does not make it explicit and instead critiques the candidate's responses indirectly. E4's question in turn 3 – "what do patients think of the computer in consultation?" – is supposed to elicit a response which covers C's understanding of research into patients' views about the role of computers – not a reporting of her own opinion on the subject. E4 gives her two clues that he is shifting to the more analytic institutional mode at turn 3. He uses the present tense and the definite article rather than asking her about *her* patients in general. C, however, fails to recognize the hidden force behind the question as she offers an opinion in the personal mode: "I think in general patients are quite happy." C continues to operate at a level of personal experience and opinion, which does not align with the expectations of the examiner. E4, finally, in turn 9, makes explicit the force of his question and this leads C to admit her weakness. It is typical of unequal encounters for the dominant participant to raise issues to an explicit level after a protracted misalignment phase and to invite the addressee to either confirm or reconfirm the propositional content of the message (what Thomas (1985) refers to as metapragmatic acts). Such metapragmatic acts often index uncomfortable interactional moments (Gumperz 1982, 1996; Roberts and Sarangi 1995).

The same topic is pursued further as they talk about how computers may eventually substitute handwritten patient records (22 turns later).

Data example 6b

34	E4	[mhm] okay (.) you mentioned going paper free [(.)] what's the legal =
35	C	[mhm]
36	E4	= position on going paper free
37	C	it's not legal at the moment you have to keep [(.)] uh written records =
38	E4	[mhm]
39	C	= (.) um (.) some people have (.) tried to bypass that by (.) uh writing in the records (.) see computer (.) erm (.) but (.) I think that's still a bit
40	E4	or what do you think about that
41	C	well I think (.) ((laughs)) I mean it's like not having written records really if you only write see computer (.) erm (.) I think the problem with records is (.) written records is that they are bulky and [(.)] =
42	E4	[mhm]
43	C	= handwriting can be difficult (.) um (.) and computers (.) can be very helpful [in] giving somebody's um
44	E4	[mhm] so although it's it's not legal you're quite happy to go along with that
45	C	well .hh (.) a- again we have the difficulties if something happened to to the computer system you could have no records [(.)] at all (.) um =
46	E4	[mhm]
47	C	= (.) so I think that perhaps (.) having both systems (.) um [(.)] is =
48	E4	[mm]
49	C	= is the best idea
50	E4	but as it's illegal at the moment do you [think] we should go on being =
51	C	[yes]
52	E4	= paper free (.) while it remains illegal
53	C	well if it's illegal you you (.) you shouldn't do it (.) I think
54	E4	okay thank you ((C laughs))

The misalignment here is in terms of the light-hearted response to a serious ethical/legal point. Indeed, toward the end, E4 corners her with the question (turns 50–52):'do you think we should go on being ... paper free while it remains illegal?" This is an instance of E4 making an over-inference on the basis of C's comments about the benefits of computers. In her turn, C does not take up a stance immediately on the question of legality, so her answer seems only partially relevant. Again it is E4 who, like E3, pushes her to produce an "objective," analytic response but uses a personal mode question to do it. This is likely to be seen as a weakness on her part to take up a stance, and we have seen such instances of her embracing opposite positions to issues of serious professional concern. Notice, however, how in turn 44, E4 reformulates C's position much more strongly than is warranted by C's previous answer. E4 wants a clear line of argumentation which is readily markable and takes up a relatively confrontational position at turn 44 to elicit this.

In the following example C not only offers a response in the personal experience mode, but also does so in a dispreferred way when it comes to giving a reason for postnatal visits.

Data example 7a

01	E3	let's go on to something (.) clinical one of your visits was a postnatal visit [(.)] there's no need [to go into great detail about it] (.) why =
02	C	[uh uh] [no right okay]
03	E3	= do you do a postnatal visit
04	C	um (.) I think one of the (.) reasons ((slightly laughing)) is because you get paid for it (.) um [(.)] (it's an item) (.) it's one of your uh (.) =
05	E3	[right]
06	C	= commitments and (.) only if you finish (the whole care of the patient) do you get full pay
07	E3	do you have to do the visit yourself to get paid
08	C	er no you can delegate like (.) to the (.) registrar [(.)] or um (.) the =
09	E3	[mhm]
10	C	= health visitor has a an obligation as well to visit [(.)] but I don't =
11	E3	[mhm]
12	C	= think you can delegate on her the actual postnatal (.) visits (.) [the]

13   E3   [okay] so let's move on for other reasons for doing
             (.) the postnatal visit (.) why do you go (.) why do
             you do it (.) what's your plan when you're going
             there

14   C   um (.) I think one would be the clinical aspect to
            (.) you know (.) make sure that they have no (.)
            post-partum hemorrhage or any other (.) actual
            you know clinical (.) complication[s] uh infection
            of the breasts or anything (.) for more social
            aspects ...

Notice E3's remark in turn 1 – "there's no need to go into great detail" – when framing the specific question: "Why do you do a postnatal visit?" This may either be because of time constraints or to act as an explicit warning to the candidate not to give a lengthy contextualizing description as with the teenage pregnancy question discussed above. The candidate's response is to give an honest and valid reason but not one which will represent her either as a caring professional or as institutionally competent in that she can reel off a list of reasons. She is basing her argument less on what van Leeuwen and Wodak (1999) categorize as "Rationalization" which emphasizes purposefulness, efficiency, and effectiveness and more on an "Authorization" category which emphasizes rules and customs. In other words, these are different bases for legitimation and what van Leeuwen and Wodak call different moralized values are used to support an argument and defend a case. Now that GP consultations are run more as businesses, the issue of payment is important. But the problem here is that she gives this as the first reason (albeit with a mitigating laugh) and the examiner's quick follow-up at line 7, "Do you have to do the visit yourself to get paid?" interrupts any listing she might be about to give and lowers the analytic level of the interaction to a simple yes/no factual question.

Again, there may be a hidden agenda here in which the examiner is looking for a defence of the candidate's position to do personal postnatal visits. There is an implied line of argument in the examiner's questioning which suggests that an institutionally accepted answer would include an acknowledgment that such personal visits were time-consuming and not always justified (in a similar vein as the nurse practitioner as administrator question earlier). And this becomes explicit in the next example. But, again, the candidate fails to make the appropriate inferences and the examiner uses a strategy which Erickson (1979) has identified as hyper explanation – that is to ask more low-level, closed, and descriptive type questions (as in turns 7 and 13).

But here, as in other instances, E3 uses the strategy of hyper questioning rather than hyper explanation in order to introduce the focus of his concern. The topic of postnatal visits is continued below (after 15 turns).

Data example 7b

30	E3	[that's right] okay (.) if I said to you (.) we really don't (.) haven't got time to be doing all these things (.) we're going to stop doing the postnatal visits (.) how do you feel about that
31	C	(2.0) um (.) I think (.) I quite enjoy doing the postnatal visits um
32	E3	is it good use of your time though
33	C	(3.0) well you could say that about everything um (.) I think you have to to (.) balance it might seem that okay most of the ladies (.) are fine (.) there's no problems at all (.) but there are probably (.) (start visit) just take five minutes (.) um (.) if if you didn't do them (.) you might find that you're having (.) after more problems and you're (.) wasting more times (.) more time
34	E3	who and is anybody else going in at the time at this time
35	C	the district nurse (.) uh the community midwife she she [(.)] goes uh every baby in =
36	E3	[mhm]
37	C	= the first ten days [(.)] um (.) and the health visitor goes as well
38	E3	[yes] do you need to go as well [or are] they able to pick up all =
39	C	[um] ((laughs))
40	E3	= these things
41	C	well they should do yes but (.) perhaps you're right there is too many people going
42	E3	*right* (.)

E3's question at line 30, "How do you feel?" is in the personal discourse mode but, given his attempts to set up a line of argumentation with C, we can interpret this question as another ambivalently framed one in which an analytic, institutional answer is expected. Once again, C offers a light-hearted response in turn 31 – "I quite enjoy doing the postnatal visits" – aligning herself to the personal experience mode cued in the question. Her response also comes as a counterpoint to the preceding discussions. It even contradicts her earlier comment that the health visitor is better placed to do the visits (not shown in the data extracts). As we can see, E3 is trying to elicit an institutional response which would argue the case for how medical personnel construe division of labor, but C continues to respond in the personal opinion mode. Interestingly, though, she gives in once again when questioned further about the economy of scale (turn 41): "perhaps you're right there is too many people going" (see also C's earlier comment (Data example 4) in connection with the nurse practitioner's workload that too many people can make things disorganized). So, C finally aligns herself with the examiner's position, but at a cost. She has not defended her position or given an analytically balanced account. She has failed professionally to have a clear line on the value of such visits, and she has failed institutionally because she has not tuned in to the cues that contextualize the preferred mode for answering this question.

Conclusion: ways of acquiring professional socialization?

At the outset we alluded to one of the examiners' remarks about C being hesitant. Although this may have been said in relation to C's lack of fluency in expression, it perhaps also embodies C's noncommittal attitude to taking positions throughout the interview, and even readily changing her stance when cross-questioned. It is arguable that for the majority of the interview she adopts a predominantly personal opinion mode in providing apparently "empty responses" to the examiners' questions. In other words, she fails to offer professionally informed responses based on her reading of published literature or clinical practice, as is required in this gatekeeping setting, or to pick up on the institutional mode expected in the answers but often not present or only implied in many of the examiners' questions. The point here is not that C is a poor general practitioner (GP) but that she has not been socialized into the hybrid discourses of gatekeeping interviews. The issue is one of a particular type of language socialization, not of professional competence.

In this chapter we have drawn upon the twofold gatekeeping function of language – indexicality and alignment – in the context of the oral examinations. Whereas indexicality is a more subtle linguistic matter, it does have implications for overall alignment and outcome of interaction. We have characterized the gatekeeping discourse as a hybrid form of institutional, professional, and personal experience modes of talk. The "more successful" candidates tend to imbed their professional discourse in the institutional discourse as a way of (re)defining the activity they are in. Although the candidates and the examiners share the same professional modalities, their performances have to be stylized to meet institutional demands. Interactional management of the hybrid discourse thus becomes a measure of socialization and a prerequisite for success. This discoursal demand undoubtedly poses difficulties for candidates from other cultural, linguistic, and social class backgrounds. They will have to acquire and display not only the linguistic and communicative competencies in generic terms, but also perform in institutionally and professionally ratified ways which align with the structure and rhetoric of the oral examination activity.

We have focused here on what might seem a rather rarified type of activity: membership of a Royal College in the UK within the field of general practice medicine. The oral exam which selects members has a particular ecology which would not be replicated elsewhere. For example, the focus on values, attitudes, and self-awareness is a particular concern of GPs, and amplifies the problems candidates have in shifting between personal experience and professional/institutional discourse modes. However, more general studies of gatekeeping have shown that hybridity of discourses is commonplace and indexes assumptions about self-presentation which require a highly sophisticated form of language socialization. The interactional management of such gatekeeping, as we have tried to show – in which both indirectness and hyper questioning are relied on – produces an environment which is as difficult to learn from as it is to succeed in, unless your own language socialization includes an apprenticeship in powerful institutional discourses.

Notes

1. Another issue that is not addressed in these debates is the level of competence of patients and clients who come from different linguistic and cultural backgrounds.
2. In the broadest sense, it is difficult to analytically separate language acquisition from language socialization. It not only poses a false dichotomy between cognitive and social dimensions of everyday life, and between what is individual and what is cultural, it even suggests a logical/temporal sequence in the way we learn a language and how we use it in social, interactional settings.
3. If we extend the notion of socialization to include the "what" and "how" of social action, it should include, within a given community of practice, decisions not to interact. This raises questions about where to look and what stance to adopt when researching socialization.

4. To dispel any sexist use of language, Becker *et al.* (1961:3) explicitly draw our attention to their focus of study: "In this book we shall talk mainly of boys becoming medical men."
5. We use "modes of talk" here in the sense that it is used by Sarangi and Slembrouck (1996). Drawing on Goffman's (1981) "forms of talk" and "footing," the notion also indexes both specific speech acts at the linguistic level and changing role relations at the interactional level, reflecting wider sociopolitical worlds than Goffman's notions tend to do.
6. It should be noted that patients can also strategically mix their experiential narratives and medical voices, e.g. use tentative medical terminology and attribute it to authoritative sources (Strong 1979; Silverman 1987).
7. The data in this case study were collected as part of some consultancy work we carried out for the Royal College of General Practitioners (Roberts and Sarangi 1996). We are grateful to Lucy Howell for transcribing the oral exam data. The following transcription conventions have been followed in this paper: dots or numericals between round brackets denote pause; texts within square brackets are glosses; vertical line (|) signals overlaps; equal sign (=) means latching; asterisk (*) signals talk with noticeably lower volume; extended colons stand for lengthened sound and untranscribable segments are signaled by [^^^^].
8. Candidates are graded on the following scale: O = Outstanding; E = Excellent; G = Good; S = Satisfactory; B = Bare Pass; N = Not Very Good; P = Poor; and D = Dangerous.

References

Atkinson, P. (1995) *Medical Talk and Medical Work: The Liturgy of the Clinic.* London: Sage.

Auer, P. (1998) Learning how to play the game: an investigation of role-played job interviews in East Germany. *Text* 18(1), 7–38.

Becker, H., Geer, B., Hughes, E.C. and Strauss, A.L. (1961*) Boys in White: Student Culture in Medical School.* Chicago: University of Chicago Press.

Bennert, K. (2000) Negotiating participation: trainee-coworker interaction in vocational placements. Unpublished PhD thesis, Cardiff University.

Bremer, K., Broeder, P., Roberts, C., Simonot, M. and Vasseur, M. (1993) Ways of achieving understanding. In C. Perdue (ed.), *Adult Language Acquisition: Cross Linguistic Perspectives, Vol 2.* Cambridge: Cambridge University Press, pp. 153–95.

Byram, M. (1997) *Teaching and Assessing Intercultural Communicative Competence.* Clevedon: Multilingual Matters.

Erickson, F. (1979) Talking down: some cultural sources of miscommunication in inter-racial interviews. In A. Wolfgang (ed.),

Research in Non-verbal Communication. New York: Academic Press.

Erickson, F. (1999) Appropriation of voice and presentation of self as a fellow physician: aspects of a discourse of apprenticeship in medicine. In S. Sarangi and C. Roberts (eds), *Talk, Work and Institutional Order: Discourse in Medical, Mediation and Management Settings*. Berlin: Mouton de Gruyter, pp. 109–43.

Erickson, F. and Shultz, J. (1982) *The Counsellor as Gatekeeper: Social Interaction in Interviews*. New York: Academic Press.

Gal, S. (1989) Language and political economy. *Annual Review of Anthropology* 18, 345–67.

Giddens, A. (1979) *Central Problems in Social Theory: Action, Structure and Contradiction in Social Analysis*. Berkeley: University of California Press.

Goffman, E. (1972/1967) *Interaction Ritual: Essays on Face-to-Face Behaviour*. Harmondsworth: Penguin.

Goffman, E. (1981) *Forms of Talk*. Philadelphia: University of Pennsylvania Press.

Goodwin, C. (1994) Professional vision. *American Anthropologist* 96(3), 606–33.

Gumperz, J. (1982) *Discourse Strategies*. Cambridge: Cambridge University Press.

Gumperz, J. (1992) Contextualisation and understanding. In A. Duranti and C. Goodwin (eds), *Rethinking Context: Language as an Interactive Phenomenon*. Cambridge: Cambridge University Press, pp. 229–52.

Gumperz, J. (1996) The linguistic and cultural relativity of conversational inference. In J. Gumperz and S. Levinson (eds), *Rethinking Linguistic Relativity*. Cambridge: Cambridge University Press, pp. 374–406.

Gumperz, J. (1997) A discussion with John J. Gumperz. In S. Eerdmans, C. Previgagno and P. Thibault (eds), *Discussing Communication Analysis 1: John Gumperz*. Lausanne: Beta Press.

Jenkins, R. (1986) *Racism and Recruitment*. Cambridge: Cambridge University Press.

Joseph, J. and Taylor, T. (1990) *Ideologies of Language*. New York: Routledge.

Lave, J. and Wenger, E. (1991) *Situated Learning: Legitimate Peripheral Participation*. Cambridge: Cambridge University Press.

Levinson, S. (1979) Activity types and language. *Linguistics* 17, 365–99.

Lockie, C. (ed.) (1990) *Examination for Membership of the Royal College of General Practitioners*. Occasional Paper No. 46. London: Royal College of General Practitioners.

Luhmann, N. (1990) *Essays on Self-Reference*. New York: Columbia University Press.

Mishler, E.G. (1984) *The Discourse of Medicine: Dialectics of Medical Interviews*. Norwood, NJ: Ablex.

Ochs, E. (1996) Linguistic resources for socialising humanity. In J. Gumperz and S. Levinson (eds), *Rethinking Linguistic Relativity*. Cambridge: Cambridge University Press, pp. 407–37.

Rampton, B. (1997) A sociolinguistic perspective on L2 communication strategies. In G. Kasper and E. Kellerman (eds), *Communication Strategies: Psycholinguistic and Sociolinguistic Perspectives*. London: Longman, pp. 279–303.

Roberts, C. (1985) *The Interview Game*. London: BBC.

Roberts, C. (2000) Professional gatekeeping in intercultural encounters. In S. Sarangi and M. Coulthard (eds), *Discourse and Social Life*. London: Pearson, pp. 102–20.

Roberts, C. and Sarangi, S. (1995) "But are they one of us?": managing and evaluating identities in work-related contexts. *Multilingua* 14(4), pp. 363–90.

Roberts, C. and Sarangi, S. (1996*) Language and Its Potential for Discrimination: The MRCGP Oral Examination*. London: Royal College of General Practitioners.

Roberts, C. and Sarangi, S. (1999) Hybridity in gatekeeping discourse: issues of practical relevance for the researcher. In *Talk, Work and Institutional Order: Discourse in Medical, Mediation and Management Settings*. Berlin: Mouton de Gruyter. pp. 473–503.

Roberts, C., Davies, E. and Jupp, T. (1992) *Language and Discrimination*. London: Longman.

Roberts, C., Sarangi, S., Southgate, L., Wakeford, R. and Wass, V. (2000) Oral examinations: equal opportunities, ethnicity and fairness issues in the MRCGP. *British Medical Journal* 320, 370–75.

Sarangi, S. (1994a) Accounting for mismatches in selection interviews. *Multilingua* 13(1–2), 163–94.

Sarangi, S. (1994b) Intercultural or not? Beyond celebration of cultural differences in miscommunication analysis. *Pragmatics* 4(3), 409–27.

Sarangi, S. and Roberts, C. (eds) (1999) *Talk, Work and Institutional Order: Discourse in Medical, Mediation and Management Settings*. Berlin: Mouton de Gruyter.

Sarangi, S. and Slembrouck, S. (1996) *Language, Bureaucracy and Social Control*. London: Longman.

Silverman, D. (1987) *Communication and Medical Practice*. London: Sage.

Stokes, R. and Hewitt, J.P. (1976) Aligning actions. *American Sociological Review* 41, 838–49.

Strong, P. (1979) *The Ceremonial Order of the Clinic.* London: Routledge.

Thomas, J. (1985) The language of power: towards a dynamic pragmatics. *Journal of Pragmatics* 9(6), 765–83.

Tomasello, M. (2000) The pragmatics of word learning in early child language. Paper presented at the 7th International Pragmatics Conference, July 9–14, Budapest.

van Leeuwen, T. and Wodak, R. (1999) Legitimising immigration control: a discourse-historical analysis. *Discourse Studies* 1(1), 83–119.

Wakeford, R., Farooqi, A., Rashid, A. and Southgate, L. (1992) Does the MRCGP examination discriminate against Asian doctors? *British Medical Journal* 305, 92–4.

Wakeford, R., Southgate, L. and Wass, V. (1995) Improving oral examinations: selecting, training and monitoring examiners for the MRCGP. *British Medical Journal* 311, 931–35.

Woolard, K. (1993) Language ideology: issues and approaches. *Pragmatics* 2, 253–59.

Commentaries

Editors: Edward Bodine and Claire Kramsch

Discourse alignments and trajectories in institutional settings

What are the methodological challenges to studying discourse hybridity in institutional settings? How can an ecological approach enable us to place hybridity in broader developmental contexts?

THORNE   From a complexity point of view, the issue of bounding units of analysis becomes especially problematic. The real value of an ecological approach to language study is its ability to explore social phenomena on a number of levels of interaction. This requires us to rethink traditional notions of unit bounding that in the past have led to rather bounded interpretations. In my opinion, the greatest challenge to doing more ecological forms of research may be in finding a suitable balance between analytic "boundedness" and phenomenological wholeness. This could not be truer than with the study of hybridity in discourse. Methodologically, I think hybridity takes us into life histories and various forms of biographical data analysis.

SARANGI   Unit bounding *can* be reductionistic. However, I think we ought to be judicious in "unbounding" our methodological practices. There is often the assumption that the more we know about people's biographical histories, the more subtle and rich our analysis. Yet data-collecting of this kind can become compulsive; in the end, you are left with a great deal of information that's not all that relevant to your basic research questions. There is always a risk of getting too deep into the narratives of your subjects. I believe the area of life history can be valuable, but it has to be looked at and understood within the particular context of the activity. Activities themselves have certain life histories that connect and configure them to other sets of activities. So it is possible for us to look at the life histories of certain discursive practices and even linguistic expressions. In order to examine hybridity *across* social practices, one must identify and commit to certain types and degrees of boundedness.

THORNE   Over the course of collecting data for a recent project, I've discovered that there were many important things about the kids in my study I couldn't answer until I got into life history interviews. Learning about all these facets of their lives had an effect of destabilizing my original unit of analysis. All the online digital communities kids take part in, are acculturated into, and in some cases help to construct – these all have very different sets of rules and involve different roles and identities. When we examine learning activities in an institutional setting – with all the boundedness we traditionally impose on them – we often disregard the noncurricular experiences kids often associate with the artifact. And without this information, we miss out on a whole range of associated meanings imbedded in the activity.

CANDLIN   These associated meanings are undoubtedly important. But in so far as many institutional settings quite often force people – learners – into certain types of language performance, the issue of socialization has to be more fully addressed. Srikant's discussion of the gatekeeping mechanism of the professional interview brings to light, I think, a critical aspect of this process: there are often multiple levels of discourse occurring – and multiple competencies being tested – in the same performance. In order to understand how this socialization works, we must look at institutional discourse in all of its complex hybridity.

SARANGI   There are, in fact, two layers of institutional talk in the data I have presented. The interview itself is one type of institutional talk, with its own specific parameters of competence. The institution of medicine is another type of talk and presents another, different set of competence parameters. So, candidates are not being evaluated on medical knowledge alone in such gatekeeping encounters. They are also being evaluated on their ability to perform within the particular social and cultural frame of the professional interview itself. Role-play during such interviews reflects precisely this kind of institutional socialization, or lack of it. And this is very much linguistically embodied. For example, such a frame might entail certain prosodic features that a non-English-speaking candidate might not pick up on because they are not lexicalized. Someone without intimate familiarity with the linguistic and paralinguistic subtleties of such an institutional frame would be at a real disadvantage. Success in these encounters depends greatly on the kind of intuitions only a candidate socialized into such culturally mediated practices as professional interviewing would possess.

RAMPTON   It seems to me that Bernstein used a similar "level analysis" in his research on classrooms and their multiple levels of content knowledge.[1] His research was very much within a particular institutional frame that distorted his data in significant ways. The research you've presented here, Srikant, seems less interactional and more structural analysis.

SARANGI   I don't think it's structural analysis, unless we are talking about the structure of the interaction itself. What I am examining is the kind of slippage between different modes of talk in the interactional frames of an institutional setting. My interest is primarily in the *hybridity* of these forms of talk. Now, it is only at the interactional level that hybridity becomes a dynamic of the socially constructed event. It allows a certain flexibility to move between modes of talk, or more generally, a freedom within and among institutional frames of interaction. What we are talking about fundamentally is a specialized sociolinguistic fluency.

GEBHARD   How do candidates come to know how to do this kind of delicate weaving of modes of talk? How can they strategically prepare for these hybrid discourses and ultimately for such gatekeeping encounters?

SARANGI   Candidates need to develop a sense of framing. In other words, they must know which interactional frame is being signaled and what interactional role and script this frame requires. A great deal is in the timing. Interview role-plays are perhaps the greatest test of interactional hybridity. They require a high degree of fluency, agility, and experience. How do educators help, in this case, prospective candidates develop a fluency in maneuvering between institutional, professional, and personal frames? Over the course of our project, we had our informants look at video recordings of interviews and analyze the talk and interaction. In some sense, they were doing the work of discourse analysts. I think the task of educators should be finding ways of training candidates in practical forms of discourse analysis. They need linguistic tools for self-diagnosis that discourse analysis can offer them.

GEBHARD   Aren't these self-reflective practices also a matter of having them confront their own ideologies surrounding language? Also, might these practices ultimately lead to institutional change in, say, standard interview practices?

SARANGI   These practices would certainly reveal a great deal about both linguistic and cultural ideologies. And they would be useful in identifying potential areas of social alignment and misalignment. That being said, it is a very naive assumption that there is a one-to-one correspondence between research findings and institutional change. I would not go so far as to claim that our work will have any substantive institutional consequences. So, I wouldn't call it institutional change. I think there may be a sense of reflexivity, or at best, a context of dialog that such research helps to foster. I would characterize change more in terms of communities of practice than in terms of institutional norms.

CANDLIN   We've been discussing the issue of training learners in discourse strategies, but we haven't yet touched on the issue of *expertise* and its relationship to the use of discourse. What we are essentially interested in here, I think, is the acquisition of an expertise. This maneuverability between frames is not merely or even essentially a matter of being able to diagnose one's language moves in terms of some knowledge-based expertise. Most successful students say that they are "just good at talk." Educational success means moving toward a more interaction-based notion of expertise. As Srikant has suggested, it is through interaction that hybridity is realized. The central question, then, becomes, what is the relationship between expertise and discourse management? I believe we ought to be thinking of discoursal hybridity according to a model of *communicative expertise*. Such a model would enable educators to teach learners to better navigate the multiplicity of communicative frames in institutional discourse.

What roles do biographical and institutional histories play in language analysis? In what ways can ecological theory-building be a process of narrative interpretation and (re)construction?

LEMKE   Elinor Ochs has already suggested that PG's initial experience in the Chinese audiolingual classroom was an instance of culture shock. I'd like to follow up on that and speculate that PG's reaction to the social order of the classroom might stem from a deep conflict of cultural frames. Perhaps she is responding to perceived threats to her individualistic sensibility as an American. This culture shock may have roots in the very different expectations of status and authority assigned to student and teacher in each culture.

LANTOLF   To be sure, culture played some role in the difficulty PG faced throughout the course. The instructors were deploying a methodology reflecting in some sense a "Chinese approach" to language learning. However, there were other powerful forces conspiring against PG's efforts to learn Chinese. The foreign languages department at this university (where PG was working on her doctorate at the time) has a particular methodological history dating back to the 1950s. All foreign languages had traditionally been taught according to "the army method," which emerged during the Second World War and appeared in civilian educational settings soon after. Gradually most of the languages in the department, especially the European languages, evolved away from this method and toward more communicative-based approaches. Chinese, however, was not one of them. The reason for this is very much reflected in a remark by the director of the Chinese language program: "Asian languages are so different, they can't be learned by European communicative methodologies." Now, it so happens that that institutional culture of this program meshes in certain ways with a Chinese cultural–ideological frame of education and instruction. For PG and her classmates, the social order of the classroom presented some fairly rigid, uncompromising rules and relations of power. As a result, PG and some of her classmates countered these through various maneuvers of resistance. I should also mention that PG is a full colonel in the US military. So she is not used to being a docile body – in fact, quite the opposite. From the beginning, she tried very hard to challenge the rules of the community but without success. She didn't become a docile body right away, but she ended up that way. Ultimately, she and other students were up against a pedagogic culture and institutional history reaching back 45 years.

KRAMSCH   I have a fundamental methodological question about your own data collection and analysis, Jim. In your presentation, you report on PG's report on her own narrative accounts of her experiences as a student in the classroom. What's more, both you and PG are research colleagues and co-authors, examining interpretative data whose *only* source is PG's own experiences. There is a great deal of narrative complexity here. We have at least three different layers of mediated discourse: i.e. a report of a report of a report. It is not entirely clear from which perspective(s) we as the research audience are supposed to understand the social practices this study is examining. We are not dealing with the immediate perception of the events but a narrative of them that has been filtered at least three times. What we are talking about here is further narrative (re)construction of a *story* about language learning and power in the classroom.

LEMKE   Is PG writing a story of herself as a *heroine*? Is she perhaps authoring her classroom experience in the vein of a canonical narrative in which she's struggling against authority?

LANTOLF   I hope not. Though, I think it's interesting that in an earlier version of this document she had more heroic qualities. I suppose both of us have been victims of our own histories and beliefs about what good and bad language teaching is. But in our research, we have tried to filter all this out. For the record, what I quoted in my presentation is exactly as she wrote it in her diary or what was tape-recorded by her shortly after the classroom sessions. Some of the data also consist of her end-of-course reflections.

CANDLIN   In order to pursue a more ecological approach to analysis, it seems that one would want to go beyond the singular perspective of PG. I would be especially interested in what her teacher thought about his own instructional practices. Of course, instructional methodology may be shaped through cultural and institutional forms of mediation. But there may be other forms as well. For example, students bring to the classroom a whole host of expectations that may help to shape pedagogic culture. Often this results in markedly different understandings of what counts as competence in a foreign language classroom.

GEBHARD   One could also look into the individual histories of teachers. What trajectories have their personal and professional lives taken? From this perspective, it might be asked how the pedagogic culture of the language department in part derives from individual teachers' biographical histories.

If educational success depends on the alignment of certain attitudes and values between the institution and the learner, what are the implications for the development of educational identity? What moral rights do educators have to impose on students particular sets of normative identities?

LEMKE   This whole process of socializing students into various academic identities involves a great deal of imposition. Often, it means impressing on them particular attitudes, values, and affective stances that may run counter to their own cultures. If one would like to think of this in terms of the ecology metaphor, then the question becomes: How do we maintain a balance between the needs of the individual organism and the ecological system? Or, to problematize the situation even further, what happens when what's good for the institution is not so for the life of the individual or the group? It seems to me that we run up against a paradox regarding educational *empowerment.*

WEINBERG   I believe that educational success depends on socializing children into certain social and institutional identities, but which ones? This question is at the core of a passionate debate over deaf education. Over 90 percent of deaf children are born to hearing parents, most of whom have no prior experience with deafness. Parents with a deaf child must choose among philosophically different approaches to educational placement, ranging from mainstreaming the child in a regular classroom to enrolling the child in a residential school for the deaf. Most parents choose the latter. In these schools, deafness is regarded as a marker of identity, defining the group as a cultural and linguistic minority based on their common use of American Sign Language (this community defines itself as Deaf with a capital "D"). Language acquisition and language socialization in this setting are inextricably linked; the very process of placing the child in a school that uses ASL both socializes that child to the ASL community and enables the child to acquire ASL him/herself. Educational success, beyond standard measures of achievement, is defined by the extent to which the child develops a strong sense of identity as a Deaf person.

Another educational option for parents, called "mainstreaming," involves socializing the deaf child according to the hearing person's identity. The objective is to reduce the cultural "effects" of deafness as much as possible and to encourage deaf students to behave as much as possible like their hearing peers. Now, which type of educational setting is the best one? Each promotes dramatically different kinds of identity and is pushed by groups with contrasting views on deafness in society. I believe what we need is a more flexible, multilayered approach to teaching language since The Language is only one of the many things we are actually teaching. What are the implicit beliefs, values, and social norms that come with learning and using language? How do our teaching philosophies imply potential memberships in new communities, themselves requiring the development of new identities?

LARSEN-FREEMAN In talking about identity and educational socialization, I think it's important to recognize that identity is not necessarily a fixed or static entity that remains unchanged once it is acquired. We need to begin to see learner identity in all its *mutability*. The lives of learners take place in a number of varying contexts, from school to community to family. Our theoretical models must be able to capture the shifting nature of experience and the malleability of identity that comes with it.

LEMKE The word "identity" tends to get saddled with a lot of meanings. We probably need a little more slippage between the notion of identity and the notion of *role behavior* in specific social practices. Are we talking about the mutability of identity or the fluency of role behavior? Claire Kramsch has pointed out the need to distinguish between such concepts as identity, role, voice, and status.[2] Others have suggested doing away with the term "identity" altogether. I think the notion of identity, however, can still be useful in the way it serves as a nexus for the social and the individual. But we ought to use the term with a greater degree of self-reflexivity. I believe our notions of identity are very much tied to the kinds of master narratives we construct about our own place within cultures. At the same time, it is these cultures that are telling us we have to make these consistent stories about ourselves.

Notes

1. Bernstein, B. (1990) *The Structuring of Pedagogic Discourse, Volume IV: Class, Codes, and Control.* London: Routledge.
2. Kramsch, C. (forthcoming) Identity, role and voice in cross-cultural (mis)communication. In J. House, G. Kasper and S. Ross (eds) *Misunderstanding in Social Life.* London: Longman.

Part Four

Classroom rituals
and their ecologies

Ritual, face, and play in a first English lesson: Bootstrapping a classroom culture

9

Jet van Dam

Introduction

While most research on language acquisition continues to consider the individual learner largely in closed system terms, the extent to which learners' linguistic development is interdependent with their participation in specific communities of practice is now increasingly recognized. Formal language learning at school engages a *group* of learners both as social actors and as acquirers in institutional events of the type 'lesson.' Since each lesson discursively builds upon the previous one(s), an inquiry into the interdependence of socialization and acquisition inevitably leads us to 'first settings': where did it all start? How is a shared world bootstrapped in the classroom as a social multiparty situation? How does it affect the learning that goes on there?

In this chapter I present an in-depth analysis – on an incremental, almost moment-by-moment basis – of what takes place in the course of a first English as a foreign language (EFL) lesson in a Dutch secondary school, on the first day of the academic year. It is part of a small corpus of similar lessons (van Dam van Isselt 1993) and involves a group of 12- or 13-year-olds who are new to the school, new to each other, and new to the teacher. At the time of the recordings, English was not yet a compulsory subject at primary school in Holland. Some students have had two years of formal instruction in English, others one year, and some none. So, while the group was fairly homogeneous in terms of linguistic and sociocultural background (students were middle-class monolinguals, or at least fluent in Dutch) the differences in prior school knowledge were considerable.

Since my concern was with the emergence of a classroom *culture*, not with any specific teacher or student behaviors in terms of a communicative (or other) SLA orthodoxy, I adopted an approach that is multidisciplinary and *ecological* (cf. Leather and van Dam, forthcoming). It acknowledges the extent to which people in classroom situations become environments and (sometimes) resources for one another; emphasizes the need for precise, fine-grained observation and minimal *a priori* assumptions about what can be ignored; and shows how multiple cultural (sub)systems affect participation and learning (cf. Bronfenbrenner 1979; van Lier 1996, 2000). The discourse framework I use allows contexts for the interpretation of utterances and behavior to be recursively embedded, overruled, and reintroduced on a moment-by-moment basis, articulating a dynamic and complex notion of "current context" (Polanyi and Scha 1983; van Dam van Isselt 1993, 1995).

Interacting systems: a structural discourse perspective on 'the lesson'

Lessons at school are multiparty situations in which multiple cultural systems are operational and mutually interdependent: institutional systems, language systems, power systems, interactional systems, politeness systems, etc. (cf. Scollon and Scollon 1995). They can be looked upon as *cultural games* that regulate and punctuate the complex stream of events: as sets of instructions for, or constraints on, what constitutes a legitimate move in a particular game currently being played (Wittgenstein 1953).

In the classroom socialization system under scrutiny here the interaction between participant roles (cf. Goffman 1967, 1979) and politeness systems (Brown and Levinson 1987; Scollon and Scollon 1981, 1995; Goffman 1972) turned out to be especially salient. The asymmetrical role relationship that is conventionally *given* between teacher and students in institutional settings predicts that teachers may impose tasks or issue directives *bald-on-record* (Brown and Levinson 1987:60), without mitigating or indirectness strategies (Cazden 1988:166; but cf. Poole 1992). Similarly, students' errors in the classroom should not, *in principle*, endanger their claim to competence: by virtue of their classroom role they are ritually supposed "not-to-know" (Seedhouse 1997). However, displaying ignorance that is not shared by others in the social situation almost inevitably raises the issue of cultural competence at the level of classroom identities and current peer groups. Lessons at school turn out to be intrinsically face-threatening situations and, especially in the language classroom, embarassment and anxiety are common (cf. Bailey 1983; Cazden 1988:162ff.; McDermott and Tylbor 1986; Tsui 1996; MacIntyre 1999). Moreover, learning to communicate in a new language involves adopting a new speaker role (cf. Kramsch 1993). Being (partially) inarticulate in this new role or anticipating failure in expressing oneself appropriately in the public classroom situation may negatively affect opportunities for feedback – and thus slow down linguistic development. How effective face and feedback conditions are negotiated over time as a result of the organization of multiparty interactions – rather than residing in discrete speech acts – is worth investigating (cf. Arundale 1999).

A few brief words on the dynamic discourse model I use to address these issues will have to suffice here (Polanyi 1988; see also Chapter 10 in this volume). When the bell rings, a set of *specific* conventions for speech events of the type "lesson" and *specific* constraints on who can do or say what, overrule default cultural conventions for the co-ordination of utterances and interactional behavior. But ongoing lesson units may also be interrupted for "other business" or recursively embedded (nested), allowing the role relationship between participants to shift or become more complex accordingly. Conversational turns at talk may be imbedded within lesson turns-in-progress; "selves" (current speaking roles) within other "selves." These changes in "footing" (Goffman 1979) at microlevels of the interaction ("Who is currently speaking to whom in what role? Who else is addressed? Who act as if they are not present?") may strategically reconcile the sometimes contradictory demands of lesson situations by realizing different moves in *stacked* frames for the interpretation of events.

What is "the" context in which an utterance is to be interpreted is resolved on a moment-by-moment basis. The model accepts incomplete utterances (turn segments) as meaningful units ("discourse constituent units" or "dcus"), and also reads nonverbal, paralinguistic and prosodic features of talk as input (laughter, whisper, loud voice, changes in tempo, intonation and timing; cf. Scollon 1982). These often signal the structural changes referred to above ("discourse POP and PUSH markers"). Understanding a situation may involve the reanalysis of a move or series of moves in terms of a different set of contextual parameters that are selected online (see sections below on spelling games and virtual dialog). Such *emergent readings of the situation* are implied in the way participants undertake their next moves.

A first English lesson: bootstrapping a classroom culture

The detailed analysis of this particular lesson was undertaken because I had the impression that participation and motivation had been high throughout; that no one had failed or had been excluded and no one had been bored – and that a lot of learning had taken place. I wanted to verify these intuitions, or at least try to articulate what they were based on: they might have relevance beyond the single case. I revisited the same group twice later in the same year (after three weeks, and at the end of the school year) and will venture some tentative remarks on the longer-term evolution of this particular classroom socialization system below. The teacher is an experienced EFL teacher, friend, and ex-colleague of the researcher.

Pre-lesson business: emergent feedback and face systems

First day of the school year, sixth lesson, 1.30 PM. When the bell rings, the new students come in noisily and look for their allocated places, according to a seating plan they were given in the morning. There is some confusion because two large pillars in the middle of the room obstruct the unambiguous matching of students and places in the conventional rows of twos and threes. The teacher walks over to the trouble area and addresses some students there: "Uh – may I ask you something? – do you all sit according to the seating-plan?"[1] Together they solve the problem. The use of indirectness strategies here (ask whether she can ask) may seem odd for a teacher who has the right to ask these types of questions. However, she is addressing total strangers and pays them due respect when interrupting their talk. Presumably, then, this is not yet "the lesson."

When student names have been checked and the coursebooks are on the desks, the teacher walks up to the front of the class. She briefly explains the organization of the coursebook and introduces some routines to be followed in lessons to come. Procedural business is rounded off by a precloser in the nature of a comprehension check (line 1) and an emphatic urge to please speak up if there is a problem:

1   Teacher   OK? – is that clear to everybody? – [looks around] do not
                 hesitate to ask if there's anything you don't understand
                 – it's just been a long STORY on my part and if I haven't
                 been QUITE clear about things you should always ASK
5   – DON'T go home thinking [pseudo student voice]
                 "GOODness knows what that creature has been
                 gibbering about – but as for me – I really haven't got a
                 clue!" – [back to own voice; emphatically] – PLEASE ask
                 – I just LOVE children who ask questions!
10 Class   [chuckle]

In almost any situation it is dispreferred to explicitly, verbally display a lack of understanding. A procedural reason for this is that such displays are implicit questions which, in calling for an answer (explanation), constitute an interruption: they disrupt the smooth continuation of the discourse-so-far. Normative expectations for what would have been a relevant next move in the current game are temporarily overruled. They must be stored or saved to be returned to as soon as the embedded trouble is over (cf. "where were we?"). Misunderstandings and repair sequences – both inside and out of the classroom – by definition introduce this structural complexity in the discourse; hence their dispreferred status (cf. "system constraints"; Goffman 1967).

But there are also "ritual constraints" (ibid.) on public displays of nonunderstanding. These differ from culture to culture and from situation to situation. The teacher's closing remarks highlight her awareness of how important it is to get the feedback mechanism in this new learning group in good working order. If students are reluctant to speak up for fear they are the only ones "not knowing,"[2] misunderstandings may persist. This is particularly important for first lessons: gatekeeping events (Erickson and Schultz 1982) that set the norm for lessons to come.

The teacher employs various strategies to get the students to speak up. She herself is to blame, she says, if anything was unclear, because she delivered this long monolog ("story"; line 3). For extra authenticity she borrows an imaginary student's irreverent voice, symbolically modeling rather than addressing the subgroup of students targeted (lines 6–8; cf. Goffman 1981:149ff.; the concept of heteroglossia or "double-voicing," Bakhtin 1981:360; Rampton 1995:222): those who are at a loss and reluctant to say so but brag about it outside class. Note, however, that no specific student is implied.

The proposition about herself ("I just love children who ask questions") is uttered in yet another theatrical stance: a parody on slightly hysterical ladies who are hooked on chocolate, for instance. Uttered in tongue-in-cheek manner, it raises the expectation that spontaneous, publicly displayed instances of not-understanding, in this lesson and in lessons to come, will be appreciated and attended to rather than meet with irritation or ridicule. More importantly, perhaps, it introduces an element of play and affection in the classroom (cf. Sullivan 2000). The students chuckle. They have learned to be skeptical about these types of claims – and rightly so. Inopportune questions disrupt the lesson agenda (see above) and are often strategically ignored or negatively assessed by both teachers and peers. Unless validated over time by successful teacher strategies these are empty claims that *suggest* but do not *guarantee* that one is safe "not knowing" in this emergent community of learning.

A moment later, in yet another digression that delays the beginning of the lesson proper, the teacher topicalizes the differences in target language proficiency that exist among the students:

11 Teacher u::hm – YES well perhaps we'd better just REALly start
                with something now – let me see – unDOUBTedly there
                are some people among you who have had some
                English at primary school – but also people who
                HAVEN't – people who have had ONE year – or TWO
17   years – so you all start from unequal positions – but
                that usually adjusts itself soon enough ...

The teacher emphasizes that differences in target language proficiency are the *normal*, logical outcome of circumstances beyond one's personal control. They do not reflect on anyone's social identity. Moreover, the effects of their different schooling histories will soon wear off, she assures them. Them? Again, her remarks primarily address the hypothetical anxieties of the less proficient members of the classroom population – without identifying them as such. And again, these assertions can only be verified over time.

The teacher brings up these issues as an aside in the context of the beginning of the actual lesson being imminent. They are the cultural backdrop that contextualizes the learning that is to come. Differences between students are not on the agenda.[3] They are taken for granted as a normal fact of life that will be accommodated in lessons to come, not something to hide or worry about. A context-sensitive face system is introduced (cf. Arminen 2000).

The first class question: interaction of face and turn systems in the discursive construction of competence

The first class question is framed as probing "common ground" (Edwards and Mercer 1987, Chapter 5) and continues the theme of the unequal distribution of knowledge. In this new group the teacher has no way of knowing "who knows what." She uses a bid-for-the-turn procedure to recruit a competent next speaker. This may be considered both a deference and a solidarity politeness strategy (Scollon and Scollon 1981): it does not oblige any specific student to speak up and at the same time minimizes the risk of an incompetent answer. It merges conversational and institutional turn exchange systems and produces "mixed values" for next speaker selection: the students self-select (default egalitarian roles); the teacher allocates within that subset (classroom roles). The invitation to self-select does not yield a volunteer:

18	Teacher	let's just see who knows what – for instance who would uh – be able to COUNT – [low pitch] something simple in English [fast] you may find that a stupid question but still – [back to normal pitch; looks round] from ONE to TWENTY – WHO can do that in English?
23	Class	[no volunteers]

Most Dutch children have been exposed to some English in what is perhaps mistakenly called a monolingual society, and counting is among the first routines to be learnt at a very young age. But that observation leads us to the other horn of the dilemma: the constraint on asking trivial ("stupid") questions. They can be an insult to addressees' face – and in multiparty situations need not be responded to (McHoul 1978). The teacher's *sotto voce* aside (lines 19/21) implicitly addresses these issues, but she asks the question anyway – fine-tuning it to the competencies of different subsets of students. It is presented as both a challenge and a safe ride:

24	Teacher	with a MAGNIFICENT pronunciation – [laughs] a ROTTEN one is OK too
26	Class	[still no volunteers]

Mispronunciations are more face-threatening than other types of errors. They have the status of cultural "faux-pas" as well as classroom errors and are more likely to elicit laughter or ridicule. When the attempt to defuse even that hypothetical fear is unsuccessful, the teacher makes use of her ritual classroom right and nominates a next speaker. But the delay testifies to the *dispreferred* status of the allocation:[4]

27	Teacher	Well – I'll just pick someone uh – from the class list
	Class	[buzz; whisper]
	Teacher	[looks up from class list] Uhm – MARK – can YOU do it?
	Mark	[starts counting] *ONE – TWO – THREE* =
31→	Teacher	= [interrupts] CAN you?
	Mark	uh: – well – uh up to ten only
33	Teacher	up to ten – OK – then someone else will take over – just try

The turn allocation is marked as dispreferred not only by being delayed, but also by being *mentioned* as well as *used* (line 27; Levinson 1983:247) and by the marker "well" which often indicates a breach of normative discourse expectations (Schiffrin 1987:126). Also, it is made optional on the nominee's ability to answer the question by spelling out the *felicity conditions* (Searle 1969) under which the allocation becomes operational (lines 29; 31): the nominated student may still opt out.

But Mark has already embarked on his answer. He has interpreted the teacher question as a classroom command to do the relevant next action, not a request for information. The ambiguity of the question is brought home by a marked interruption on the part of the teacher (line 31) of a turn-in-progress that is completely unproblematic so far: she insists on a "real" answer to her "real" question. It turns out the interruption had a point;[5] it addressed a virtual error, not a current one. Mark is only partially competent in the context of the question. His feedback causes the parameters of the task to be reset; someone else will do the second part. Owing to the teacher's intervention, a student's not-knowing did not surface as an interactional *event* in the classroom situation, but as a metacommunication about classroom events: a self-assessment that is neutral with respect to face.

The teacher's violation of the *conversational* constraint on interrupting turns-in-progress has resulted in an update of classroom expectations for the upcoming turn. There is now a *discursively constructed* expectation that Mark can do the job. He resumes his interrupted turn:

35	Mark	*one – two – three – four – five – six – seven – eight – nine – teen* [D. tien?] =
→	Teacher	[latching; very fast, *sotto voce*]=ten=
	Mark	=ten
39	Teacher	very good – who can go on?

Mark's mistake in the last item of the list has a different status from errors produced in unnegotiated speaking slots. In the context of a claim to competence even a minor slip may endanger one's face. A teacher invitation to self-correct – the preferred format according to many classroom studies (McHoul 1990) – would have topicalized the error without yielding self-repair. Mark's "teen" is probably an overgeneralization based on compounds like "eigh*teen*"; "nine*teen*" – a rational hypothesis, not a fault. One just has to be told.

The teacher again uses a structural strategy. The snappy timing and *sotto voce* production of "ten" mark it as a change in footing in which she briefly distances herself from her teacher role. It is framed as an off-record move (much like peer prompts) that we are not supposed to notice – not an other-correction that occupies "next turn." It enables Mark as the overhearer of the correct answer to "overwrite" his error (cf. Hockett 1973:100) in the same turn segment that a singly-authored self-correction would occupy. His updated answer is followed by a conventional third-place teacher evaluation move: he has done well (line 39).

Other students are now recruited more easily, and count from 10 to 20, and in decades up to one hundred. Occasionally they make mistakes. Since all turns consist of *lists* of English numbers, any errors that are produced occur in *subunits* of turns. As before, they are framed as minor, *partial* errors in the context of overall competent answers.

As we have seen, the teacher consistently uses *structural discourse strategies*: what constitutes a turn at talk, who authors it and what is a correct answer is context-dependent. It is an *emergent* feature of interactional situations that crucially involves prosody and timing as well as the words that are spoken (Scollon 1982). According to Ochs (1992:353) the collusive co-authoring that frames a learner move as a single-author accomplishment is typical of Western models of socialization that minimize the asymmetrical distribution of knowledge between acquirers and caregivers or teachers.

Chorusing the alphabet: affordances for phonological learning

The "counting" episode went very well and the whole class is praised. There is a suggestion that their doing well precipitated the transition to a next, "more difficult" topic. Again the bid-for-the turn procedure fails to yield a volunteer, but there is now a change in strategy:

40	Teacher	WELL – that's going REALLY well folks – we can push on at once to a more difficult topic – SPELLING – can anyone do that?
	Class	(…) [mumbling; frowns]
44	Teacher	yes that's tricky – that's REALLY quite tricky [looks worried]
	Ss	[laughter]
47	Teacher	OK then – I'm going to say the alphabet out loud – if anyone KNOWS it
49	→	and thinks "AH I can do that too" – then you – then that person joins in – OK? [looks around] – I start – and if you know how to say something you
52	→	join in – and then you keep quiet again – and then you join in again and keep quiet and so on – just see what you can do –
55	Teacher and Class	$A : B : C : D : E : F : G :$ [fast, low pitch] well done $H:$ (etc.) =A =B =C [simile; just off-beat] – =H

Probably cued by observable signs of anticipated difficulty in class (line 43), the teacher decides to repair the dyadic participation structure (cf. "OK *then;*" line 47). They are going to "say the alphabet" all together and she will take the lead. Her detailed instructions emphasize that all students are able to participate in this collective chorusing. This time (cf. lines 6–8, cited earlier) the voice of a *competent* student is modeled (line 49): choir leaders are needed to scaffold wavering voices.

Participation in the choir is defined entirely in terms of *self-selection*, and self-selection on a split-second, local basis across modalities: even silent participation modes are possible (lines 52–54). Students are free to decide *whether* to participate, *when* to participate, and *how* to participate (loud voice; whisper voice; no voice, silent lip-modeling), in accordance with self-monitored measures of competence and confidence. There are no public evaluation slots in this ritual speaking format: *everyone* is "the speaker."

The routine is repeated three times, preceded by brief comments: "those people who couldn't – try and join in now – see what you can do – it doesn't matter if you make mistakes." Indeed it doesn't. Individual errors are not publicly noticed but drowned or made anonymous in the chorus – except, perhaps, for an occasional glance from a neighboring peer. But this occasional noticing of mismatches is mutual. It also enables students as overhearers of the output of more competent others in their immediate environment to do peer-scaffolded self-corrections and "first tries," by coming in late at the fuzzy edges of speaking-slots-in-progress.

In between reruns, the teacher comments on some particularly troublesome letters that show up as persistent, collectively-authored "false notes." For the last round ("now EVERYONE will be able to join in") she requests "a nice FULL CHOIR please!" – which she gets. The increased volume is evidence that more students participated all of the time (and I daresay *all* students participated *some* of the time). Of course, we cannot exactly measure the learning for each student, or count how many diffident students "became speakers" in the third round. Interactional modifications take place in off-record subfloors: whatever learning occurs is screened off from public inspection.

As far as I know the redeeming features of "chorusing" – a stigmatized participation frame in communicative methodology – have not been explored in depth.[6] It is often reductionistically thought of in terms of *speaking roles* only, and inauthentic ones at that. In fact, as in a real choir, tempo and rhythm are crucial (Scollon 1982). It is a performance mode that combines hearing, speaking and overhearing roles in cultural ensembles that create their own discourse world.

"False notes" do not really matter and their instant repair does not disrupt the rhythm: they are done before "next slot" becomes "actual" in the collectively-authored performance. The complex sound-clusters are evidence of participation and learning but they cannot be unravelled: Charles Ives[7] would have been delighted and would have composed them in – as the teacher did.

The participation structure affords differential opportunities for students to do "inner speaking" (Ohta 2000), to become speakers or better speakers, to repair and update within and across participation modes. Learning is synchronized in a format that provides for both the involvement and the independence needs of individual students.

Time out. "Wasp hunt:" cultural and classroom scenarios

Before the last round the teacher invited the students to look at the grammar section of the coursebook and the symbols of the phonetic alphabet (see also section on spelling games 3 below). When she asks them what "grammar" is, a wasp circles around the teacher's head and she interrupts herself: "Go away –YOU!" The wasp doesn't comply. Some students get up and start chasing it across the classroom. After a dramatic "Yes – I'm afraid there'll have to be a dead body here!" from the teacher, classroom order is really in jeopardy. The teacher now raises her voice: "IN YOUR SEATS – all of you – we have ONE murderer among us – WHO volunteers to do the job?" A contract killer is appointed (turn allocation!) and cheered on by all, the teacher included. The "kill" elicits various comments from the other students, both in Dutch and in English ("*wasp soup!*"). The teacher joins in: "nice prodding," thanks the wasp killer and then resumes the lesson where it had been interrupted: "we were – TALKing – [looks pointedly at some students who are still talking] about GRAM-mar ...." The class slowly settles down and they do one more round of the alphabet.

The whole episode took under two minutes. A classroom incident has been reframed and dramatized as a cultural scenario that involves teacher and students on equal terms (for a more elaborate discussion of this episode, see van Dam van Isselt 1995).

Spelling games 1: classroom face and shared linguistic metasystems

The next activity is framed as a suggestion rather than agenda business (cf. Poole 1992:609; "teachers *have* agendas but avoid implementing them in a direct manner"): "Shall we try and see if we can make up some English words?" The teacher slowly spells the letters of some simple English words and writes them on the blackboard. Then they start "for real:" "of course you do not yet know all of the – uh – pronunciations, but we'll see how far we get – you'll probably all have different answers." She slowly spells /biː/ - /ou/ - /diː/ - /wai/ and the students write down what they hear.

The first three letters of the English word "body" are very similar in pronunciation to their Dutch equivalents; the last one, however, does not exist as such in the Dutch alphabet. English *y* is a predictable source of trouble for Dutch learners because its initial sound resembles that of Dutch *w* [/weː/]. When she has finished, the teacher asks whether any outcomes look like a possible English word. Some students enthusiastically shout: "body!" The teacher continues:

58	Teacher	RIGHT – this is what should have been there [writes *body* on blackboard]
	Sx	=[enthusiastic] *body*! – a match!
	Sx	=[fall-rise tone of surprise] OH?!
62	Teacher→	were you more or less able to cope? – [looks around] – or not at all?
	Ss	//NO! // hè – hè [tone of self-reproach]// that last letter (that wasn't ..) //
66	Ss	//the last one // the last letter// (last … funny)

By contextualizing the correct answer as "what should have been there" (line 58) the teacher implies that she does not think this is what actually is *there*, i.e. in the exercise books of the students. Her remark sets up incorrect or partially incorrect answers as the norm. The request for feedback in line 62 reinforces that impression: it implicitly addresses the subset of students who had minor or major problems with the task. The others are momentarily framed as outsiders. It may not be accidental that the students *en masse*, spontaneously, report their errors. The teacher turns to one of them:

67	Teacher	[turns to Sx] did you get it? – or didn't you?
	Sx	NO – I had the last letter a "w" [/weː/ (Dutch *w*)]
	Teacher	OH – you got mixed up of course – because I said "y" – you naturally thought it was a "w" [/weː / (Dutch *w*)]
	Sx	Yes
72	Teacher	Yeah – I see – makes sense – ALL RIGHT – we'll do another one.

The turn allocation (line 67) is again phrased in such a way that the student addressed can opt out: she does not *have to* say she got it wrong – but she does. This paves the way for the teacher to do an attribution (Scollon and Scollon 1981:178ff.) or make an "expressed guess" ("OH – you naturally thought …") of the mindset that caused the error (Ochs 1992:352). When linguistic metasystems are shared, attributions may be done with some confidence. The teacher's guess was right and together they reconstruct the processing strategies that led to the production of the error. It acquires the status of a "good fault" when its rationality in terms of the two linguistic systems that are simultaneously accessed is recognized. It is perfectly natural for this beginning learner – and the indirectly addressed others who had the same problem – to confuse the two systems at this stage. Learner errors do not matter if their unmarked status that is ritually *given* for classroom situations is also locally, interactionally confirmed.

Spelling games 2: reframing learner errors

There are considerable "technical" difficulties involved in transcribing classroom acquisition data. Interlanguage errors, mixed forms, inaudible and incomplete contributions may make it difficult to tell even what language an utterance is in (cf. Scollon, Chapter 5 of this volume). Clearly these problems do not exist for the analyst alone; they also have to be resolved online by the participants themselves in classroom situations. The following episode is particularly difficult to transcribe and I will render it anecdotally. It addresses the status and effect of bald-on-record negative evaluations of learner answers: "no" or "wrong" + teacher feedback.

Seedhouse (1997) deplores the fact that direct negative evaluations of student answers in form-and-accuracy contexts are rare in classroom talk. He argues that indirectness strategies and mitigating strategies in following up learner errors *interactionally* transmit the message that making errors is embarrassing, and raise the issue of face-loss rather than resolving it (567). Mitigated forms of feedback are therefore inefficient, he says, both pedagogically and in terms of class time. In the lesson under scrutiny here I found only two instances of direct unmitigated negative evaluations on the part of the teacher. In order to find out whether they support Seedhouse's argument I will analyze one of them below. It occurs toward the end of the spelling episode and involves a series of such negative evaluations.

The letters of the word "library" (where the protagonist in the coursebook, the ill-fated anti-hero Arthur works) had just been read out in class. A girl volunteered to say what she had made of this. It turned out she had analyzed each of the letters as one-syllable English words: i.e. "*I*," "*be*," and "*are*" for the letters *i*, *b*, and *r* respectively. The teacher responds to each answer-segment with an unmodulated other-correction: "no, it's just a b;" or "no, just r" (how she understood that the girl was saying the words "*be*" and "*are*" rather than the names of the letters *b* and *r* is still unclear to me). In any case, near-homophones are involved and it was some time before the teacher realized the structural nature of the misunderstanding.

Apparently the teacher, in rejecting each incoming turn-segment, had simultaneously inspected it for its underlying systematicity in the series as a whole. Having identified under what assumptions all of these answers would have been correct, she now *retrospectively* constructs face for all of them. They are recognized as possible and rational answers in some noncurrent context: "Oh I see! – quite – it *could* have been that way yes – but – in spelling we usually take each letter separately ... [further explanations] you see what I mean?" The negative evaluations are overruled. The errors are made subunits in an emergent larger discourse unit, which is constructed online, and which recontextualizes all four of them as "culturally correct" under different presuppositions: after all, when spelling words over the telephone we often use names to refer to letters.

Seedhouse only has half a point. Immediate direct feedback to learner errors can be combined with the construction of face in a higher-order cultural domain. The effect of feedback strategies cannot be investigated without considering *emerging interpretations* in the discourse contexts in which they occur. Just counting instances will not tell us their social "meaning:" how they may realize complex values in more than one face system.

Spelling games 3: notions of normativity in the construction of excellence

One may wonder whether the consistent use of face-saving strategies and the normative status of not-knowing do justice to the more proficient students in the group. Are they framed as outsiders? Are they bored? Here's the last subunit of the spelling episode:

74	Teacher	shall I do a REALLY difficult word – with lots of "g"s and "h"s ? =
	Ss	=yes!//yes!=
	Teacher	=just to see how far you get? – a word that you do not know?
79	Ss	yes!// [nods]

Again, the transition to next class business is presented as a negotiated one: it is up to the students to decide whether they want to do a very difficult item. The challenge is accepted. Failing in the context of such a task can hardly be a threat to anyone's face. The teacher spells the word *exaggerate* slowly and says she is curious whether anyone could make sense out of it: "I told you this was a really difficult one!"

There is laughter and the students compete in self-deprecating comments ("ahum – abacadabra!") and word play with exaggerated (!) gutturals in L1-Dutch phonology. The teacher writes the monster on the blackboard, explains its meaning, and asks who got it right:

80   Ss   [some hands are raised]
     Teacher [counts] ONE TWO THREE FOUR! – VE:RY good –
                  VE:RY good=
     Ss   =I had two "j"'s instead of two "g"'s// two "j"'s//
                  instead of "g"'s// me too!
85 Teacher well that's OK – I can see why – but everyone
                  understands how it works?

The teacher is generous in her praise and seems to be genuinely surprised: this was an exceptionally difficult word and the four students who got it right did extremely well. It is clear, moreover, that the smart can be constructed as smart without constructing the nonsmart as "dumb":[8] the other students compete publicly, spontaneously reporting their errors. Given resourceful discursive contextualization, praising excellence may interactionally confirm the expectation that it is *normal* "not to know."

I mentioned that some students make fun of their utter failure to deal with this tricky word – thus creating a diversion that meets with appreciative laughter in class. Bragging about "gaffes" and blunders is part of school life. They involve a "play on face" that may enhance rather than diminish one's status in the peer group. When we blunder we want to recover with poise. But blundering may also be topicalized and recontextualized as a feat in the eyes of one's peers (Rampton 1995). Self-reported, after-the-fact, errors do not involve face-loss: they are not classroom events but metacommunications about events in a story world (cf. Bateson 1972).

Earlier in the lesson the teacher had suggested that those who already knew the alphabet might try and read the symbols of the International Phonetic Alphabet (IPA) in the back of the book at the same time: "maybe you can recognize a few." We don't know whether they did, but it is clear that tasks can be finely tuned to the differential abilities of students. The "smart ones" may do a more challenging version of the "same" task – without having to identify themselves as such.

"Ottiwell Wood": cultural frames as classroom practice

Immediately after the preceding episode the teacher rounds off the topic "English alphabet" with a rhyming chant. She writes the name

"Ottiwell Wood" on the blackboard (T: "[*sotto voce]* idiotic name!"), then turns round and surprises everyone with a sudden, *prestissimo:*

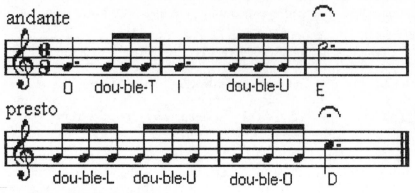

Figure 9.1 *Ottiwell Wood*

The students are stunned and laugh. She repeats the chant more slowly, and they are invited to join in. They do so with gusto. Then the graded participation cycle starts all over again: first slowly in chorus, then faster, then without the teacher scaffolding. Eventually individual students are invited to perform ("just try") – and there are lots of volunteers now. The teacher praises a student who is particularly fluent and fast, adding that "just once" there was a student who beat her at speed.

The spelling chant is made homework for the next lesson. A challenge is implied. These students may also become "better than the teacher" (a reversal of ritual classroom roles). They are not in competition with each other, but as a team against a virtual peer. And also – perhaps more importantly – they may impress siblings and parents by performing their newly-acquired L2 skills out of school. Rhyming chants are authentic cultural frames. Being able to perform them fast and faultlessly marks the emergence of a competent *L2 animator* (Goffman 1979) – even after one English lesson. In retrospect the spelling games were "communicative" after all: classroom practice for cultural speaking roles.

Reframing the "self:" emergent, virtual, and dispreferred classroom identities

The language socialization perspective on acquisition raises the question: To what degree does speaking in another language entail a reframing of the self? Some language teachers consistently assign target language names to their students, which the latter may or may not take as an imposition. Students in classrooms may also find themselves without *any* currently appropriate identity owing to ill-understood complexities that arise in classroom talk – as I will show below.

Immediately after the "Ottiwell Wood" episode, the teacher announces that they will now go on with *"what's your name, what's my name, I am so-and-so – that kind of thing"* – hardly a *communicative* way of launching introduction pairs. The questions are explicitly contextualized as "phrases one can say or ask" rather than direct speech acts. However, she rejects the one that involves the first-person form of the English possessive pronoun system on the grounds that it is irrelevant and trivial (cf. Sullivan 2000:83):

87   Teacher   WELL – I think it is a bit ODD to ask *"what's MY name"*
              – because one normally knows that – but what I CAN
              say for instance [turns to Freek] is –
90   *what's YOUR name?*

The teacher addresses a student called "Freek" who sits near her in the front of the class. He volunteered earlier in the lesson and is probably one of the students who has had English at primary school: he recognizes the classroom game. His answer in the full-sentence format incorporates a new L2-based identity, and is uttered in a theatrical stance to match: with hypercorrect British-English voice and intonation.

91   SF   *"My name is Frederic"* (low fall; caricatured British
              voice and phonology] =
     Sx   =[clearly audible dramatic stage-whisper] *M i s – t e r
              "X"!*
95   Teacher   [imitates, recitation mode] *"My name is – Frederic"* –
              [dreamily; "middle distance" look] MOO:I hè! (E.
              BEAU:tiful, isn't it) – [echoes again] *"my name is
              Frederic'*

Freek's answer is a beautifully co-operative "lesson" answer framed as a theatrical performance. The teacher acknowledges the "extra quality" in a brief instance of staged self-talk in Dutch: "BEAUtiful, isn't it?" (line 97). It is heavily marked (code switch; prosodic and visual markers; tag) as a *free ride* in the lesson sequence, an off-record aside to be overheard rather than a third-place teacher evaluation move in the dyadic interaction with Freek. She momentarily distances herself from her teacher role, accommodating her footing to his theatrical stance. The half-off-record comment constructs an *audience* that, she implies, shares in her appreciation. It sets up Freek as the overhearer of *collusive byplay* between herself and the rest of the class (Goffman 1981:134).

There is a case for interpreting the teacher's enthusiastic response in Dutch as setting up expectations beyond the current interaction with Freek: a first question–answer pair in a list often sets up normative expectations for what is to follow (Schegloff 1979). The next student, Hans, now has a problem:

99	Teacher	*and uh* – [turns to Hans] *what's YOUR name?*
	SH	[looks worried, pulls face] ja – uh God – u::h – nou ((E. yes- uh – my God – u::h – well)) [shrugs shoulders; blushes] –
103		[grunts; "low Dutch" pronunciation] uh – ↓ HANS
	Class	[grins; laughter]
105	Teacher	*I don't want to hear "HANS" – I want to hear "my NAME is Hans."*
	SH	O-OH! [high-fall "relief" tone] – [repeats] *"my name is Hans"*

Hans seems to want to give an equally "beautiful" answer: construct an L2 identity for himself to fit the English sentence frame set up by the previous student. But apparently he cannot think of an English equivalent for the Dutch name "Hans."[9] His body language and the multiple hesitation markers are evidence of his embarrassment. His answer – when eventually it is produced – is heavily marked as *dispreferred*, as a defeat, both by the delay and by being pronounced with very marked "low-Dutch" phonology and prosody. In this context his L1-based "real" name apparently takes on the value of a classroom fault.

As in the earlier "exaggerate" episode, it is precisely because Hans manages to metacommunicate about his "error" that his face is saved, and perhaps even enhanced.[10] Paradoxically, by negatively framing his default L1-based self, he increases respect for it in the peer domain. Most of the other students intuitively understood the nature of Hans' predicament, it seems. There were grins and laughter, clearly of the affiliative kind. The attempt that failed – like so many "faults" – created a welcome diversion in what might have become a relentlessly artificial classroom routine.

The teacher, however, did not join in the laughter this time. She seemed to be missing out on something. All she wanted to hear was the full-sentence format. Hans obediently echoes her model, his update-marker "O-oh!" expressing both surprise and relief: "is that all?" – evidence perhaps that he had indeed set himself a more difficult task.

As this was the *only* overt instance of student embarrassment in the lesson, it may have the status of a "fault" in this particular classroom socialization system and is worth investigating in more depth. The teacher apparently was not aware that her embedded aside in Dutch could be read as having structural implications *beyond* the local interaction with Freek. She therefore did not understand the "double bind" it could create for subsequent speakers like Hans. It is often overlooked that student "errors" – and jokes – may have their origin in linguistic sophistication and an awareness of structural discourse issues – not the lack of these. Again, this was a "good" fault.

Up to this point I have followed the perspective of the teacher – and of much classroom research – in ignoring the spontaneous contribution in English from the overhearer floor: the dramatically-whispered but clearly audible "Mis-ter 'X'." In terms of the classroom game it does not *count* as a turn at talk: it was not sollicited by the teacher and she has the right to ignore it (McHoul 1978). But teachers and students both exploit the interactional niches of classroom talk for realizing their agendas (Mehan 1979: van Dam, forthcoming). The play on frames implied in this utterance is "on topic" as well as beautifully coherent at all levels of the interaction: it is a perfectly correct "English lesson" answer; it solves the dilemma that results from having to refer to one's Dutch identity in an English sentence frame; it is a play upon the artificiality inherent in ritual classroom question–answer sequences: it may be unclear what one's currently-relevant identity is (see above), or one may wish not to disclose it. Nonlesson frames and speaker roles can be playfully introduced in off-record speaking slots, that, being illegitimate, do not require a response.

Ritual dialog: grammar as conversational prefabs

The "what's your name; what's his/her name" episode caused a great deal of confusion and repair work. Sometimes the students *really* did not know each other's names; they came up with short form answers and then "forgot" which name to insert in the full-sentence frame; referentially wrong names in correct sentences were positively evaluated by the teacher – faults that, as shown above, were a source of great hilarity.

The teacher soon abandons the dyadic format and starts an all-class dialog. The phrases that had been introduced in the conversational interactions are now decontextualized and drilled, cued by L1 prompts:[11]

109	Teacher	U:HM – so what have we heard so far – if you say
		"het is MIJN naam or MIJN boek" then you say it's – ?
	Class	[together] *MY name*

	Teacher	*MY name or MY book or MY house* – and if I ask
113		"wat is HAAR naam?" then we say – ?
	Class	[together] *HER name*
115	Teacher	*HER name or HER book or HER car* – but I also asked (etc.)

The English possessive pronoun system is taught in an utterly noncommunicative drill: L1-based prompts elicit L2 translations, not "answers." The teacher continues:

117	Teacher	now I CAN say *my name is Mrs van Polanen* but I can also say *I AM Mrs van Polanen* and – u:h – if I want to say JIJ bent uh Jan then I say – ?
	Class	[together] *you are* =
120	Teacher	= *you are Jan* – uh::m let me see – what other names do I know …

It does not matter now what real-world persons are referred to. The teacher introduces fixed discourse entities that are mentioned in formulaic phrases containing forms of the English pronoun system and forms of "to be" (also: "you are pupils"; "we are people"). She thus builds up a small corpus of stock phrases which are elicited "on cue" as "*prefabricated chunks*" in various repetition-with-minimal-variation frames. The students as collective speakers have to monitor "when is a context" (Erickson and Schultz 1981) but right now they need not worry *what* it is. Conventional speech act and pragmatic implications or ambiguities are temporarily overruled in this ritual classroom dialog. The phrases must be produced in the appropriate slots in time with the classroom interactional rhythm: "a teething ring for utterances" as well as a ball game (Goffman 1981:151, on primary language socialization). The cues for producing the appropriate second-pair-parts are locally introduced and the variety of the elicitation frames (L1 question-L2 question; L2 question-L2answer; L2 prompt-L2 paraphrase) is gradually increased. In the end the response formats are cued by gesture only, without mediation by the L1.

At age 12 one does not have to relearn social life from scratch: these are "meaningful answers" only in the ritual sense. In order to keep up one's end of the conversation game, retrieval of the appropriate L2 phrases must be prompt and automatic. Contexts for utterances change on a moment-by-moment basis and the cues that index these changes must be attended to (cf. Erickson and Schultz 1981). That is what seems to be "learnt" in this form-focused lesson episode.

Lesson closure: cultural and classroom games

The last item on the lesson agenda – listening to a song and co-singing its refrain – had to be abandoned because the tape-recorder broke down. The cacophony of sounds elicited spontaneous comments from the students, in different languages: "kaput!" (German for "out of order") and *"it's ONE BLUR"* can be heard on the tape. The teacher calls in the help of an expert student – to no avail. She resets the agenda: they will do a guessing game instead. One student leaves the classroom and, on re-entering, has to guess which object the class has chosen to be "it." The teacher now is very strict and insists they follow the rules of the game: "No" is an incorrect answer; it has to be "No, it isn't."

As in some of the earlier episodes, the students seem to be totally involved and there is evidence of great "flow"[12] (Csikszentmihalyi 1990): "WARM! – WARMER! – HOT-HOT-HOT – CO:LD – CO:LDER – ICECREAM [laughter] – ICE – ICE" (overtaken by the bell). Again the ritual game allows for linguistic creativity and play in the margins of conventional answers (Sullivan 2000:126).

The evolution of a lesson system

I revisited the same group after three-and-a-half weeks, in September (lesson 7), and again toward the end of the school year. In both lessons student participation was consistently high, but the participation frames themselves had changed. In September there were fewer all-class recitation episodes. The students now acted out scenes from the coursebook, having intensively rehearsed each text in previous lessons. Weaker students were assigned verbally less demanding (but comical, and therefore rewarding) parts. Book in hand, the actors performed their semi-memorized roles with great enthusiasm and remarkable "authenticity" (fluency, intonation, phonology). There is great hilarity in the audience when an actor fails to co-ordinate his verbal and nonverbal behavior and says "Here you are, Sir" without putting the bottle on the restaurant table. Once in a while the teacher does *sotto voce* repairs or prompts. After three performances with different sets of actors, followed by all-class applause, the students demand yet another rerun and burst out into collective rhythmical chanting: *"an-O-ther-TIME - - an-O-ther-TIME"* – but they are bribed into doing some routine class work first: then the performances will be resumed.

The lesson in May contained more dyadic teacher–student exchanges, some play-acting, and some pair work. The all-class format is shifted to mainly for repair, for instance for rehearsing (in recitation mode) some irregular verbs that proved particularly troublesome.

Comments from the sidelines (in English and Dutch) have increased and are selectively responded to, rebuked, or ignored. Politeness strategies have become much more direct for instructions and corrections of behavior, but turns and tasks are still delicately tuned to the abilities of individual students. And – there is always an element of play. Verbal dueling, mild teasing, and creative frame play in the margins of lesson activities are frequent. They are initiated by both the teacher and the students and extend the notion of what is "the lesson" by exploiting all available linguistic codes and registers: the "interactive juggling between play and seriousness" (Rampton 1995:75) that is such a defining feature of this teacher's professional style (cf. Cook 1997; Sullivan 2000).

Concluding discussion

> Almost all of what takes place in this class is group centered. Learning is a social event, not an individual endeavor. The activities in this classroom are *unlike those in most others* (my italics), where the typical learning strategy matches one learner with a text: [...] ; where individuals compete against each other [...] and where students [...] learn without the assistance of teacher or other students. Learning in this class is structured as social activity (Foster 1989:25).

Foster here talks about a black woman teacher in a culturally mixed urban community college in the US, but her remarks globally apply to the lesson that has been analyzed in this chapter. My motive for undertaking the analysis was to find out where the cultural baselines are: how are classrom cultures bootstrapped in institutional multiparty situations? What can they tell us about normative expectations in classroom research? What is seen and heard, what is ignored? What is "ours," what is "theirs?" An ecological approach to these issues addresses the extent to which classroom cultures are emergent in everyday practices, and seeks to reveal how the – cultural, linguistic, pragmatic – systems that are both firmly institutional and inherited from the world outside the classroom interconnect. The analyses also raise questions about how teaching strategies "translate" across settings and populations. Clearly ESL classroom settings create very different conditions for *metacommunicating* about classroom events, which turned out to be such a consistent feature of this teacher's classroom style.

Apparently it is not *impossible* to negotiate the paradoxes of face and learning in emergent communities of learning. Discursive practices in this first English lesson excluded no one and caused no one to fail, or be *noticeably* less competent than any of his/her peers. Student participation was high throughout and almost wholly organized on the basis of self-selection. The considerable differences in prior knowledge among the students were accommodated in off-record teacher interventions that allowed same-turn self-corrections or teacher-and-peer-scaffolded collective speaking formats associated with cultural "games:" rhymes, chants, recitation and performance modes, ritual dialog. Structural dimensions of these collective ritual "speaking slots" (which construct subunits of turns) can mediate the role shift from overhearer to co-speaker while allowing the already-competent to improve their output. Thus the learning of students of different ability and confidence can be *synchronized* in off-record niches of multiparty lesson floors that are also exploited for language play and metacommunication – thus fostering both socialization and acquisition.[13]

The emphasis on linear, dyadic interaction in mainstream (Western) linguistic theory has greatly restricted our notion of where to look for evidence of learning and empowerment in classroom settings. Researchers who aim to establish the effectivity of a specific task or activity in language lessons need to take into account the instructions that locally contextualize them (e.g. see the section on Chorusing the alphabet) in order for the results to be empirically, *ecologically* valid (Cole *et al.* 1997). If singly-authored, context-free, monolithic turns-at-talk are considered the building-blocks of "inter-action",[14] the framing practices, linguistic play and emergent face work that occur in the course of discourse-units-in-progress remain invisible.[15] But they are *part* of "what's going on:" "life was never meant to be an adjacency pair" (Wajnryb 1997). Experienced teachers who interpret the complex input of 20 or more students in classroom situations know this: they create affordances for individual voices in the off-record "interstices" of institutional talk, as well as keeping different circles "on hold" and in play.

Transcription conventions

T	: teacher
S	: student
Sx	: unidentified student
SF	: identified student, initial indicates first name
Ss	: several students simultaneously
Class	: (nearly) all students
HOT	: capital letters indicate strong stress or emphasis
↓	: marked fall in pitch

Jet van Dam

–	: unmarked pause (± 0.3 seconds)
—	: marked pause
=	: immediately adjacent utterances, sometimes having the status of interruption
[ ]	: contextual information; prosodic and nonverbal features of talk; author's comments
:	: lengthening of preceding sound
/ /	: "primitive" phonetic transcriptions
( )	: unintelligible vocalizations
(( ))	: English translation of utterances in Dutch
name	: English in the original; imbedded code-switches
?	: rising intonation, not necessarily a question
// //	: turn boundaries in overlapping turn

Notes

1. All teacher and student utterances were originally in Dutch, both in the text and in the transcripts, unless explicitly marked as *English original* by *italics*. Readability and space concerns prevent my including glosses throughout the paper. They will be given in later sections when necessary for understanding what's going on.
2. Cf. "kids spend most of their time at school trying not to get caught not-knowing something" (Ray McDermott, personal communication).
3. In another lesson in my corpus these differences were "agenda business." The teacher asked each student whether (s)he had had any English at primary school and entered their answers in her diary: two years ++; one year +; "nothing." The "nothing" answers were often accompanied by embarrassment markers.
4. Whereas in the literature on linguistic pragmatics dispreferred or delayed acts are normally discussed in connection with second-pair-parts or responses (cf. Levinson 1983:308), I extend the notion to encompass options in the turn exchange system.
5. Upon being shown the transcript of this episode, the teacher at once made a derogatory remark about herself: "How just like me, always interrupting people." Practitioners may not be aware of the non-local relevance of their actions.
6. Exceptions are e.g. Poole 1992; van Lier 1988; Cook 1997, but these authors do not focus on the internal structure of speaking slots as much as I do. Donato (2000) draws attention to the related phenomenon of "private speech" in classroom settings: "it is unwise to assume that all classroom talk is composed of 'between-person' meanings to be sent and received" and suggests that "a fruitful line of enquiry within the private speech research agenda is to examine more fully the concept of private speech during teacher-fronted instruction" (33). For "scaffolding," see e.g. Bruner 1983; van Lier 1996, 2000.

7. The American composer Charles Ives (1874–1954) was fascinated by the clusters of false notes he heard around the "harmonic centers" in his father's church choir and composed them in in his *Psalm 24* (1897).

8. cf. McDermott and Tylbor (1986): "The smart–dumb continuum is constantly applied in classrooms and much interactional delicacy must be organized to apply the continuum only in cases where someone can be called smart. The application of the continuum to instances of dumb behavior does occur, but participants usually work hard to have it not noticed" (132/33).

9. How Hans knew or supposed that his name could not be "translated" into English by just transferring phonological features is an interesting question.

10. He is an Athabaskan: "for one to be able to keep one's face one has to renounce one's fear of losing it" (Scollon and Scollon 1981:160).

11. Sato (1990) reminds us of the limitations of "conversation as the driver of syntax." Recent lexical and corpus-based research on language use and language learning suggests that drawing ready-made and largely unanalyzed prefabricated phrases from memory may well be a basic strategy of language learners (e.g. Ellis 1998; Harley 1995; Williams 1999). Williams recommends elaborative training by repetition or rote rehearsal. The ready-made chunks may provide the building blocks for the development of more complex and more creative language behavior. On the role of play and focus on form in language teaching, see e.g. Cook (1997:230); Sullivan (2000); on repetition as a strategy in primary language socialization see Pallotti (1996, forthcoming).

12. In search of a more dynamic view of motivation, Csikszentmihalyi (1990) coined the construct of "flow:" "an experience, in work or play, when time seems to be suspended [...] and one is totally involved in the activity" (van Lier 1996:106).

13. Having analyzed the lesson, now let us count. I calculated that, not counting individually authored turns, a "good" student could have produced 102 mini-utterances (3 × the alphabet; 3× Ottiwell Wood); 18 mini-phrases, and several "no, it isn't" and "warm, cold, hot": all in all, about 140 "speaking times." A more diffident student might, say, have produced none in the first round to half in the third one, which, together with the games, would still amount to 40–50 vocalizations in English – not a bad score for a 50-minute first English lesson. But, of course, we *cannot* give exact figures: we just do not know.

14. For a critique of these views in Brown and Levinson's politeness proposals, see Arundale 1999.

15. For a detailed discussion of the ill-understood and self-reflexive nature of repair in "low-ability" reading groups, see Collins 1996.

References

Arminen, I. (2000) On the context sensitivity of institutional interaction. *Discourse and Society* 11(4), 435–58.

Arundale, R. (1999) An alternative model and ideology of communication for an alternative to politeness theory. *Pragmatics* 9, 119–54.

Bailey, K.M. (1983) Competitiveness and anxiety in adult second language learning: looking *at* and *through* the diary studies. In H.W. Seliger and M. Long (eds), *Classroom-oriented Research in Second Language Acquisition*. Rowley: Newbury House, pp. 67–102.

Bakhtin, M.M. (1981) *The Dialogic Imagination*. Austin: University of Texas Press.

Bateson, G. (1972) *Steps to an Ecology of Mind*. New York: Ballantine Books.

Bronfenbrenner, U. (1979) *The Ecology of Human Development*. Cambridge, MA: Harvard University Press.

Brown, P. and Levinson, S. (1987), *Politeness: Some Universals in Language Usage*. Cambridge: Cambridge University Press.

Bruner, J. (1983) *Child's Talk: Learning to Use Language*. New York: Norton.

Cazden, C.B. (1988) *The Language of Teaching and Learning*. Portsmouth: Heinemann.

Cole, M., Hood, L. and McDermott, R.P. (1997) Concepts of ecological validity: their differing implications for comparative cognitive research. In M. Cole, Y. Engeström and O. Vasquez (eds), *Mind, Culture, and Activity. Seminal Papers from the Laboratory of Comparative Human Cognition*. Cambridge: Cambridge University Press, pp. 49–57.

Collins, J. (1996) Socialization to text: structure and contradiction in schooled literacy. In M. Silverstein and G. Urban (eds), *Natural Histories of Discourse*. Chicago: University of Chicago Press, pp. 203–29.

Cook, G. (1997) Language play, language learning. *ELT Journal* 51(3), 224–31.

Csikszentmihalyi, M. (1990) *Flow: The Psychology of Optimal Experience*. New York: Harper and Row.

Donato, R. (2000) Sociocultural contributions to understanding the foreign and second-language classroom. In J. Lantolf (ed.), *Sociocultural Theory and Second Language Learning*. Oxford: Oxford University Press, pp. 27–50.

Edwards, D. and Mercer, N. (1987) *Common Knowledge: The Development of Understanding in the Classroom*. London: Methuen.

Ellis, N.C. (1998) Emergentism, connectionism and language learning. *Language Learning* 48(4), 631–64.

Erickson, F. and Schultz, J. (1981) When is a context? In J. Green and C. Wallatt (eds), *Ethnography and Language in Educational Settings*. Norwood, NJ: Ablex, pp.147–60.

Erickson, F. and Schultz, J. (1982) *The Counselor as Gatekeeper: Social Interaction in Interviews*. New York: Academic Press.

Foster, M. (1989) "It's cookin now": a performance analysis of the speech of a Black teacher in an urban community college. *Language in Society* 18, 1–29.

Goffman, E. (1967) *Interaction Ritual: Essays on Face-to-Face Behavior*. New York: Doubleday Anchor.

Goffman, E. (1972) On face-work: an analysis of ritual elements in social interaction. In J. Laver and S. Hutchinson (eds), *Communication in Face-to-Face Interaction*. Harmondsworth: Penguin Books, pp. 319–47.

Goffman, E. (1979) Footing. *Semiotica* 25, 1–29 (reprinted in Goffman 1981).

Goffman, E. (1981) *Forms of Talk*. Oxford: Basil Blackwell.

Harley, B. (1995) *Lexical Issues in Language Learning*. Philadelphia: John Benjamins.

Hockett, C. (1973 [1967]) Where the tongue slips, there slip I. In V. Fromkin (ed.), *Speech Errors as Linguistic Evidence*. The Hague: Mouton, pp. 93–120.

Kramsch, C. (1993) *Context and Culture in Language Teaching*. Oxford: Oxford University Press.

Leather, J. and van Dam, H.R. (eds) (in press), *The Ecology of Language Acquisition*. Dordrecht: Kluwer Academic.

Levinson, S.C. (1983) *Pragmatics*. Cambridge: Cambridge University Press.

MacIntyre, P.D. (1999) Language anxiety: A review of the research for language teachers. In D.J. Young (ed.), *Affect in Foreign Language and Second Language Learning: A Practical Guide to Creating a Low-anxiety Classroom Atmosphere*. Boston: McGraw-Hill, pp. 24–45.

McDermott, R.P. and Tylbor, H. (1986) On the necessity of collusion in conversation. In S. Fischer and A. Todd (eds), *Advances in Discourse Processes* 19. Norwood, NJ: Ablex, pp. 123–39.

McHoul, A.H. (1978) The organization of turns at formal talk in the classroom. *Language in Society* 7, 183–213.

McHoul, A.H. (1990) The organization of repair in classroom talk. *Language in Society* 19, 349–77.

Mehan, H. (1979) The competent student. *Sociolinguistic Working Papers 61*. Austin: Southwest Educational Development Laboratory.

Ochs, E. (1992) Indexing gender. In A. Duranti and C. Goodwin (eds), *Rethinking Context*. Cambridge: Cambridge University Press, pp. 335–58.

Ohta, A.S. (2000) Rethinking interaction in SLA: Developmentally appropriate assistance in the zone of proximal development and the acquisition of L2 grammar. In Lantolf, J. (ed.), *Sociocultural Theory and Second Language Learning*. Oxford: Oxford University Press, pp. 51–78.

Pallotti, G. (1996) Towards an ecology of second language acquisition. *Toegepaste Taalwetenschap in Artikelen* 55, 121–35.

Pallotti, G. (forthcoming) Borrowing words: appropriations in child second language discourse. In J.L. Leather and J. van Dam (eds), *Ecology of Language Aquisition*. Dordrecht: Kluwer Academic.

Polanyi, L. (1988) A formal model of the structure of discourse. *Journal of Pragmatics* 12, 601–38.

Polanyi, L. and Scha, R.J.H. (1983) On the recursive structure of discourse. In K. Ehlich and H. van Riemsdijk (eds), *Connectedness in Sentence, Discourse and Text*. Tilburg, Tilburg University Press, pp. 141–78.

Poole, D. (1992) Language socialization in the second language classroom. *Language Learning* 42(4), 593–616.

Rampton, B. (1995*) Crossing: Language and Ethnicity among Adolescents*. London: Longman.

Sato, C. (1990*) The Syntax of Conversation in Interlanguage Development*. Tübingen: Gunter Narr Verlag.

Schegloff, E.A. (1979) The relevance of repair for syntax-for-conversation. In T. Givon (ed.), *Syntax and Semantics 12: Discourse and Syntax*. New York: Academic Press, pp. 261–80.

Schiffrin, D. (1987*) Discourse Markers*. Cambridge: Cambridge University Press.

Scollon, R. (1982) The rhythmic integration of ordinary talk. In D. Tannen (ed.), *Analyzing Discourse: Text and Talk*. Washington, D.C.: Georgetown University Press, pp. 335–50.

Scollon, R. and Scollon, S.B.K. (1981*) Narrative, Literacy and Face in Interethnic Communication*. Norwood, NJ: Ablex.

Scollon, R. and Scollon, S.B.K. (1995*) Intercultural Communication*. Oxford: Blackwell.

Searle, J. (1969*) Speech Acts*. Cambridge: Cambridge University Press.

Seedhouse, P. (1997) The case of the missing "No": the relationship between pedagogy and interaction. *Language Learning* 47(3), 547–83.

Sullivan, P. (2000) Spoken artistry: performance in a foreign language classroom. In J.K. Hall and L. Stoops Verplaetse (eds), *The Development of Second and Foreign Language Learning through Classroom Interaction*. Mahwah: Lawrence Erlbaum, pp. 73–90.

Tsui, A.B.M. (1996) Reticence and anxiety in second language learning. In K.M. Bailey and D. Nunan (eds) *Voices from the Language Classroom*. Cambridge: Cambridge University Press, pp. 145–68.

van Dam, J. (forthcomming) Language aquisition behind the scenes: collusion and play in educational settings. In J. L. Leather and J. van Dam (eds) *Ecology of Language Aquisition*. Dordrecht: Kluwer Academic.

van Dam van Isselt, H.R. (1993) *"Her name is – uh dat weet ik niet." Authenticity in the L2 classroom*. Unpublished PhD dissertation, University of Amsterdam.

van Dam van Isselt, H.R. (1995) "Where is the lesson in all this talk?" In E. Huls and J. Klatter-Folmer (eds), *Artikelen van de van de Tweede Sociolinguistische Conferentie*. Delft: Eburon, pp.125–39.

van Lier, L. (1988) *The Classroom and the Language Learner*. New York: Longman.

van Lier, L. (1996) *Interaction in the Language Curriculum: Awareness, Autonomy and Authenticity*. New York: Longman.

van Lier, L. (2000) From input to affordance: social-interactive learning from an ecological perspective. In J. Lantolf (ed.), *Socio-cultural Theory and Second Language Learning*. Oxford: Oxford University Press, pp. 245–61.

Wajnryb, R. (1997) Death, taxes and jeopardy: systematic omissions in EFL – or life was never meant to be an adjacency pair. *international education-ej* 1(2)

Williams, J.M. (1999) Memory, attention, and inductive learning. *Studies in Second Language Acquisition* 21(1), 1–48.

Wittgenstein, L. (1953) *Philosophical Investigations*. Oxford: Basil Blackwell.

10 Negotiating the paradoxes of spontaneous talk in advanced L2 classes

Anne Bannink

Introduction[1]

Since the early 1980s numerous publications on L2 teaching have appeared which recommend teachers to use "communicative" methods. In the communicative paradigm the focus is on language use and the goal of the foreign language class is primarily communicative competence. This has consequences for classroom practices: the materials used should be "authentic," taken from "real life" and not be especially designed for the foreign or second language learner; the tasks set to the students should be meaningful and related to the world outside the classroom, should emphasize communication through interaction among students and be learner-centered (cf. Brown 1994). The baseline for meaningful communication in this setting is seen as "doing conversation" (van Lier 1996). This view of the talk that should be going on in L2 classes fits in with the prevalent idea among linguists that conversation is the prototypical form of language use. Levelt calls conversation: "the most primordial and universal setting for speech and the canonical setting for speech in all human societies" (1989:29). Heritage and Atkinson argue that it is "the most pervasively used mode of interaction in social life and the form within which ... language is first acquired ..." (1984:12–13).

Along more or less similar lines Levinson states:

> It is not hard to see why one should look to conversation for insight into pragmatic phenomena, for conversation is clearly the prototypical kind of language usage, the form in which we all are first exposed to language – *the matrix for language acquisition.*
>
> (1983:284; italics added)

Van Lier (1989) proposes a list of features that characterize conversation: it is face-to-face interaction which is locally assembled (although it may contain planned elements, for instance, a request or a proposal); the sequence and outcome are unpredictable; there is a potentially equal distribution of rights and obligations in talk, and there is reactive and mutual contingency. If this list is mapped onto the characteristics of the discourse in traditional teacher-fronted class-rooms, major discrepancies surface. The organization of talk in this sort of classroom implies more or less strict hierarchical speaker–hearer roles and teacher–student role obligations. The majority of teacher questions in these lessons are so-called display questions and the teacher is the addressee of all student turns. This means that doing conversation in the classroom is problematic, since this has to do with the right to initiate topics and talk. In the classroom setting, as McHoul (1979) rightly argues, only the teacher can direct speakership in any creative way. So it seems that traditional classroom environments do not lend themselves very well to conversation: by definition the classroom is a formal, institutional, and asymmetric setting. And, paradoxically, in this setting the informal, unpredictable, spontaneous "conversational" interactions which should lead to communicative competence of the learners somehow have to be accommodated.

In this chapter I argue that the frame complexity of the communicative L2 classroom as described above has been under-analyzed. The multiplicity of discourse levels obtained may lead to conflicts and dilemmas for all participants, and results in a number of paradoxes which have not been recognized. This has led to assump-tions about tasks, materials, and classroom organization which are widespread and commonly accepted but which have not been empirically investigated.

I will begin with a brief introduction to the theoretical framework followed by data from two advanced oral proficiency classes which yielded results that I – as the teacher – had not expected when I planned them and in which I identified both positive and negative instances of "real" negotiation for meaning that emerged during the talk.

Theoretical framework: discourse analysis

For the analysis of the data a structural discourse framework will be employed which derives from Goffman's work on participation structures and face-to-face communication (1974, 1979, 1981), and from proposals by Polanyi and Scha (1983; Polyani 1988) and van Dam van Isselt (1993, 1995) on discourse units and operations which allow for the recursive imbedding of talk of various types within one another.

Anne Bannink

Participation framework: speaker and hearer roles

In *Footing* (1979) Erving Goffman argues that the notions of "speaker" and "hearer" have been grossly underanalyzed both for dyadic and for multiparty interactions. A social occasion will have official, ratified participants, but there might also be nonratified participants, co-present others, in the roles of overhearers or eavesdroppers. Besides, participants may be addressed or unaddressed recipients within a particular section of talk. In his analysis of the notion of "speaker," Goffman distinguishes three different roles: "*principal*, someone whose position is established by the words that are spoken, a person active in some particular social identity or role; ... *animator*, the talking-machine, a body engaged in acoustic activity; and ... *author*, the one who has selected the sentiments which are expressed and the words in which they are encoded" (1981:144).

Structural dimensions of social situations: floors and subfloors

Most interactions are experienced by participants as belonging to a certain socially recognizable occasion, e.g. an informal conversation, a lesson, a business meeting, and so on ("speech events"; Hymes 1964). At speech-event level, a set of specific conventions is defined about: who are the participants, what is their role, what is the business at hand, and what are the ritual attributes and procedures. These interactional conventions should be seen as a tool to help people reach consensus on the definition of a current situation. Interactions, however, may be imbedded in other interactions and interrupt one type of business for another. We may, for example, tell a story which is part of a conversation that takes place before the beginning of another activity, like getting down to business at a meeting. In that case, our talk is involved in at least three types of interaction: a "premeeting small talk," a "conversation," and a "storytelling." The assignment of utterances to the category "same sort of talk" and preceding utterances to "different sort of talk" prompts Polanyi and Scha (1983) to argue that the actual flow of talk is properly seen as separable into various discourse units to which individual utterances are seen to belong. Such units, strung together, make up the actual discourses which are produced. In their model Polanyi and Scha distinguish three types of discourse units. These units range from one word "echoes," response cries (Goffman 1979), and nonverbal acts through minimal clauses and sentences to very large discourse structures. Type I are small, local structures involving turn-taking, i.e. adjacency pairs (greetings, question–answer). These have traditionally been studied within the framework of conversation analysis. Type II structures are coherent semantic structures built up through sustained talk, such as stories, reports, arguments, and so on. Type III structures are socially defined, recognizable occasions for talk, often of a highly focused sort, defined as speech events above. These discourse units may be *recursively* embedded. This means that stories may be embedded in stories, but also that a speech event (e.g. a service encounter) may be embedded in a story (if a person pauses in the middle of a story to buy something). An embedded episode is signaled by structural discourse operators, so-called PUSH and POP markers (Polanyi 1988; cf. Goffman 1981: "changes in footing;" Gumperz 1982: "contextualization cues"). PUSH markers signal the beginning of an embedded subordinated constituent or an interruption of the dominant discourse unit. A communicative assignment to be done in groups, for example, creates as many subfloors as there are groups. When the task is done, the discourse will have to be shifted back to the embedding interactional level: the collective classroom floor. A POP marker will effect this return to the embedding level. POP and PUSH markers may be linguistic, para-linguistic, prosodic, or nonverbal. Examples of verbal realizations of POP markers are "okay," "right," "anyway," and code switches. Verbal realizations of PUSH markers are particles like "for instance," "like," "by the way;" tense or pronoun shift, deictic shifts, and code switches.

The question addressed in this chapter is: How do students and teacher negotiate the multiplicity of potential discourse formats and the variety of speaker and hearer roles in the communicative L2 classroom?

Method and data collection

When I taught advanced oral proficiency I found that some classes were not a success and some assignments simply did not work, although they met the criteria for communicative materials and tasks (see below). This experience prompted me to take a closer look at the frame complexity of fluency classes. This study should thus be seen as an attempt on my part, as a teacher of English as a foreign language, to make sense of my own everyday practice. What follows, then, is the result of *action research* (cf. van Lier 1988): my roles of teacher and researcher coincide in the study, and the data analyzed are grounded in participation in and knowledge of the specific real-world settings involved.

The data to be discussed emerged from a proficiency course I taught to first-year students of English at the University of Amsterdam.[2] The aim of the course was to improve students' essay writing and oral fluency. At the end of each fluency assignment I conducted an informal evaluation in order to receive feedback on the particular task. Three of the classes were taped by graduate students who had to prepare a paper for the specialization course *Topics in Applied Linguistics*, which – among other subjects – dealt with classroom discourse. I subsequently used their transcripts and analyzed data from the tapes they had made for the purpose of this study. The feedback my students gave me during the evaluations and my own observations of the classes serve to complement the data.

The communicative language class: speech event context

The organization of talk

Looking at the communicative language class, it may be argued that the type II structure "fluency assignment" is imbedded in the type III speech event "lesson." This means that during the assignment, even if it entails "doing conversation," teacher and student roles and tasks are inherited from the imbedding speech event, although a number of these ritual rights and obligations may of course be suspended during a particular lesson episode. Let us look more closely at these teacher and student roles. Classroom roles and tasks are defined in terms of the supposedly asymmetrical distribution of knowledge between members of the category "student" and their ritual "other," the teacher. The teacher is there precisely because she is the one who knows or knows more. In principle the teacher is in control of the lesson agenda, and the organization of turns and activities. She initiates tasks and allocates and evaluates pupil turns. Students, on the other hand, do not have the right to speak up in class unless they are invited to do so by the teacher. In teacher-fronted classes the teacher orients toward all pupils, but the pupils do not orient toward each other. All legitimate student utterances are directed toward, if not solicited by, the teacher. In this type of lesson all students are ratified participants of the social occasion "lesson," but they may be addressed recipients, unaddressed recipients, or even overhearers. All students are supposed to attend to what is said without having (spontaneous) access to the floor. This means that not all ratified participants have the same status and role in the lesson at any moment in the state of talk: the participation structure is nonlinear and dynamic. As soon as the teacher allocates a turn to one student, however, this person is the addressed recipient of the teacher's utterances and therefore the next speaker; the others are confined to their ritual social role of listeners. Therefore, the participation framework of teacher-fronted classes results in little opportunity for individual students to practice their oral language skills, and does not create affordances for conversational interactions.

The communicative language teaching paradigm claims to have found a solution for this problem: it advocates pair- and group-work to insure not only equal distribution of language practice among the students, but also favorable conditions for "conversational" practice. Students working on tasks in pairs or small groups leads to an informal classroom format and therefore creates the right conditions for successful language learning (Long 1996). When students work in small groups the teacher is not the addressed recipient of students' turns: the collective classroom floor splits up into a number of subfloors. With groupwork, students orient toward each other and this makes it possible to have symmetrical interactions in class, based on the principle of self-selection. Moreover, feedback and evaluation moves are managed by the students themselves. This way the participation framework of the communicative language class moves in the direction of the ideal dyadic model of generic conversation. This does not mean, however, that fluency tasks in small groups automatically create contexts for conversation. The episode is still imbedded in the speech event "lesson" and therefore during the assignment the teacher retains her social right to break in and interrupt ongoing "conversations" and comment upon procedural matters, topics, etc. Moreover, fluency assignments lead to the pragmatic paradox (Watzlawick *et al.* 1967) "be spontaneous" being achieved. Students are obliged to talk, and not allowed to sit in silence, they are given a topic to talk about, and are not allowed to shift topic, they are often instructed to make sure the other members of the group get a chance to contribute to the discussion, etc. Students receive instructions about the topic of their conversation, about the length of time they are supposed to talk about the topic, and about the expected outcome of their conversation. All this is clearly not conversational. As we have seen in van Lier's definition: *authentic conversation typically has more fluent boundaries.* It seems, then, that the solution to this paradox cannot be found in just another teaching methodology: it is inherent in the pedagogical situation of the classroom. Genuine conversational interactions cannot be the outcome of preplanned lesson agendas, they have to *emerge* – and so, by definition, cannot be planned.

The role of the teacher

With the introduction of groupwork the collective classroom floor is split into several subfloors. The members of each group enter into and maintain a distinct spatial and orientational arrangement by which the members of this particular group are delineated from those who are outsiders, and body posture and spatial orientation are used to collaboratively frame participation for the duration of the task (Kendon 1992). In this interactional arrangement the teacher has organized herself away, so she is merely a bystander. This has consequences for the way she is expected to behave. As Goffman states: "Much of the etiquette of bystanders can be generated from the basic understanding that they should act so as to maximally encourage the fiction that they aren't present; in brief that the assumptions of the conversational paradigm are being realized" (1979:8).

However, since the fluency assignment is embedded in the speech event "lesson," the ritual rights and obligations of teacher and students are inherited from the higher-order discourse unit. This means that the teacher still has the right to interrupt, correct, or evaluate student performances. Moreover, the teacher will feel the need to know how the students are doing: are they on task; is the activity suitable, of the right level, and so on? In order to get information about these issues, the teacher has to "maneuver" herself, albeit temporarily, into the position of eavesdropper in order to be able to hear what is going on in a group. In one of the lessons that will be discussed in this chapter, it was observed that as the teacher approached a group, the student who sat with her back to the teacher, and therefore did not notice her approach, continued talking as if for her the situation remained the same. Students who saw her coming, however, began to talk in a different, "funny" tone of voice. This is the result of a change of "footing" (Goffman 1979), which "implies a change in the alignment we take up to ourselves and the others present" and which occurs when the participation framework of an interaction changes. If the teacher really wants to know what is going on the only strategy that is left is to use the "disattend track," which Kendon defines as "consisting of events that are officially treated as irrelevant to the activity in progress" (1992:328). The teacher will ostensibly adhere to her role of bystander and enact a show of disinterest. She will not hover and by her gaze and bodily position she will try to sustain the illusion that she is not there (Goffman 1979).[3] So it may be argued that the communicative language classroom makes paradoxical demands on the teacher: she will have to maneuver among various "footings" since she needs to play multiple roles at the same time (teacher, conversational partner, stage director, etc.).

I will now go on to discuss the data.

The data

Task 1: preprogrammed meanings

During one of the classes the students worked on a questionnaire on childhood experiences. In it were items like: do you come from a noisy family? did you receive any pocket money? did you watch television a lot? etc? The task was to be done in groups of four and was aimed at encouraging the students to exchange "stories" on childhood experiences. In my instructions for the assignment I explicitly addressed interactional dimensions:

Example 1

T   what I want you to do is to talk about your childhood

Cl   [unintelligible noises]

T   je jeugd ((your childhood)) ... your childhood

                    [

Cl   oh [unintelligible noises]

T   it's always interesting I think to talk about each other's childhood

Sx   it's personal

SSS [laugh]

T   yes well uhm I've made I've come up with some questions to talk about some things to give you material to talk about ... IF you think one of these topics is a bit too uh too personal you don't want to talk about these things you can just skip the question or you could even make up another childhood if you uh want to

     [

SSS [laugh]

T   that's okay with me

......

T   now remember it's not supposed to be a sort of Ivo Niehe [Dutch talk-show host] conversation if you know what I mean

SSS nee ((no))

T   Ivo Niehe has this list of questions those sort of TV people they just ask a question and their guests answer the question and they go on to the next question because they are not really interested in the answer but you are all interested in each other ... OKAY? *[hands out questionnaire]*

In some of the groups, however, the activity organized itself as follows: one of the students would introduce the question by reading it aloud. She would then give the floor to the next person, often after first having answered the question herself.

The group of four in Example 2 was seated around an oblong table, one student on each side. S1, who read the questions aloud, had appropriated the paper with the questionnaire, which was supposed to set the agenda for the interaction, by placing it right in front of her, thereby virtually denying the others physical access to the questions.

> *Example 2*
> S1   did you get pocket money? [nonverbal turn allocation: gaze direction S2]
> S2   I did=
> S1   =yeah
> S3   I did
> S4   I didn't until I found out [unintellible] then I demanded to get it
> SSS [laugh]
> S1   why didn't you get it?
> S4   I just got the things I wanted but you want candy uh uh ... and uh you want to go to the shops [unint] you want to buy clothes and later I found out that
>   [
> S1   it can't have been much
> S4   everyone else got it
> SSS [silence; S1 reads next question]
> S1   when did you go to bed? ... what time? ... when my older brothers went to bed *I could* go to bed
> S2   no I only remember I always had to go too soon

The data show that there were hardly any interruptions, although they are the norm, even in story-type turns (e.g. appreciative noises, back-channeling) and no collaborative floors (Edelsky 1981). There was hardly any overlap and the turn-taking organization was atypical for "conversation" in groups of three (cf. Kerbrat-Orecchioni 1997). There were no "struggles for the floor:" the resulting distribution of turns strongly resembled the participation framework in the teacher-fronted lesson: S1 asks the questions, the others provide the answers.

Task 1 revisited: emergent meanings

At one point, however, the students did what they were supposed to do. It occurred when the group involved had decided they had finished doing the assignment. The "stand-in" teacher said: "Okay, that's it, *we've done all the questions,*" which ended the formal question–answer sequence. This remark unequivocally proves that the students interpreted the assignment as "doing the questions" and also, clearly, that they felt they had completed that task. Because of their interpretation of the task instructions, they had finished long before the time allocated to the assignment was up, before I told them they could stop talking. After a short pause the students then resumed their talk:

Example 3

S3   and well I was always the boss of our street so I made out what happened

                                        [

SSS   [laugh]

                                          [

S2   yeah you ruled the street

S3   where we were going to play and uh it made me quite uncomfortable it really did – I don't wanna be the boss of those children they do everything I say

    [

S4   I can imagine

S3   I felt really stupid

    [

S2   they did that to me as well

    [

SSS [laugh]

    [

S2   I I I remember when you when you got in fights with your friends or the neighbor – the children next door you know you'd always say from uh I'LL GET

    [

SSS yeah yeah

S2   MY OLDER BROTHER if you don't stop teasing me=

    [

SSS yeah yeah [laugh]

S4   = everybody [high pitch] my daddy's a policeman=

SSS = [laugh]

The students now did exactly what I had intended them to do: they shared their childhood experiences. This time there were story-type turns, there were overlaps and interruptions, there were collaborative floors. There was no *need* for them to continue on this topic: here the questions functioned as lead-in to authentic conversation and sharing in a classroom context. There were no leading questions: there was a real conversational flow.

It might be concluded then that this group found a way to negotiate the paradox of planned–unplanned communication in the language class: they spent a minimum amount of time on "doing the questions" and so created a space for unprogrammed meaning to emerge.

Task 2: enacting the script

The second task I would like to discuss concerns an assignment from the book that was used in the course. It was to be done in groups of three. The type of activity is well known in the communicative language teaching syllabus: students are supposed to plan a weekend together but receive instructions to make sure that they have divergent aims and agendas and need to negotiate compromises. Below is the set of instructions they received.

> Your two friends have agreed to spend the weekend with you. Here are your ideas on what to do:
> Saturday: Spend day on the beach – enjoy sun and relaxing
> Take picnic lunch (tell them what food you'll take)
> Evening: party at Michael's (tell them about Michael's last party, which was really great)
> Sunday: Meet rest of class at railway station
> All go to London for the day (tell the others what you can see and do there)
> Stay till late – go to a restaurant (tell the others what they can eat there)
> Take it in turns to present your plans to each other. Be enthusiastic![4] Then decide which plan sounds best. If necessary, work out a compromise plan.

The assignment meets the criteria Clark (1987) formulated for the activities and materials needed for a communicative, task-based approach to language learning: "The learner must participate in meaningful interaction in the target language, so that information-processing mechanisms can be involved at some depth. For this to occur there must be some sort of information gap" (1987:63–4).

The assignment itself, however, was not a success. When I observed the groups I noticed that the students were not really focused on their task. When they had finished I asked them whether they had enjoyed doing the assignment. They were unanimous in their view that it had not been inspiring. They felt it was highly *artificial*. During their discussions they had found it hard to remember what they were supposed to want to do so eagerly in their assigned pseudo-identities, which necessitated frequent looking at their instructions to "remember their text."

Task 2 redesigned: inserting unpredictability

On the basis of student feedback on the above task, I decided to redesign the speaker roles of the assignment. My goal was to make the task more "authentic," which meant changing the production format of the resulting conversation. In the new design I enabled my students to be the *author* of their utterances – a role which has clear connotations of creativity and authenticity – by giving them the opportunity to set their own agenda for the discussion, within the framework of the task. I used the revised version in another group I was teaching at the time. The text of the new assignment read as follows:

> Write down individually how you would like to spend your ideal weekend (Saturday and Sunday; morning, afternoon, and evening). If you plan to go to a restaurant for a meal, specify the restaurant; if you plan to go away for a break, specify where to, etc.
> Make groups of four.
> Decide which member of your group will report the discussion to the entire class.
> Discuss your plans with the others and try to come up with one plan you all agree on.

There are two important differences between the original and the revised assignment. First, a preactivity or advance organizer has been inserted: the students first have to make up their minds on their ideal weekend and put their ideas down on paper before discussing them with the other members of their group. This means that during this preactivity the students have the opportunity to invent their own "personae" to be enacted and, indeed, can be the authors of their talk during the discussion. Moreover, it added a certain unpredictability to the negotiation stage of the task and therefore allowed more unprogrammed meaning to emerge in the group interaction within the context of the task.

Second, I announced that one member of each group would act as an official spokesperson, who would report the group's discussion to the entire class in order to force the groups to really reach agreement on their joint plans. The redesigned assignment thus consisted of an advance organizer, followed by the original activity, and was rounded off by a postunit, the class report.

This exercise provoked lively interaction among the members of the groups. Students presented their ideas with passion, and long discussions ensued. The reporters mentioned quite a few heated arguments. The introduction of the preactivity clearly made the assignment more realistic for the students: in the problem-solving group discussion, they presented and defended their own ideas and therefore felt more involved in the outcome of the decision-making part of the activity. There were no constraints on memory, which meant hardly any "gaps" and more conversational overlap, so the task resulted in rich interaction and a wide participation among the students.

Task 2 redesigned: reflecting on the task

The reporter role that I had introduced to make sure the students would take the assignment seriously, and give them the opportunity to widen their practice to the genre of "reporting a discussion," made it necessary for the students to reflect on what "exactly" was being said.

In one of the groups, the students agreed to have dinner in a Chinese restaurant and one of the students mentioned that he wanted to eat Peking duck there. At the time none of the others asked for an explanation of this. The participant-reporter, however, fulfilled a double, "relay" role, which necessitated not just an approximate but a perfect understanding of what was said. Thus she was trying to "rehearse" what was said so as to be a competent reporter in the public classroom follow-up of the groupwork episode. This resulted in a prolonged episode of negotiation of meaning, during which default conversational conventions were overruled, as is shown in Example 4:

Example 4
1   S1   so, what do you want to eat there?
     S2   uh, I'll have the Peking duck please
     SSS   [laugh]
     S1   the what?
5   S2   Peking duck
     S1   what's that?
     S2   [fast; Dutch] Peking eend ((Peking duck)) – uh – [laughs]
     S3   Peking duck=
     S2   =Peking [ei: Dutch value for vowel]
10   S1   Peking [ei] – OH!

	S2	Peking
		[
	S3	Bejing=
	S2	=Bejing duck
	S3	Bejing duck
15	S1	you mean that? – duck?
		[
	S2	Donald Duck
	S3	duck, ja ((yes))
	S1	Peking duck – alright
		[
	S3	Bejing
20	S2	serieus ((seriously))
	S1	[nonverbally allocates turn to S3]
	S3	uhm, I'll decide when I see the menu I really don't know what I'll have
		[
	S4	it's Chinese
		[
	S2	I really recommend it

In line 1, the reporter comes back to a topic that had been nominated before: the dish S2 has stated as his preference earlier in the discourse. In his response to this question S2 adopts a different "footing." He recontextualizes S1's question as a move in the "script" of another speech event: "ordering a meal in a restaurant," which accounts for the laughter of the others in line 3. S1's problem, though, remains unsolved and she reports her trouble source once more. This time her effort is interpreted as a mishearing or a request for a rerun by S2 (line 5). An explicit clarification request is the only option left to her to fulfill her need, and this move follows in line 6. The clarification request triggers extensive repair work and language play. Communication strategies (Poulisse 1990; Mitchell and Myles 1998) are employed to achieve understanding: the students go back to L1 (lines 7 and 9) and use a L2-based segmentation strategy (Peking # Duck), which solves the problem for the reporter. This is indicated by the update marker "OH" in line 10, which might have ended the repair sequence. This does not happen, however. In line 15 there is a confirmation check by the reporter which receives a positive response in line 17. In line 18 the reporter rounds up the discussion by repeating the correct name of the dish. It is clear that a POP to the interrupted task-in-progress would be sequentially relevant, but even a second update marker ("alright" in line 18) does not cause a return to the imbedding floor. In line 21 the reporter makes a nonconversational move and nonverbally allocates a turn to a member of the group who has not yet stated his preference. But even then the POP is not entirely successful: there is still overlap with the previous business (lines 24–25: "it's Chinese;" "I really recommend it"). The group goes beyond the task considered: the item for the list has been delivered, but it is reframed for real-world evaluation. The result of the reporter role in this case has led to imbedded language play, which is very much "on task:" students help each other choose a dish they think is delicious.

It turned out, then, that the two alterations in the format of the task allowed for emergent meaning. This was done by inserting unpredictability – through the pretask – and by introducing the necessity for students to step out of the system of the task to reflect upon what was meant – through the reporter role.

Discussion

The data investigated show that "doing conversation" in the communicative L2 classroom is a recommendation that is complicated to follow. Whatever task is set to the students, in whatever way the classroom is organized, the fluency episode will always be imbedded in the speech event "lesson" and a lot of work is needed to overrule the classroom frame. Example 2 shows that, with groupwork, there is the risk that the teacher role is taken over by one of the student members of the group, who nominates the topics, handles transitions, allocates turns, and generally takes charge of the organization of talk. The distinct spatial configuration of the members of the group in the example may play an important part in this respect. Student 1 is the only member of the group who has physical access to the questions supposed to set the agenda for the "conversation," which makes it more or less "logical" for her to adopt the role of teacher. The question–answer format of the task might also have caused discourse ambiguity: the questions in the questionnaire may be interpreted as the first part of a question–answer adjacency pair instead of prompts for story-type turns. In the latter type of talk the question functions as a "story preface" that creates an answer slot which necessitates a "PUSH" to an imbedded "story-telling" floor. After the "point" of the story, a "POP" will occur to the imbedding floor and the storytelling world. In the teacher-fronted lesson frame, however, the unmarked, default student response to questions is a simple answer, not a story-type turn. The instructions I gave the students made clear that they should not take the questions as short-form questions, but I had not anticipated that a mini-classroom would be created, imbedded in the speech event "lesson," a frame within a frame, which inherits ritual classroom roles, and results in formal discourse with fixed procedures.

The task eventually yields interaction of the type intended, as is shown in Example 3. This occurs when the students have rounded off the official assignment. Now they are finally "on task" while they are at the same time – paradoxically – "off task." The group has created a time out that still orients to the higher-order "lesson" context: the students are doing conversation while practicing their English fluency. This means that "authentic conversation" may only occur, so to speak, in the "cracks and seams" of the lesson. This then may lead to yet another paradox in communicative L2 classes: if we accept that, ideally, talk in these lessons should be conversation, then it might be that *the task of the teacher is to plan unplanned discourse*. It shows at least that it is important for teachers to be *aware* of the potential for off-record interactional metafloors which might emerge within the context of current tasks. This "awareness," however, should not be "conceived as a private internal state, but as a constantly shifting active relationship between the [teacher] and [her] surroundings" (Fettes, forthcoming). Successful language teaching is not simply the result of making the "right" methodological decisions, it requires *metareflection* on what happens in class on the parts of both teacher and students through learner logbooks, feedback sessions, teacher diaries, lesson observations by colleagues, action research, etc.

Task 2 was meant to be a role play. The student evaluations of the assignment, however, show that, in order for this type of activity to result in "conversation," it is important to know how much information can be stored in students' short-term memory so that it can be immediately accessed. The student feedback shows the weak points of the assignment: because they do not succeed in remembering their list of activities, they have to "cheat" to remember what they are supposed to want and have to take long time-outs which is typical for formal classroom contexts of talk ("gap;" McHoul 1979), but is incompatible with the flow of authentic conversation. The result is disfluency and inauthentic speaking roles. If we contend that fluency assignments should contain information gap and problem-solving type elements, we usually consider the *content* level of the task. The problem here has to do with *speaker–hearer roles*. This task does not allow the students to be, to use Goffman's terms, the *authors* of their words; they are merely the animators or, we might even say, the principals: actors-in-function. It might be argued that this sort of role-play is normal practice in communicative L2 classes, but for a successful simulation of "conversational" contexts of talk, students should be able to sustain the illusion that they are "acting out themselves." This means that *framing* (Goffman 1974) is all-important: classroom realities and roles need to be temporarily overruled. Students are asked to construct a make-believe or pseudo-identity in an imaginary story or text world, while discourse world parameters and values are temporarily suspended (cf. Werth 1999). As Breen (1985) argues, one of the conventions assumed to be honored by participants in the culture of a language class is the willingness and capacity to suspend disbelief, to participate in simulated communication within classroom specific interaction. If this fails, the result is not *conversation*, it is saying one's part as *reading aloud* in a rehearsal for a play. Some of these negative results might have been avoided if I had given the students time to study their "role." I wonder, however, whether this would have solved the problem: the activities listed for each participant in the text of the assignment were hard to memorize: they seem to be chosen randomly and do not create "rounded characters."

In Example 4, the students actively negotiate for meaning, which traditional SLA research tells us is crucial for second-language input to become intake and to result in learning (Corder 1967; Ellis 1985). Long argues that "... environmental contributions to acquisition are mediated by selective attention and the learner's developing L2 processing capacity, and these resources are brought together most usefully, although not exclusively, during negotiation for meaning" (1996:414).

Negotiation of meaning supposedly bestows three benefits on L2 learning: improved comprehensibility of input, enhanced attention to form, and the need to produce output. Pica (1994) claims that negotiation of meaning may lead to manipulation of form which may be noticed by learners because it interrupts conversation. Swain (1985) proposes that a function of negotiation of meaning may be that the learner is pushed toward the delivery of precise, coherent, and appropriate messages.

Interactional modifications such as comprehension checks and clarification requests are seen as evidence that negotiation of meaning and thus "learning" is taking place. However, the assumption that in everyday interactions noncomprehension *always* results in comprehension checks and clarification requests is too strong (cf. Firth and Wagner 1997). This is a consequence of the conversational preference for self-correction, as Schegloff *et al.* (1977) have shown: explicit clarification requests and comprehension checks are dispreferred, since they create disfluency which interrupts the smooth ongoing flow of talk and do not move the agenda forward. So according to SLA research, the norm should be "negotiate repair"; in natural conversation zero or nonverbal clarification requests are the norm – the norm is "don't negotiate repair." It is therefore not surprising that the claim that learners, when engaged in communicative language tasks, will automatically initiate negotiated interaction (cf. Clark 1987) is not corroborated by classroom studies. Foster (1998) found that the students in her communicative language class employed a different communication strategy when they confronted a gap in understanding: they pretended to understand, and hoped that a future utterance would explain things to them, which concurs with the tolerance for uncertainty that is quite normal in everyday conversation. Paradoxically, the traditional language classroom, with its focus on accuracy, might be better suited to create the conditions for negotiation of meaning. The affordances for the prolonged interaction reported in Example 4 are created by the introduction of *a nonconversational* speaker role. The reporter is determined to grasp the exact meaning of her interlocutor's words, because exact understanding is made conditionally relevant by her formal role on the imbedding classroom floor. The negotiation of meaning occurs because the outcome of the discussion is *made consequential* for what is to happen in the classroom frame: after the POP to the imbedding discourse unit "lesson" she will be expected to report faithfully on the (outcomes of the) discussion in the public domain of the class. So the introduction of the reporter role introduced a reflexive element in a communicative activity that was designed to be nonreflexive. The reporter broke the homogeneity of the "community of practice" and therefore served as a mediator between two incompatible discourse genres – informal conversation and formal report.

A final point that is worth making is that to achieve mutual understanding in the negotiation of meaning sequence reported in Example 4, the students employ code-switching, repetition, and parallelism. These are instances of *language play*, which is beneficial for language learning in a number of ways. Cook (1997) argues that in language play the introduction of patterns of linguistic form (e.g. rhythm, rhyme, parallelism) beyond those demanded by meaning and purpose, destabilizes the relation of meaning and form, allowing changes in the range of possibilities open to both. Exploiting such destabilization may be important for creative thought, and for adaptation in general, including the adaptation involved in second-language acquisition. Sullivan (2000b) points out: "in a second language classroom, storytelling and wordplay can increase motivation, serve as mediation in expert–novice interaction, and encourage a focus on form" (2000b:74). Real-life language of native speakers includes form-focused and playful language as well as task-based language. Storytelling and wordplay, therefore, may contribute toward preparing students for the demands of the multiple forms of communication outside the classroom (cf. Polanyi 1985; Chapter 9 of this volume).

At this point, it might be appropriate to explore the reporter role in more detail. Levinson (1988), in a paper in which he attempts to further systematize Goffman's analysis of participant structures, proposes two levels of organization of participant roles: those related to the utterance event (type I unit in the Polanyi and Scha model) and those applicable to the larger, more inclusive speech event (type III). But, to fully analyze the participant roles of the reporter, we need to add a third level (type II), the level of the language assignment imbedded in the speech event "lesson." In Example 4 the reporter shares the roles of speaker and hearer with the other members of her group on an utterance event level. On the level of the language assignment she has to do the "minutes," she has to make notes of what is being said during the discussion. On the speech event level, when she reports on the discussion on the official classroom floor, she functions as narrator of a coauthored "story." The participant roles the reporter fulfills on language assignment and speech event levels provide an important contextualization frame for the utterance events in Example 4. In this way Example 4 can be said to represent "one moment in a diachronic chain of discourses, a moment which presumes earlier moments and in which later moments are already envisaged" (Irvine 1996:153). The communicative acts in Example 4 are related to other acts, including those that occurred in the past and will occur in the future, and these intersecting frames inform the participation structure of the moment. The result is an intricate lamination of participant roles and an opportunity for the learners to transcend the "flat" interactional objective of the communicative language class of simply "doing conversation."

Concluding remarks

The data discussed show that a number of paradoxes were found in the communicative L2 class under investigation which have not been accounted for in traditional SLA theories. Negotiation of meaning and language play, rather than being features of informal conversation, were brought about by importing a formal speaker role into an informal, conversational setting. Authentic conversation, rather than being the result of carefully planned group tasks, occurred in a post-task time-out environment. It might be concluded that the fluency class yielded complex interactional domains.

Analysis of the data suggests that the metaphor of the formal–informal, conversational–institutional, authentic–inauthentic dichotomies, on which SLA research has been built, should be challenged. The distinctions SLA theory has drawn between speech events and discourse genres in the classroom are too rigid. In the classroom "game" the speech event "lesson" does not contextualize monolithic discourse structures with invariable speaker and hearer roles and ritual business only. Frames can be imbedded in or superimposed on one another. Interactional arrangements, current roles, and identities may be shifted into and out of at will. The classroom may be viewed as an ecological environment in which "lesson" and "conversation" are relational to each other, needing one another for ecological balance. The L2 class might be reframed as a stage for "performance" which includes events like "storytelling," "conversation," "language play," "role play," "chorus work," etc. The teacher then should be prepared to act out several scenarios, to try various parts, and to introduce new protagonists when needed. Rather than trying to "plan unplanned discourse" she should perform the role of stage director in the context of current class tasks – to inspire and direct the student-actors. Ultimately it is up to them to impose their style on the script and enact a variety of participant roles.

It might be argued that the frame complexity of the classroom has not been sufficiently recognized in theories on L2 pedagogy to date. A precise analysis of what actually happens in the classroom may bring us to re-examine a number of assumptions underlying L2 learning research and ensuing recommendations for L2 teaching methodology. This involves re-examination of the data to be investigated and an unraveling of the cultural, institutional, and interactional dimensions of the contexts in which they are nested.

Notes

1. I gratefully acknowledge the very helpful comments of Claire Kramsch and Jet van Dam on an earlier version of this chapter.
2. When freshman students in the Netherlands arrive at university, they are relatively fluent in English, since by that time they have attended English classes at school for a minimum of eight years.
3. In my data I found that when I, as the organizer of the activity, felt obliged to interrupt a group's interaction, I also oriented to the conversational rules for bystanders: I stood at a distance from the group involved, waited for a pause in the talk and apologized for breaking in ("Sorry to interrupt but could you ..."). In this way I did my best to sustain the illusion of the conversational frame of the talk that was going on in the group.
4. Here the pragmatic paradox is spelt out in the instructions.

References

Breen, M.P. (1985) Authenticity in the language classroom. *Applied Linguistics* 6(1), 60–70.

Brown, H.D. (1994) *Teaching by Principles: An Interactive Approach to Language Pedagogy*, Englewood Cliffs, NJ: Prentice Hall Regents.

Clark, J.L. (1987) *Curriculum Renewal in School.* Oxford: Oxford University Press.

Cook, G. (1997) Language play, language learning. *English Language Teaching Journal* 51(3), 224–31.

Corder, S.P. (1967) The significance of learners' errors. *International Review of Applied Linguistics* 5, 161–9.

Edelsky, C. (1981) Who's got the floor? *Language in Society* 10, 383–421.

Ellis, R. (1985) *Understanding Second Language Learning.* Oxford: Oxford University Press.

Fettes, M. (forthcoming) Critical realism and ecological psychology: foundations for a naturalist theory of language acquisition. In J. Leather and J. van Dam (eds), *The Ecology of Language Acquisition.* Dordrecht: Kluwer.

Firth, A. and Wagner, J. (1997) On discourse, communication, and (some) fundamental concepts in SLA research. *Modern Language Journal* 81(3), 285–300.

Foster, P. (1998) A classroom perspective on the negotiation of meaning. *Applied Linguistics* 19(1), 1–23.

Goffman, E. (1974) *Frame Analysis.* Cambridge, MA: Harvard University Press.

Goffman, E. (1979) Footing. *Semiotica* 25, 1–29.

Goffman, E. (1981) *Forms of Talk.* Oxford: Basil Blackwell.

Gumperz, J.J. (1982) *Discourse Strategies.* Cambridge: Cambridge University Press.

Heritage, J. and Atkinson, J.M. (1984) Introduction. In J. Heritage and J.M. Atkinson (eds), *Structures of Social Action: Studies in Conversation Analysis.* Cambridge: Cambridge University Press, pp. 1–15.

Hymes, D.H. (1964) *Language in Culture and Society: A Reader in Linguistics and Anthropology.* New York: Harper & Row.

Irvine, J.T. (1996) Shadow conversations: the indeterminacy of participant roles. In M. Silverstein and G. Urban (eds), *Natural Histories of Discourse.* Chicago: University of Chicago Press, pp. 131–59.

Kendon, A. (1992) The negotiation of context in face-to-face interaction. In A. Duranti and C. Goodwin (eds), *Rethinking Context.* Cambridge: Cambridge University Press, pp. 323–34.

Kerbrat-Orecchioni, C. (1997) A multilevel approach in the study of talk-in-interaction. *Pragmatics* 7, 1–20.

Levelt, W. (1989) *Speaking: From Intention to Articulation*, Cambridge: MIT Press.

Levinson, S.C. (1983) *Pragmatics*. Cambridge: Cambridge University Press.

Levinson, S.C. (1988) Putting linguistics on a proper footing: explorations in Goffman's concepts of participation. In P. Drew and A. Wootton (eds), *Erving Goffman: An Interdisciplinary Appreciation*. Oxford: Polity Press, pp. 161–227.

Long, M.H. (1996) The role of the linguistic environment in second language acquisition. In W.C. Ritchie and T.K. Bhatia (eds), *Handbook of Second Language Acquisition*. San Diego: Academic Press, pp. 413–68.

McHoul, A.W. (1979) The organization of turns at formal talk in the classroom, *Language in Society* 19, 349–77.

Mitchell, R. and Myles F. (1998) *Second Language Learning Theories*. London: Arnold.

Pica, T. (1994) Research on negotiation: what does it reveal about second-language learning conditions, processes, and outcomes? *Language Learning* 38, 45–73.

Polanyi, L. (1985) *Telling the American Story: A Structural and Cultural Analysis of Conversational Storytelling*. Norwood, NJ: Ablex.

Polanyi, L. (1988) A formal model of the structure of discourse. *Journal of Pragmatics* 12, 601–38.

Polanyi, L. and Scha, R.J.H. (1983) On the recursive structure of discourse. In K. Ehlich and H. van Riemsdijk (eds), *Connectedness in Sentence, Discourse and Text*. Tilburg: Tilburg University, pp. 141–78.

Poulisse, N. (1990) *The Use of Compensatory Strategies by Dutch Learners of English*. Dordrecht: Foris.

Schegloff, E.A., Jefferson, G. and Sacks, H. (1977) The preference for self-correction in the organization of repair in conversation. *Language* 53, 361–83.

Sullivan, P. (2000a) Playfulness as mediation in communicative language teaching in a Vietnamese classroom. In J.P. Lantolf (ed.), *Sociocultural Theory and Second Language Learning*. Oxford: Oxford University Press, pp. 115–31.

Sullivan, P. (2000b) Spoken artistry: performance in a foreign language classroom. In J.K. Hall and L. Stoops-Verplaetse (eds), *Second and Foreign Language Learning Through Classroom Interaction*. Hillsdale, NJ: Lawrence Erlbaum, pp. 73–90.

Swain, M. (1985) Communicative competence: some roles of comprehensible input and comprehensible output in its development. In S. Gass and C. Madden (eds), *Input in Second Language Acquisition*. Rowley, MA: Newbury House, pp. 235–56.

van Dam van Isselt, H.R. (1993) *"Her name is – uh dat weet ik niet": authenticity in the L2 classroom*. Unpublished PhD dissertation, University of Amsterdam.

van Dam van Isselt, H.R. (1995) "Where's the lesson in all this talk?" Structural features of classroom floors. In E. Huls and J. Klatter-Folmer (eds), *Artikelen van de Tweede Sociolinguistische Conferentie*. Delft: Eburon, pp. 125–39.

van Lier, L. (1988) *The Classroom and the Language Learner*. New York: Longman.

van Lier, L. (1989) Reeling, writhing, drawling, stretching, and fainting in coils: oral proficiency interviews as conversation. *TESOL Quarterly* 23(3), 489–508.

van Lier, L. (1996) *Interaction in the Language Curriculum: Awareness, Autonomy and Authenticity*. New York: Longman.

Watzlawick, P., Beavin, J.H. and Jackson, D.D. (1967) *Pragmatics of Human Communication*. New York: Norton.

Werth, P. (1999) *Text Worlds: Representing Conceptual Space in Discourse*. New York: Longman.

Commentaries

Editors: Edward Bodine and Claire Kramsch

Classroom rituals and their ecologies

What is the relationship between systems of typification and ritualized language use? What does "ritual" mean from an ecological perspective?

RAMPTON During my research on groups of adolescent Londoners "playing around" with German, I found the analytical frame of interactional *ritual* to be especially useful.[1] Ritual provides a tool for looking into the participatory structures in social practice. It gives one a handle on the "flow" of structured collective activities, be they artistic performances, games, or religious practices. Ritual also involves a state of immersion in the moment; it can open up a dimension of play and improvisation. For example, in a school corridor as students and teacher are entering the classroom, a student blurts out: "Schnell, schnell!" The teacher responds with "Schnell, schnell, exactly! – vite, vite!" The interchange happens before the lesson starts so it is outside of the typical lesson frame of interaction. What the student is doing here is essentially mocking or ventriloquating the teacher. He is acting out a role in a kind of a *ritualistic* performance. Now, this use of Deutsch is not part of the rites of institution. Rather, it is a spontaneous response to a momentary situation. In this respect, it is much more Goffman than Durkheim, Bernstein, or Bourdieu. But it is also more than *just* interpersonal face-work between friends. It is also a play on institutional power relations.

OCHS The concept of *ritual* may be even more productive for our research if it is understood as intersecting with the broader concept of *typification*. Perhaps, with the "Schnell, schnell ..." example you cited, what we have is a student invoking or indexing a typification that those words are connected to. Of course, to pin down exactly what that typification is in each instance would take quite some time. Perhaps it was gleaned from another context, such as a popular film in which German was spoken. Wherever it may have originated from, the short interchange initiated by the student may in fact be casting the teacher in a kind of typification that those words are evoking. In other words, there is a linguistic and a cultural ideology connected to those words and that may recast this situation paradigmatically. The real motivation for the remark might be disruption, given the context of establishing order before the start of the lesson. There is also an element of teasing. We should also recognize that such disruptions are also a way of creating and strengthening alignments with peers.

RAMPTON   Not only does an analysis of typification reveal patterns of social alignment, it also shows how through various kinds of ritualized language use people will refigure ethnic relations. Typification is a kind of invocation; it's a model of society. Moments of interactional disjuncture, such as the one I detailed, open up interesting opportunities for ritualistic play. These playful moments display, in a very performative sense, unconventional and unexpected social alignments. I think considering both ritual and typification together is especially useful in exploring the interactional nesting of indexical activities. In this sense, such an approach is quite *ecological;* it lends itself to a clustering of analytic perspectives, which I should say, sometimes gets lost when people talk about indexicality in general.

KRAMSCH   You might interpret the teacher's rejoinder "Schnell, schnell, exactly! – vite, vite!" to the student's "Schnell, schnell!" as an act of ritual *resignification*. It may be that the teacher is echoing the student's utterance with the intention of institutionally repossessing it. We have the teacher in some sense recognizing the student's act of subversion and then re-establishing institutional relations of power. Interestingly, the teacher adds the synonymous French expression to the German. How do we make sense of this? What typifications are evoked through this maneuver? In what ways might the teacher's and the student's respective typificational evocations be connotatively different? This may have to do with the "French-ness" or the "German-ness" each associates with these expressions. Linguistic and cultural ideologies are intricately intertwined and are shaped according to one's cultural exposures.

RAMPTON   I think you've touched on an interesting aspect of ritual events, which I would call social symbolism. There are certainly many layers to such symbolism that lend themselves to literary-critical types of interpretation. I would caution, however, that this kind of analysis also opens itself up to a fair bit of speculation with respect to the social and cultural experiences of our research subjects. The first steps to take, I think, should involve a more ethnographic approach to understanding how these practices are distributed. It's imperative that we build a large corpus that would help to give us a sense of the potential resonances *across* social practices. It would also help constrain the ways in which one makes such interpretations of evocations.

POLANYI   I think your observation about the important role of a comprehensive database is apt. There are already of number of systems that might be relevant to your data. In particular, the Dubois system would seem especially well suited for your purposes. On the other hand, the ritual analysis framework you've outlined could also be productive for thinking about social-interactive phenomena in broader terms. For example, instead of just considering the particularistic circumstances of this German classroom in London, ritual analysis could enable us to look at second language acquisition and socialization processes in ways that cross scales and give us a more comprehensive picture.

RAMPTON   Indeed, Peter McLaren, the cultural critic, has talked about schooling itself as a ritual process.[2] While this certainly appears to be an intriguing direction for ritual analysis, I question its promise, at least in terms of the sociolinguistic research I'm interested in. One can very easily overextend the notion of ritual until it becomes useless. After all, Goffman has remarked that *all* social-interactive activity has a ritual dimension. Now, Goffman does provide us with a mechanism for examining larger social patterns. Yet, when the concept of ritual itself becomes so broad and diffuse, it begins to lose its utility as an analytic tool. I think you always have to ask where a particular concept is going to get you. If it's simply a broad label that loosely guides your data collection, it's not going to serve you all that well.

POLANYI   This may indeed be the case with the kind of microsociolinguistic analysis that you've presented here. But an important question is how can the researcher make sense of broader interactional patterns that cut across contexts with this kind of analysis?

VAN LIER   I think we need to further problematize the notion of ritual. On the one hand, ritual can be understood as fairly predictable, fixed, and conventional. It defines a dimension of social normativity. On the other hand, ritual can be understood as ambiguous, unpredictable, disjunctive, and improvisatory. This is the side of ritual we saw displayed with the "Schnell, schnell" exchange. Now with this incident, we might say the student was trying out a sociolinguistic experiment. He didn't know quite how things would turn out. How would the teacher respond? There seems to be a kind of deliberate ambiguity on the student's part. Bourdieu and Tannen both talk about the role of ambiguity in discourse, and I think it is instrumental here.[3] So, are we dealing with two contradictory dimensions of ritual: the predicted and unpredictable?

RAMPTON   No rituals are totally predictable. Rituals are events constructed online, in response to particular situations.

VAN LIER   But there clearly is a tension between the predicted and the unpredictable nature of ritual.

RAMPTON   Perhaps we can look at rituals in much the same way we often look at rites. We talk about the difference between consensual ·rites, differentiating rites, even antirites. Similarly, I think there are multiple constructions of ritual. Perhaps we need a way of categorizing this multiplicity – a way that captures both the predicted and the unpredictable and allows us to understand how learners quite often play between the two.

VOLLMER   To return to your linguistic data, I think it's significant that your focal interaction constitutes 63 turns distributed among five male students to four turns by a singular female student. I'd like to argue that an important dimension to ritual is *gender*. Unfortunately, gender has been under-researched in the area of second language development; yet, such a great deal of social practice is gendered! For example, the sociolinguistic phenomenon of "discourse syncopation" – that is, the deliberate upsetting of order – is a very male-gendered practice. With this in mind, is "Schnell, schnell ..." just another intersubjective tool, or does it serve as a gendered response within this classroom context? If we're going to take a more ecological view of language acquisition, many of the interactional dynamics we're talking about, such as face-saving mechanisms, footing, politeness, and rituals, must be looked at in terms of gender as well.

How we can achieve a methodological balance between describing the conventional while remaining sensitive to the creative? To what extent can multiply-embedded contextualizations allow for an interplay between the two? Finally, in what ways can creativity be developed in the language classroom?

OCHS   Mihaly Csikszentmihalyi's work on creativity – or perhaps on the *flow* of creative experience – highlights a particularly important feature of all creative endeavors.[4] In order to be truly creative, you have to be well versed in the traditions that have come to shape the field of your activity – and then be able to go beyond them. In other words, it's not enough just to do something new or unconventional without regard for what came before. You must be steeped in certain traditions yet without letting them blind you to novel ways of seeing the world. I'd like to suggest that this view of creativity might hold for successful language learning environments as well. Language learners need to possess the knowledge of certain paradigmatic dimensions of language within an environment that allows for individual creativity. The challenge is how to balance the conventional with the creative. In the classroom, how do we make sense of shifting forms of agency – and all the metapragmatic complexity – within institutional and social paradigms? Let me illustrate this with an example from Jet van Dam's data. The "What is my name?" episode clearly shows the student known as "Freek" fulfilling a conventional lesson requirement (responding to the teacher's initiation) but in a playful, improvisatory way – complete with mock British accent. In such a way, his response takes the interaction into a new and unexpected context – or in Goffman's terms, the interaction is "keyed," (it is shifted to a new interpretative schema). Freek's response is both institutionally co-operative *and* interactionally playful. It serves two functions and involves two different types of interpretation. Then, another student adds, in a dramatic stage whisper, "Mister 'X'!" which keys the interaction to yet another context. We have here a number of semantic–pragmatic contexts in this very short interaction. I would suggest that a way of making sense of them all is by analyzing these contexts from the perspectives of the different participants. The whole interaction is a complex of these shiftings or "keyings" from multiple viewpoints.

VAN DAM   What we have with this interaction is double or even multiple layers of contextualization in ritual work. I think Goffman's theatrical metaphor is a useful way of understanding the modulations of ritual work and role-play that make up these contextual frames.[5] The teacher is playing her part; so too is the student. Freek is really playing *multiple* parts – in some sense he is playing roles off one another.

POLANYI   We often think of the creative process as an act of authoring. But attributing authorship is often more complicated than our customary analytical tools might suggest. When learners speak, *whose* words issue forth? With all the performative shifting in the classroom, how does one locate turns at talk? How does one attribute authorship? Jet's research brings this dilemma to the surface and problematizes the notion of turn at talk.

VAN DAM   The phenomena of ventriloquation cannot really be dealt with through typical discourse analysis. We have to look to Bakhtinian analysis for this. Ventriloquation really challenges our traditional notions of turn structure and management because it introduces the idea of someone speaking *for* someone else. Suddenly, a turn becomes a multidimensional unit; it is carrying more than one voice. When a teacher corrects a student's Dutch "tien" with the English "ten," and the student follows with "ten," we can see this process at work. A great deal of error correction follows this pattern. Yet, it is not merely ventriloquation. The teacher is doing more than just talking for the student. She is also scaffolding the learner's response, showing how the words to the part get properly spoken. This scaffolding, I think, explains a good deal of the performative shifting in classrooms between students and teachers. In that sense, creativity is often less individual and more co-constructed.

LEMKE The notion of layers of embedded contextualizations with certain imperative properties could go far in advancing our understanding of the ecology of social interaction. For me, it's in the dynamism of or the very *shiftability* between these contextualizations where we find learner creativity. This shiftability needs to be built into our research models. It's not enough to describe the layers of contextualizations alone. We must be able to describe how learners spontaneously reorder them in particular situations. Of course, describing learner creativity and teaching the learner to be more creative are two very different tasks. Whether, in fact, the latter is possible is an age-old dilemma. How do we, as educators, encourage playfulness and plan for creativity within the constraints of an institutional setting? I believe the answer may be found in making institutional spaces, in effect, less institutional by removing normative constraints and thereby enlarging the space for playfulness and creativity. At its core, this is really a control issue.

OCHS I would disagree that creativity involves the removal of constraints, *per se*. All social interaction is constrained in various ways, whether institutionally or socially. Rather, creativity entails the changing or transformation of constraints. It's not that we are freeing ourselves from constraints exactly but that we are shifting to a different configuration of them, which also entails different interpretive schemas.

LEMKE Let me redefine "constraint" here. I've already suggested that the shiftability between and among contextualizations describes creative activity. This between-ness is important and something we have seen learners quite often take advantage of. It seems apparent that creativity tends to grow where there is slackness between frames of contextualizations. I believe educators can help to encourage creativity by "building in" a certain degree of slackness. I think this is done by creating an interactive space where there can exist a greater number of possible or potential legitimate moves than would be otherwise sanctioned in a more constrained institutional space.

OCHS Encouraging creativity in educational settings is not a matter of destructuring but *restructuring*. This can happen on any number of levels. Two important levels are the participative and the propositional framework. Now, in terms of the first, restructuring for creativity might involve a certain loosening of the role system. And on the propositional level, this loosening might lead to an opening up in the turn management system, resulting in more opportunities for topic shifts. But this loosening process also requires putting in place new structures or reconfiguring the original structure. This brings to mind Judith Irvine's work some time ago on defining the features of informality.[6] I think what we are really talking about here is moving from formality to informality. This movement toward informality involves a fundamental restructuring of opportunity in the institutional setting.

KRAMSCH   I don't think we should throw out the idea of formality altogether in our drive toward informality. The two, it seems to me, define one another, perhaps play off one another. We need both the relationship and the tension between the two.

POLANYI   This interplay itself between formality and informality may be a critical element of creativity. Spontaneity, in a very symbiotic way, thrives on normative expectations by playing on them, twisting them, eschewing them. Formality and informality form a dialectical relationship. In the classroom, the teacher needs first and foremost to try to set the conditions in which talk can exist at all. But then, getting students to speak in the target language requires a more controlled, formal setting. Creativity may arise out of the space between these two sets of context and educational intention.

How do we weigh authenticity in the development of learners' educational identities? How might the ways we define educational success constrain learners or even force them to misrepresent themselves through typical forms of classroom expression and self-expression?

VOLLMER   In American ESL classrooms, heavy emphasis is placed on expressing feelings, quite often through writing, and then sharing them with other students. The motive behind such practices – which are by no means atypical – is a desire to make the students authors of their own experiences. This involves a great deal of selecting particular sentiments and putting them into language. There is, of course, a danger in this. In such classrooms you tend to find a very consistent framing of ESL students as "new immigrants to America." Since this is often the dominant frame of expression, the process of authoring is constrained and shaped in ways that accentuate their immigrant experiences. This may have disturbing implications for the shaping of educational identity and attitudes about learning in a new culture. In such classrooms, all of their perceptions as immigrants are ratified. Yet, learners' other roles, i.e. as teenagers, sons, daughters, and workers – both here in the US and in their home country – go unacknowledged and unexplored. It is the very narrowness of role ascribed to these students that I find so disconcerting. In my own research on ESL classrooms, I found that students resist this dominant frame in a variety of ways. Many develop a clear distinction between what is true and what is fictional and would frequently point this out when talking about their writing. Quite often, it's these kinds of immigrant stories, tailored for classroom presentation, that were made up. What's more, students would borrow freely from each other's immigrant narratives – so much so, you would repeatedly hear the same kinds of stories coming up in the classroom, sprinkled with the same phrases about "my new life" and "the challenges I faced" and "hard work brings rewards," etc. Now, I'm not saying there's no truth in their narratives. But what struck me was the clear lack of *investment* in them by the students. For them, I believe, this was "doing" school, playing the part. What does educational success mean if the socialization frame is so limiting with respect to the real lives of learners? If we as researchers are claiming interdependence between the socialization and the acquisition of language, how does lack of authenticity influence acquisition of the language itself?

VAN LIER   I think you have touched on a particularly worrisome side of ESL classroom culture in this country – an aspect that rarely gets much critical examination. How does this culture – even in the best interests of *empowering* the learner – unwittingly filter out those aspects of their symbolic worlds that are essential to how they identify themselves? We ought to question more aggressively the limits to access we place on these cultural worlds in the classroom.

KRAMSCH   Educational success should perhaps be thought of in terms of both empowerment and critical awareness. This is where an ecological approach may help us understand this dialectic. In other words, an ecological view toward pedagogy might alert the teacher to the link between language and identity and at the same time signal the value of validating certain experiences. Our research can at once essentialize student experiences and warn against an excessive manipulation of them.

BODINE   In the pursuit of authenticity, I think it becomes easy to underestimate learners' protean abilities to shift in and out of performative roles. When the classroom imperative becomes telling one's "real" story, the chameleon aspects of learning tend to get devalued, and the space for creativity crowded out. How is the capacity to author one's life – not in any premeditated and indelible sense but as spontaneous activity – an adaptive response to new environments? This shape-shifting dynamic has educational value too. I take these students adapting each other's narratives, even each other's language, as an interesting point of departure for teaching.

RAMPTON   I think assessing the quality of authenticity is itself problematic. We are attributing all sorts of ideological representations to learner talk, suggesting that certain educational efforts limit educational identity. Who knows whether these kids might feel constrained by these narratives?

VOLLMER   My concern is not so much over the validity of the stories but the quality of narration. Though the pedagogical aim was to make them into authors, the activity seemed to make them mere "animators" of others' discourse. The effect for most of them was like "Oh, this is easy!" There is no effort there and few incentives to be novel. They are merely fulfilling an institutional prerequisite and going through the motions. What is the consequence for language acquisition where language production occurs as an endless recycling or reanimation of the same narratives?

LEMKE   I think this presents us with an interesting methodological opportunity and challenge. You get a strong sense that in the cracks, around the edges, and behind the seams of standard institutional frames of classroom interaction, there are all of these marginalized things going on. Perhaps an ecological approach here has pushed us to the realization that there exists a hidden world between the paradigmatic frames themselves. And it is in these spaces that we are beginning to find some very interesting and important implications for educational practice.

Notes

1. Rampton, B. (1999) Inner London *Deutsch* and the animation of an instructed foreign language. *Journal of Sociolinguistics* 3(4), 480–504.

2. McLaren, P. (1993) *Schooling as Ritual Performance*, 2nd edn. London: Routledge & Kegan Paul.

3. Bourdieu, P. (1990) *The Logic of Practice*. Stanford: Stanford University Press; Tannen, D. (1987) *That's Not What I Meant*. London: Dent.

4. Czikszentmihalyi, M. (1990) *Flow: The Psychology of Optimal Experience*. New York: Harper & Row.

5. Goffman, E. (1974) The theatrical frame. In his *Frame Analysis*. New York: Harper & Row, pp. 123–55.

6. Irvine, J. (1979) Formality and informality in communicative events. *American Anthropologist* 81, 773–90.

Index

Entries in bold refer to tables. Italicized entries refer to figures.